Paths of
Neighborhood Change

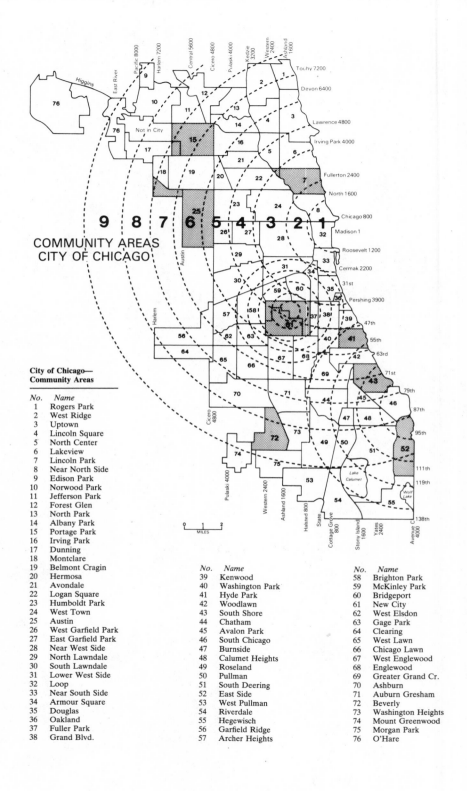

COMMUNITY AREAS
CITY OF CHICAGO

**City of Chicago—
Community Areas**

No.	Name
1	Rogers Park
2	West Ridge
3	Uptown
4	Lincoln Square
5	North Center
6	Lakeview
7	Lincoln Park
8	Near North Side
9	Edison Park
10	Norwood Park
11	Jefferson Park
12	Forest Glen
13	North Park
14	Albany Park
15	Portage Park
16	Irving Park
17	Dunning
18	Montclare
19	Belmont Cragin
20	Hermosa
21	Avondale
22	Logan Square
23	Humboldt Park
24	West Town
25	Austin
26	West Garfield Park
27	East Garfield Park
28	Near West Side
29	North Lawndale
30	South Lawndale
31	Lower West Side
32	Loop
33	Near South Side
34	Armour Square
35	Douglas
36	Oakland
37	Fuller Park
38	Grand Blvd.

No.	Name
39	Kenwood
40	Washington Park
41	Hyde Park
42	Woodlawn
43	South Shore
44	Chatham
45	Avalon Park
46	South Chicago
47	Burnside
48	Calumet Heights
49	Roseland
50	Pullman
51	South Deering
52	East Side
53	West Pullman
54	Riverdale
55	Hegewisch
56	Garfield Ridge
57	Archer Heights

No.	Name
58	Brighton Park
59	McKinley Park
60	Bridgeport
61	New City
62	West Elsdon
63	Gage Park
64	Clearing
65	West Lawn
66	Chicago Lawn
67	West Englewood
68	Englewood
69	Greater Grand Cr.
70	Ashburn
71	Auburn Gresham
72	Beverly
73	Washington Heights
74	Mount Greenwood
75	Morgan Park
76	O'Hare

Paths of
Neighborhood Change

Race and Crime in Urban America

Richard P. Taub
D. Garth Taylor
and Jan D. Dunham

The University of Chicago Press
Chicago and London

Richard P. Taub is professor of social sciences and director of the Program for Urban Neighborhoods at the University of Chicago and a research associate of the National Opinion Research Center. **D. Garth Taylor** is assistant professor of political science at the University of Chicago and a research associate of the National Opinion Research Center. **Jan D. Dunham**, a doctoral student in sociology, was project coordinator of NORC's Crime and Urban Neighborhood Study.

The University of Chicago Press, Chicago 60637
The University of Chicago Press, Ltd., London
© 1984 by The University of Chicago
All rights reserved. Published 1984
Printed in the United States of America
93 92 91 90 89 88 87 86 85 84   5 4 3 2 1

Library of Congress Cataloging in Publication Data

Taub, Richard P.
  Paths of neighborhood change.

  Bibliography: p.
  Includes index.
    1. Crime and criminals—Illinois—Chicago.   2. Crime
and criminals—Illinois—Chicago—Public opinion.
3. Public opinion—Illinois—Chicago.   4. Neighborhood—
Illinois—Chicago.   5. Chicago (Ill.)—Social conditions.
6. Chicago (Ill.)—Race relations. I. Taylor, D. Garth.
II. Dunham, Jan D.   III. Title.
HV6795.C4T38   1984   364.3′09773′11   84-2488
ISBN 0-226-79001-0

For
Neela and Zach
T-Sue
Dave

Contents

Illustrations

Acknowledgments

A project as complex as this one requires the efforts of many. Consequently, there are more people to thank than can even be recalled. However, some individuals still stand out.

The original research on which this manuscript is based was supported by the National Institute of Justice. Its representatives, especially Alan Wallace and Richard Titus, were particularly helpful and supportive during the stages of research design and writing. Alene Bycer and Kathi Rose played important roles during the early stages of design and implementation of the project. The NORC field staff, led by Paul Sheatsley, Shirley Knight, and Barbara Campbell, deserves commendation for the fielding of a complex and demanding project.

Jim Lucas, Bruce Peterson, and Patricia Wittberg all made valuable individual contributions during the production of our NIJ report. Stan Merrill sensitized us to salient issues in crime research, and Steve Garry joined Peterson and Lucas in data preparation.

Al Hunter, Dan Lewis, and Wes Skogan of the Northwestern University Reactions to Crime Project were singularly collegial and helpful, providing support for the view that the community of scholars here in Chicago surmounts institutional barriers.

Student research assistants Doug Dow, Jeff Elton, David Kendall, Tom Lombardo, Mark Matthews, Valerie Morrow, Erol Ricketts, and Tom Rief all provided valuable help.

Colleague readers who were helpful include Chris Achen, Mark Granovetter, Russell Hardin, Morris Janowitz, Peter Marsden, Gary Orfield, John Padgett, Benjamin Page, Paul Peterson, Thomas Schelling, Robert Shapiro, Duncan Snidal, and William Julius Wilson. They all provided helpful comments.

Wendy Guilfoyle, Susan Tepas, and Debra Sutherlin provided typing assistance at various phases of the project. Lisa McIntyre supplied the original illustrations.

Because there were three coauthors, a word should be said about the allocation of responsibility among them. All chapters were read, reviewed, and altered by all authors. Taub designed the project and, with Dunham, guided it through to completion. Taub and Dunham are primarily responsible for the text and ideas in chapters 1–5. Taylor has primary responsibility for the text and ideas in chapters 6–8; he also wrote appendix E. All of us were equally involved in chapter 9. Dunham had the major responsibility for seeing to it that there was a completed manuscript and that all the parts held together.

In a real scholarly community, the diverse contributions of one's colleagues and students are important in subtle ways. We gratefully acknowledge their presence.

1
Introduction

The relationship between crime and neighborhood deterioration is a peculiar one. We know that American cities are, relatively speaking, the loci of serious crime problems. We also know that within these cities crime is not equally distributed. There are places that are known for being dangerous and others that are known for being safe.

In addition, most of our cities, particularly those in the North and East, are losing both population and industry as well as the taxpayers and jobs that go with them. The consequence is that cities are in physical decline as well as population decline; more to the point, the more deteriorated areas are high-crime areas.

For many people, visualizing the most deteriorated areas of a city calls to mind images of roving youth gangs; unemployed people standing on street corners; vacant buildings, some scarred by arson; and uncollected litter blowing in the wind. They are the sorts of areas in which drivers passing through roll up their windows and lock their doors. In these areas, crime does seem to contribute to deterioration quite directly—windows are broken, buildings are burned, many people are afraid to rent or purchase housing.

For people observing such a situation, the relationship between crime and deterioration is obvious—crime causes deterioration. Nonetheless, three important points have to be made. The first is the old statistics adage that correlation is not causation. The presence of deterioration and crime together does not necessarily mean that one caused the other. Nor does it mean that causal relations only go one way. Deterioration could either cause crime or create the conditions that allow crime to flourish. Arson by property owners is one dramatic example.

Second, neighborhoods, and in fact cities, have deteriorated without the presence of particularly high rates of crime. Some of the old mill towns in New England are striking examples of this process. The mills, the major employers of the area, moved away for reasons quite unrelated to crime. Without the jobs they provided, the residents of these small cities did not have the money to maintain their houses or to shop in the commercial areas. Without income, these areas could not be maintained. The absence of employment opportunities meant that there were no newcomers to purchase houses and, in so doing, keep up the housing prices. Supply exceeded demand, and the final result was deterioration. Similarly, the classical theorists of urban society explained that urban areas had natural lifetimes and that, in the normal course of events, some would decline.

Finally, as we shall see, there are neighborhoods that are not deteriorating even though their crime rates are dramatically high. In fact, they are doing just the opposite. Their properties are improving, the quality of maintenance is being upgraded, and judging by the levels of property appreciation, many people want to live there—that is, demand exceeds supply.

The apparently obvious relationship between crime and deterioration is thus not so obvious at all. That there is some sort of connection, one would be foolish to deny. But the connection is more complex and subtle than it appears at first glance.

City Growth and Neighborhood Deterioration

To understand the relationship between crime and neighborhood deterioration, one must first have some understanding of the other forces that contribute to changes within the city, because American cities are and always have been locations of rapid change. During the late nineteenth and early twentieth centuries, many of them grew dramatically as they became the nation's manufacturing centers, producing many of the world's industrial goods. They were ports of arrival for migrants, both from across the sea and from America's rural areas, as well as the launching pads for their progeny.

Most theories of urban structure and change are premised on the growth characteristic of that era (Molotch 1976). Early theories emphasized the fact that as cities grew, the most prosperous residents would locate on the periphery, the distance from the center being determined by some combination of cost and time. As the city grew outward, the more affluent would be able to purchase new housing, and, because there was less congestion there than toward the center, dwellings could be located on larger lots (Burgess 1925; Hawley 1981). In contrast, the poorest would be crowded into the land near the center of the city, and each group, in turn, would move into older housing vacated by those who were moving outward and upward. In such cases, the housing of the better off becomes subdivided or the land becomes more intensively used in some other way. The process is known as filtering. It was expected that the oldest housing would continue to be for the poorest people and that new immigrants would continue to arrive in order to fill it up.

According to the older theories, however, not all housing was oriented solely to the center of the city. Distinct centers of economic activity, or nodes, might develop as well (Harris and Ullman 1957). Around these nodes, patterns might develop in a similar fashion, with the poorest housing closest to the economic activity and the more expensive housing farther away.

Another variant on the theme of growth and change should be briefly mentioned. The sectoral theory (Hoyt 1937; Berry and Kasarda 1977) suggests that there may be bands of persistent-use patterns as one moves out from the center of the city. For example, high-income housing may expand along a relatively narrow strip moving northward. Certain kinds of light industry may expand along another narrow strip moving westward, and so forth.

Several assumptions are embedded in this model. The first is that cities would continue to grow as they had during the preceding century. The second is that much of this growth would result from the influx of poor immigrants who would fill the housing left behind by those moving farther toward the periphery. The third is that transportation systems would continue to function as spokes to a hub, carrying the population to and from the central business district.

For the period during which the theory was developing, these were valid assumptions. Cities did grow during this time, as new poor migrants arrived. With fixed-rail transportation, many cities grew outward alongside the railroad tracks, the sections in between the railroad lines remaining relatively undeveloped. But conditions changed, at both the city level and the national and international levels, and with these changes, the assumptions no longer held.

First, the automobile largely replaced fixed-rail systems. This made it possible for residents to spread out rather than to hug the radii formed by the rail lines. People were then able to move farther from the center of the city, and commercial and industrial activity followed as well. Cheap land and federal subsidy made possible not only the suburban tracts, but also shopping centers with the vast parking areas cars require. Inexpensive property also made possible industrial and wholesale production and handling, processes that benefited from operations located in a single-story building spread over a wide area.

Polycentrality then became possible in truly dramatic forms, and, because of this, the central business district no longer had reason to grow (Molotch 1976). At the same time, in-migration to the central cities lessened. Restrictions had been set for migrants from abroad, and the black migration from the South slowed to a trickle. Thus there was no population available to fill the lowest levels of housing stock left behind by people moving upward and outward. Consequently, the central areas of the city, particularly those ringing the central business district, became increasingly empty. The city began to develop a hollow core as housing abandonment became a gritty fact of urban life.

At the broader national and international levels, northern cities in the United States have been affected by a worldwide shift in which many industrial activities have moved to less-developed areas both here and abroad. Simultaneously, new kinds of jobs associated with electronics and information processing have moved to the American South and West (Kasarda 1982). Northern cities are thus becoming more exclusively specialized service centers—centers of legal, financial, and governmental activities—as well as more exclusively entertainment centers, being important stops for tourists, conventioneers, and aficionados of the arts.

Northern cities as a whole, then, have shown signs of decline not dissimilar from those fading New England towns. Traditional kinds of urban jobs have moved elsewhere, taking with them employment opportunities. Such shifts do not affect all cities equally, nor do they affect all neighborhoods equally. Those neighborhoods whose raison d'être was traditional industrial activity may suffer disproportionately; in Chicago, neighborhoods built around the stockyards and the steel mills fit into that category. Other neighborhoods may become newly attractive to participants in the growing service sector. Even against a background of general urban economic decline, such areas show growth and redevelopment.

In spite of these changes, however, there is a core set of ideas in the theory that appears to apply broadly (Hawley 1981; Berry and Kasarda 1977). As one moves out from the center of the city, any concentric band does have much the same density, ownership, and family patterns. At the same time, along each axis, economic characteristics are relatively uniform, demonstrating the sectoral nature of the process. The exception, Berry and Kasarda suggest, is in patterns of segregation, which tend to take their own special forms in different cities, but which disrupt the pattern we have described.

In addition, the early Chicago theorists called attention to the fact that neighborhoods have a kind of life cycle. They begin new and full of promise, then tend to deteriorate and become less desirable.

There is ambiguity in much of the earlier literature about the extent to which urban residents are drawn to the residential areas at the fringe and the extent to which they are chased. Burgess (1925) makes clear that the urge to move away from the center of the city comes from a desire to escape the congestion, noises, and fumes associated with manufacture. Beyond that, he and his immediate followers are not too explicit. The Duncans, on the other hand, report that a high status group "often vacates a residential area, as the area ages and its housing becomes less desirable" (Duncan and Duncan 1957, 109). Much has been written about the fact that the wealthier like to move away from the center of the city, with emphasis on their desire for new housing and the amenities associated with decreased congestion. Even with these ambiguities about the general process, however, there is a powerful model of neighborhood change that can be understood to contribute to it.

The concept of invasion and succession was drawn from the field of biological ecology. In the biological model, a new kind of plant invades a habitat. Initially, the plant has some difficulty taking hold. But over time it does succeed and, in so doing, creates conditions that make the habitat more attractive to others like it, and perhaps less so for the indigenes. A pine tree invading a prairie, for example, sheds its needles; the resulting increased soil acidity is attractive to pine trees. Their shade discourages prairie grasses, which in turn makes it easier for new pine seeds to take root. These ideas, transferred to urban theory, can be used to cover a wide range of conditions. The arrival of industry may drive away residential inhabitants, for example, because of the associated noises and smells as well as the increased traffic that industry may bring.

Nevertheless, the concept has been used most consistently and powerfully to characterize racial change in urban neighborhoods, and almost all the literature that discusses the spread of minorities in urban settings makes use of it. The Duncans (1957) consider four stages in the process. The first is "penetration," the stage of initial entry. The second stage is "invasion," when a substantial number of blacks enter the area (defined by the Duncans as 250 per census tract). "Consolidation [the third stage] refers to the continued increase in number and proportion of Negroes in an area, after invasion has been accomplished" (p. 115). And finally, after the area has turned racially, there may be a "piling up" stage in which densities increase dramatically as housing is subdivided or small units become home for large families.

Although time tables may vary, most theorists believe that once the process begins, it will not come to a halt until racial change has been completed. "It is, of course, logically possible for the succession process to come to a halt at an early stage. . . . However, there is nothing in the history of Negro succession in Chicago to indicate that this is a likely outcome" (p. 113).

In the 1950s and early 1960s when, in fact, most of the important systematic research on succession was conducted, that position seemed reasonable. However, numerous changes—in the housing market, in the class distribution of minorities, in attitudes of tolerance toward minorities, and in the increased sophistication of institutional actors who are able to manipulate the marketplace—all contribute to the possibility that penetration of an urban neighborhood by a minority may not lead to total racial transition. Below, we look at these changes which make theories about the inevitability of racial change more qualified than they have been in the past.

Changes in the Housing Market

The well-developed empirical analyses of housing-market forces and racial change were done in the 1950s and early 1960s. This period was one of pent-up housing demand for most Americans, and particularly so for urban blacks. Directly after World War II, there was an acute housing shortage for everyone. New household formation had greatly exceeded housing starts during the war, and many urban residents were living in tightly cramped quarters, in many instances sharing space with relatives. The difficulty of the situation was amplified for blacks. Confined to small sections of the city, the northern black communities had grown massively during the war, because many blacks had moved up from the South to get war-time industrial jobs.

Subsequently, as the suburban housing boom got under way and white families began to move to the suburbs, the ghetto was allowed to expand on a block-by-block basis, since blacks hungry for space were willing to pay almost anything or to put up with almost any conditions in order to improve their residential position. This often meant that they moved into formerly spacious apartments broken up by landlords who saw that, if they were to make profits from relatively low-income blacks, they had to create additional units in the same amount of space. Whites were often willing to sell their houses and other buildings for low prices because they feared the neighborhood was changing and, in the classic mode of the self-fulfilling prophecy, property values went down. As a result, much money was to be made by buying houses at low prices from whites and selling them for high prices to blacks. Some real estate companies were willing to pay good prices for multiple-family dwellings as well because they saw the opportunity for a good return on investments by subdividing and undermaintaining. Subsequently, subsidized low-downpayment FHA mortgages made it possible for fleeing whites to leave single-family-home areas easily, often selling their houses to low-income blacks who could not afford them. Because these mortgages were FHA guaranteed, banks and mortgage companies had little incentive to screen mortgage applicants.

The entire process could be understood by the classic theories of urban change, although it took place in a somewhat heated-up form. Whites were moving out to the periphery of the city, which now meant the suburbs, and their houses were "filtering down" to lower-income groups, many of whom made more intensive use of the property. This process of succession was so dramatic and visible that it became the way people understood change in the city—blacks hungry for space spreading out, and unscrupulous real estate interests exploiting both them and the whites who moved away.)

What is important to bear in mind, then, is that the events of that period are in part a consequence of pent-up demand for housing and that theories of racial change developed during that time reflect this fact. One important illustration is the concept of "piling up" found in the older theories of succession. Piling up was possible, indeed necessary, because housing was in such short supply, which made subdivision of rooming housing and other subleasing arrangements profitable (Duncan and Duncan 1957).

Since that time, however, conditions have changed. And it is the change from a very tight housing supply to a much looser one that has led to lower urban densities, and in particular to housing abandonment. Suburban construction was so successful that that trend—coupled with the population shifts to the South, West, and nonurban areas, the decreases in fresh migration to the cities, and the growth of public housing for the very poor—took the pressure off the housing market. Under these circumstances, congestion and undermaintenance have become less profitable to those involved in urban real estate. It became more difficult to make money by crowding blacks into undermaintained buildings. Also, many of the buildings were so deteriorated that renovation would not pay an acceptable rate of return at the rents poorer blacks could afford (Stegman 1972). With many of the poorest blacks in public housing, others could choose among the growing range of housing that white middle- and working-class residents had left behind. The simultaneous failure of central business districts to expand as they lost out to suburban shopping centers, the departure of light industry, and the decline of pressure on the housing market led to the hollow core we have already discussed. It also took some of the profit out of encouraging racial change.

Changing Class Distributions of American Blacks

The period under consideration also saw the growth of a substantial black middle class. The growth of the economy, particularly the corporate and governmental sectors, combined with various forms of equal-employment legislation, made it increasingly possible for well-educated blacks to enter the mainstream American economic world (Wilson 1979; Farley 1979). The numbers tell the story. Only 16.4 percent of black males were employed in middle-class occupations in 1950. By 1970, that figure was just under 30 percent (Wilson 1979). In 1960, only 15 percent of the black population had family incomes above the median for whites; this figure now is over 25 percent (Taylor 1982). For blacks who have achieved middle-class levels of education, large numbers of mainstream middle-class occupations are available. These changes have given blacks economic power to buy into more expensive housing and political power to maintain pressure against discriminatory activity in housing. Higher levels of education also have helped to make blacks less culturally distinct from their white neighbors than they once were.

Changes in Attitudes of Whites toward Minorities

Repeated waves of survey research since the 1940s have documented a long-range, steady decline in white prejudice toward blacks (Hyman and Sheatsley 1964; Taylor, Sheatsley, and Greeley 1978). In addition, growing numbers of white Americans, particularly in the educated middle-class, report that they are willing to live in neighborhoods in which black families are present (Farley et al. 1978). Thus, under appropriate conditions, the social forces that used to keep blacks and whites separate have become somewhat attenuated.

Working-class whites, however, are still more often likely to feel threatened by the arrival of blacks than are middle-class whites (Taylor 1979). Because working-class homeowners are closer to the economic edge, a weakening of property values is particularly threatening, and property values do weaken with the threat of racial change in our Chicago communities. Since, by definition, housing prices are lower in working-class neighborhoods than they are in middle-class ones, the housing is within the reach of a large proportion of the black population, making the arrival of large numbers of blacks probable in a generally weak housing market. And thirdly, in the working-class community there is a weaker underpinning for the general-tolerance values we have already discussed. Among our survey respondents, more working-class whites (and working-class blacks) than middle-class whites believe that black entry into a community brings higher crime rates and lower property values. Compared with some middle-class experiences, this is probably true.

What is important to understand, then, as a first step in the modification of a theory of invasion and succession, is that the class position of both the white resident population and the arriving blacks does make a difference in how the process works. Middle-class whites are somewhat more likely to accept middle-class black neighbors than are working-class whites to accept black neighbors of their own class.

We have now discussed three changes that necessitate revision of the original theories of succession. The first is in the nature of the housing market. The second is the rise of the black middle class. The third is increased levels of tolerance, particularly by the better-educated white public. A fourth component is the increased sophistication of institutions that choose to intervene in communities in which racial change is a prospect.

Sophisticated Community Interventions

Large-scale institutions, tied to communities by large investments in those communities, are showing increasing levels of success at managing integration. Earlier efforts may have failed because the important changes we have just described had not yet come about (for example, see Molotch 1972; Goodwin 1979). In addition, skills have improved for dealing with some of the problems associated with initial entry. Paid staff members of community organizations supported by these institutions are able to discourage blockbusting and allied activities; manipulate the real estate market by making crucial investments; deploy urban renewal and similar government programs; focus public concerns on improved education; deal visibly with crime issues; and promote integration as a valued social goal (for example, see Goodwin 1979; Greeley 1977), all in the service of promoting integration or halting the process of racial change.

For this effort to work, sufficient resources must be available to provide for full-time paid staff, because the effort is a full-time one. The capacity to relate to those in power, both in order to make use of such special federal programs as urban renewal and to see that city services continue to be adequate, is also essential.

In short, where conditions are appropriate in ways that we shall define later, institutional application of sophisticated skills can enter the process and help to alter what seemed to be a predetermined set of outcomes.

Gentrification

These emendations in the theory of racial change can be seen working themselves out in a large number of empirical contexts. Perhaps the most dramatic of these is the process of "gentrification." One of those unfortunate misnomers that have stuck, gentrification is the process by which older neighborhoods near the city's core are discovered and renovated by young professionals (usually with small families), and ultimately become substantially upgraded, attractive areas for the young professional middle class.

Although the model of succession has been used primarily to describe neighborhood declines of one sort or another, the general theory applies to gentrification as well. The penetrators, known as urban pioneers, are often singles or individuals living together who are in some way connected with the arts. In another period, they would have been called "bohemians." With little money, flexible time, and taste, they identify deteriorated, but attractive, older housing that seems to be moving into the cycle of abandonment. They begin to renovate. As the pine trees dropping their needles make the soil more attractive to new pine trees, the urban pioneers begin to make the area more attractive, dropping boutiques, new-style bars, and other gathering places along the way. Word gets out that this is a coming area where housing bargains are to be found. Full-scale invasion begins. Young professionals who are interested in decent housing at low prices and who are willing to undertake the burden of renovation become involved. Speculative investors and developers also begin to enter the area. During the period of consolidation, the area gets a reputation for being "hot." Residents and large institutional actors form neighborhood organizations to promote the area and to create conditions attractive to the middle class. They begin to work on the schools, the quality of city services, and the local police. Simultaneously, they attack "undesirable" uses that appeal to "elements" who detract from the neighborhood. Parks that are meeting places for drug addicts or homosexuals, "game rooms," buildings that lag in the renovation process as landlords rent to prostitutes and other "disreputables"—all are placed on the reform agenda.

In this process, we see in sharp relief the changes we have discussed.[1] The housing is initially cheap because it is located near the declining urban core. The price advantage is particularly helpful to lower-income members of the middle class—young professionals and those in the arts—who find owning homes in the suburbs often out of reach, both directly because of housing costs and indirectly because of transportation expenses. The more general issues of tolerance we have discussed are relevant here as well. The invaders often move into minority residential neighborhoods. A successful gentrification effort, it is true, will drive poor minority residents out of the area. Nonetheless, the initial decisions to move into such locations are made possible by generally declining prejudice. The fact of the rising black middle class is also relevant, since gentrifying groups, as we shall see, are often integrated.

Young black professionals face the same set of housing problems as their white counterparts. Their problems are often exacerbated by the uncertain welcome they might receive in all-white suburban areas. (Significantly, blacks use the word "pioneer" to refer to being the first black in the neighborhood.) Consequently, gentrifying neighborhoods, particularly after they acquire the reputation of being desirable, have special attraction for blacks. The broader white tolerance that focuses on class instead of race makes the whole effort more harmonious, although, as we shall see, some tensions are generated when the poor residents of such an area are also black.

Two final points about the gentrification process should be made. First, institutional actors often are able to deploy resources with skill in such settings. Second, the growth of the service sector provides both the troops and the necessary levels of income to make gentrification possible.[2]

The Role of Individual Decisions

Although our discussion so far makes change sound like the impact of a tidal wave washing over a beach, change is in fact the consequence of large numbers of individual decisions. Individuals must decide, one by one, whether to stay in the community or to move away; whether to spend money maintaining their buildings or to let them slide; whether to join community organizations to help protect the neighborhood from blight or to withdraw, cutting themselves off from their neighbors and, perhaps, barricading themselves behind locked doors.

The forces that help shape such decisions are both economic and social. Inadequate demand in a rental market, for example, may lead to lack of maintenance and related deterioration when landlords perceive the future of the neighborhood to be degeneration. This perception feeds upon itself. Conversely, if landlords perceive that their neighborhood has a future, they respond with reinvestment to improve their properties and with other aggressive market behaviors to attract new tenants.

Inadequate demand (or excessive supply) in single-family-housing markets leads to rentals rather than purchases, the breakup of houses into rooming houses, purchases on contract, and the growth of FHA financing with its attendant problems. It should be added that demand is not always determined by the concerned actors in particular localized settings. There may be others, such as mortgage lenders or insurance companies, who, through their control of resources, can reduce the flow of capital to a community. Such a reduction in capital may also reduce demand.

Research that focuses on the role of demand in the maintenance both of property values and of property itself will inevitably focus more heavily on white behavior than on black. At the macro level, it is the fact of white flight (or white avoidance) that has softened urban housing markets, increasing the supply of such housing and reducing, almost by definition, the pressure of demand. Market demand requires that there be enough people with enough money who want to live in a place to keep the price of property up. Where property prices are not maintained, the forces that lead to deterioration are set into play. The long history of discrimination against blacks means that in most cities, their incomes, on average, are substantially lower than those of whites; hence, there are not enough blacks with enough resources to keep prices up along a broad front.[3] The shortage of blacks with adequate resources in cities is heightened by the fact that many of those with middle-class incomes have followed their white counterparts to the suburbs.

To gain insight into the decision-making process of individuals, we focus on a type of social theory that might in shorthand form be called the theory of individual rationality and public choice (Olson 1965; Riker and Ordeshook 1973; Schelling 1978). One core idea of this theoretical approach is that individual decisions, based on the calculation of short-term self-interest, can produce collective outcomes that are actually worse for everybody than one might expect or, at the very least, collective outcomes that are surprising when looked at from the perspective of the individual actor. Book titles such as *Rational Man and Irrational Society?* (Barry and Hardin 1982) and *Micromotives and Macrobehavior* (Schelling 1978) communicate the problems explored in such analyses.

Let us turn to one example in order to illustrate some attributes of the general class. We can do so, borrowing an example from Pareto (quoted in Barry and Hardin 1982, 19), and adapting it to the current problem.

> Suppose that if *all* individuals refrained from doing A [selling their houses in the face of racial change], every individual as a member of the community would derive a certain advantage [would maintain property values by keeping the market tight; would forestall change]. But now if all individuals *less one* continue refraining from doing A [selling their houses], the community loss is very slight, whereas the one individual doing A makes a personal gain far greater than the loss he incurs as a member of the community.

What happens, however, in this far-from-hypothetical state of affairs, is that each individual hopes to gain the maximum by being the one seller before the bottom drops out of the market. Ultimately, almost everybody loses as that which was feared becomes the most likely outcome.

One theory of individual behavior and collective irrationality that we examine is Schelling's (1978) model of racial change. He argues that even when one assumes whites to be generally tolerant toward living on the same block with blacks, the dynamics of racial sorting lead, through an iterative or recursive process, almost inevitably to neighborhood tipping. The model produces a surprising result, because the process purports to take place even where there are large numbers of very tolerant whites.

A second theory of individual rationality and collective choice that we examine is Granovetter's (1978) theory of threshold effects. We use this theory as a way of understanding when people decide to invest in household maintenance or rehabilitation. In this instance, individuals are assumed to base their decisions about whether or not to invest partly on the number of individuals around them who are making the same decisions. The aggregate outcome—the overall level of neighborhood investment—depends on how well informed people are and how confident they are about the intentions of their neighbors.

Neighborhood rehabilitation is thus a self-reinforcing cycle. Within this cycle, individuals have different thresholds for determining when the level of neighborhood investment is high enough to make it worthwhile for them to invest in their own property. Urban pioneers, for example, have low thresholds—they do not require a high level of neighborhood investment to justify making investments themselves; rather, they make the decision to invest independently of the actions of others. By contrast, elderly retired people living on fixed incomes may have thresholds so high that nothing can make them invest because "one cannot get blood from a stone." Most people have thresholds that are somewhere in between. How reinvestment gathers momentum in some areas and not in others becomes, then, a problem in the nature of the distribution of thresholds and in the availability of extra market supports, as more individuals decide to invest.

These mathemetically elegant models derive their force from the fact that they are abstracted from context. At their best, their purity helps us to understand complex reality by removing the problem under consideration from all the confusing background noise. When we use these models as tools for clarifying the process of urban change, we find that individuals act within a context that is considerably more complex. They live in neighborhoods where extra social forces operate, forces that can alter individual propensities or attract individuals with particular propensities. Attitudes toward racial differences, for example, are not distributed the same way everywhere, nor are propensities to invest. Contextual forces intercede, influencing both the distributions and the scales of costs and benefits which individuals use to make their decisions.

Let us give some examples of how contextual factors may modify the outcomes presumed in the models discussed above. We will begin with the quotation from Pareto, which can be understood as one version of the prisoner's dilemma. One reason many people may simultaneously want to sell their houses is that each fears that selling after others have sold will lead to severe personal economic reversals. But what if one introduces another actor—a university, a hospital, a commercial enterprise, perhaps a governmental agency—who will find it difficult to desert the area? Since it is not easy for this institutional actor to run, it will enter the real estate market and perhaps also attempt to influence government to ensure that the bottom does not drop out of the market. In this situation, the cost to the individual of not being one of the first to sell is reduced. Consequently, if other considerations also support the decision to stay, he or she is more likely to abide by them. Because many actors make this same decision, the market becomes stabilized, even though the large institutional actor itself could not in fact buy up enough property to achieve this end. Instead, its actions reinforce the moderate commitment of residents to their neighborhoods by reducing the potential costs of staying. Janowitz (1952) made the important point that most individuals have limited commitments to their neighborhoods. The question in producing healthy neighborhoods is how to bolster that commitment. The role of institutional actors can become important in this regard.

Similarly, when we turn to the Schelling model, we may discover that institutional actors are, in some situations, able to keep housing prices high enough so that lower-income blacks are not able to satisfy their desire to move into an integrated neighborhood. The institutional actor keeps up the property values partly by entering the real estate market, as we have already discussed, but also partly by selling the virtues of racial integration. This may mean that racial attitudes will play a role in the housing market different from that postulated by Schelling. This, in turn, undercuts the inevitable set of recursive forces that Schelling hypothesizes will be set into motion.

Corresponding forces may work in the "threshold" model. Not only do individuals differ in the predisposition to invest in their housing, but manipulation of the market may result in higher rates of return for investment. This has the effect of reducing everybody's threshhold—that is, the level at which they will be induced to invest.

The discussions are simple and schematic, but they provide the reader with some basic understanding of the interplay, not only between individuals per se, but also between them and the structural settings within which they act. It remains for us to show in detail how the forces in these settings operate. The goal in subsequent pages will be to show how these contextual forces work to produce the altered outcomes which we have suggested above are possible.

Crime

We have now come full circle, returning to the issue with which we started this chapter—crime. We noted at the beginning that crime and neighborhood deterioration are not related in a simple, straightforward manner. In fact, a perplexing problem for students of the impact of crime on urban communities is that, despite widespread concern about crime and the intense emotional heat that discussions of it generate, crime per se appears to have little effect on how cities grow and develop. Survey after survey indicates that people perceive crime as one of our most pressing social problems. Nonetheless, although a substantial proportion of the population alters its behavior because it fears crime—people install new locks, avoid walking at night, stay off public transportation, and the like—enduring collective responses to crime are difficult to discover when one attempts systematically to find them) Bradbury, Downs, and Small (1982), for example, have attempted to measure the impact of crime rates on urban growth and decline and have discovered that no measurable relationship exists on the national level. Jacob (1982) reports that it is difficult to relate increases in crime rates either to increased budgetary commitments to police forces or to increased policing activities. Other students have reported that community organizations that organize around crime-related issues have little chance of longevity unless they are linked to other goals and activities as well (DuBow and Podolefsky 1980). No scholar has been able to relate any sizable number of decisions to move away from a community to variations in the crime rate, although Skogan (1981) did find that those who themselves have been victims of crime are more likely to move than those who have not been. Finally, there is a large body of literature that shows fear of crime does not always track very closely either crime rates or the probability of becoming a victim (Lewis and Maxfield 1978; Skogan and Maxfield 1981).

These seemingly inconsistent findings become somewhat less so when we take into account the situational nature of both the perceived importance of crime and the fear of it. Although crime and fear of crime are in some sense endemic to urban communities, both their levels and their impacts vary substantially from neighborhood to neighborhood. We will see, for example, that gentrification and dramatic economic development take place in neighborhoods with very high rates of crime. Stable, successful communities may also have high crime rates. To be sure, in those settings, collective efforts are made to deal with crime; we shall see consistent patterns of intervention in our communities under consideration. Nevertheless, crime is not a deterrent to long-term community commitments, great community pride, and a willingness to make investments in the community's housing.

In other cases, crime seems to matter very much. People report a great deal of fear, and they demonstrate weakened commitment to their neighborhoods. What we shall show is that crime rates function as symptoms and symbols of the general decline of a neighborhood when residents have other reasons to fear that the area has begun to skid. Many of these fears are linked to the issue of racial change.

People who perceive that their neighborhood is threatened by racial change are more anxious about crime than are those who do not share those perceptions. Similarly, middle-class people in minority neighborhoods who perceive that they are threatened with social-class change of the sort we discussed earlier are more anxious about crime than are those who do not see the threat. In such settings, cues other than crime become part and parcel of the same package. The presence of a vacant lot, an abandoned house, large pieces of uncollected litter—all are linked to fear of crime, dissatisfaction with neighborhood amenities, and a decline in commitment to the neighborhood. In other words, once individuals decide that their neighborhood has begun to decline, they become more generally helpless and more generally fearful, and they select the evidence around them that reinforces this view. For individuals who view their neighborhood as improving—property values going up, housing renovation taking place on their block—crime rates, problems of litter, and the like are items either to be shrugged off or to be attacked through collective community action. Once the collective commitment has been made and is supported by substantial resources (often provided by institutional actors), individuals are prepared to put the crime problem behind them.

The remainder of this volume is largely an elaboration of the views put forth here. It is the report of a study of eight Chicago neighborhoods that vary in crime rates, in racial stability, and in economic appreciation. Through surveys in the neighborhoods, analysis of historical documents, field research, and systematic observation of the physical attributes of the neighborhoods, we developed our current understandings of the ways in which neighborhoods rise and fall. It is to this study that we now turn.

In chapter 2, we describe the study in more detail. We explain the selection of the neighborhoods and discuss some of the methodological issues we faced in conducting the study. We conclude the chapter with a comparative overview of the eight neighborhoods.

Chapters 3, 4, and 5 are devoted to descriptions of our communities. These are provided not only to present a backdrop for subsequent data analysis, but also to explain the contexts that help shape individual perceptions and understandings. We have divided the communities into three distinct groups. The first group (chapter 3) includes communities that in many ways typify the classical succession model of ecological theory, although each neighborhood represents a different stage in the process. The second set (chapter 4) includes predominantly working-class and lower-middle-class communities that are still virtually all white. These are areas that have avoided even the early stages of penetration. The final group (chapter 5) includes middle-class communities that are at variance with classical predictions in that they appear to be stably integrated.

Having laid out the relevant historical background and the current structure of these communities, we turn to the analysis of individual attitudes and behaviors. It is here that we begin to test our models of commitment to maintenance and renovation (chapter 6), of racial attitudes and neighborhood tipping (chapter 7), and of the ways in which crime and perceptions of it shape feelings toward one's community (chapter 8).

In the final chapter, we present a revised theoretical framework for considering urban-neighborhood change. We conclude that chapter with policy recommendations for positive intervention in the neighborhood-change process.

2
The Integration
of Multiple Methods

We turn now from the rather abstract theoretical issues raised in chapter 1 to a concrete discussion of the Chicago study. The city of Chicago has always been one of the most important laboratories for studies of urban America. Scores of neighborhood studies from the Chicago school of sociology (Faris 1970) and many years of neighborhood social-indicator reports from the *Local Community Fact Books* (e.g., Kitagawa and Taeuber 1963) give us a well-documented vantage point for reexamining the past and raising new questions about the future of urban neighborhoods, both in Chicago and in other American cities.

In the first section of this chapter, we discuss the design for the Chicago study, including the selection of the study communities. The second section is devoted to a description of the types of data we collected. This book is based primarily, but not exclusively, on data from the Chicago study; we will also briefly mention some of the other sources of survey and nonsurvey data that contribute to the conclusions reported in later chapters. Finally, as a precursor to the neighborhood chapters which follow, we present some basic results from the Chicago data in order to give the reader a general picture of each area.

Design of the Chicago Study

The Chicago Neighborhood Study is a sample of neighborhoods and a sample of individuals within neighborhoods. Each sample was chosen to allow us to study most advantageously the issues central to our concerns—the relationships among crime, racial change, and neighborhood economic trends. The sample of neighborhoods was designed to allow comparisons between areas with high versus low crime rates, changing versus nonchanging racial composition, and appreciating versus stagnat-

stagnating housing markets. Within each neighborhood, the survey data allow us to study how individuals' perceptions and experiences accumulate to produce the aggregate patterns of urban change that are the core subject matter of this book.

Selection of Neighborhoods

Neighborhood crime rates, market rates of appreciation in housing values, and rates of racial change are the aggregate-level, contextual factors that form the basis of our study design. The goal was to select a sample of neighborhoods representing, as nearly as possible, a "balanced" or "crossed" research design with respect to these three variables.

We did not know beforehand the exact score for each of the seventy-five community areas in Chicago (see Hunter 1974) for the three variables used in the sample design. On the basis of previous research in Chicago (including a similar study conducted by the Reactions to Crime Project at Northwestern University; see Skogan and Maxfield 1981), conversations with a number of expert informants, three secondary data sources, and our own "windshield surveys" of the city, we selected eight neighborhoods for study. Table 2.1 gives the names of the eight neighborhoods and shows how we expected them to fit into the balanced research design, based on the three aggregate-level contextual variables.

After choosing the neighborhoods, the next step was to make sure of the categorization shown in table 2.1. We compiled information about crime and victimization rates, property-value appreciation, and racial change for each area. With these data, we found that the study design actually achieved using these eight neighborhoods was not as perfectly balanced as we had hoped, but the results were very close.

Crime rates. The initial classification of communities as high crime or low crime was based on whether the community's index-crime rate for 1978 was above or below the city-wide average of sixty-five crimes per thousand population. Table 2.2 shows the index rates and the personal, property, and total (including nonindex offenses) rates for the eight communities. These rates are based on block-level, verified crime reports obtained from the Chicago police department. These reports, in conjunction with 1978 census-tract population estimates, enabled us to calculate crime rates for each community.[1]

When the sample survey data became available, we were able to construct a separate, independent estimate of the ranking of neighborhood crime rates. The battery of questions used to estimate household victimization levels is described later in this chapter.

We expected that the survey estimates of household victimization rates would differ from the estimates in table 2.2. The survey estimates

Table 2.1 Eight Chicago Communities Selected for Study

	Racial Stability			
	Stable		New Black Residents	
Property Values	High Crime Rates	Low Crime Rates	High Crime Rates	Low Crime Rates
Rapidly appreciating	Hyde Park–Kenwood	Portage Park	Lincoln Park	Beverly
Slowly appreciating	South Shore	East Side	Austin	Back of the Yards

Table 2.2 1978 Index Crime Rates by Community[a]

Community	Personal Crime[b]	Property Crime[c]	Total Index Crime[d]	Total Crime[e]
Low Crime				
1. East Side	1.94	26.22	28.16	69.03
2. Beverly	2.30	28.52	30.82	53.89
3. Portage Park	1.63	33.35	34.98	64.14
4. Back of the Yards	9.13	46.25	55.38	102.45
High Crime				
5. Lincoln Park	7.55	70.54	78.09	119.90
6. Austin	15.99	67.42	83.41	132.89
7. South Shore	17.42	80.48	97.90	161.39
8. Hyde Park–Kenwood	13.45	93.25	106.70	160.88

[a]Rates are per 1,000 population.
[b]Includes homicide, rape, assault, and robbery.
[c]Includes burglary, index theft, and auto theft.
[d]Includes personal and property crime.
[e]Includes index and nonindex crime.

are based on somewhat different definitions of victimization. In addition, it is frequently observed that sample surveys uncover a great deal of victimization that is "hidden" from official police-reporting systems (Sparks, Genn, and Dodd 1977).

The neighborhood estimates of household victimization rates based on the survey data are shown in table 2.3. The ranking of neighborhoods using the survey victimization data is consistent with the ranking in table 2.2 in all important respects except one. The survey results show that Back of the Yards should be classified as a high-crime area rather than a low-crime area. The Northwestern University Reactions to Crime Project found Back of the Yards to be a low-crime community. The neighborhood boundaries used in that study were more restrictive than our own, however, which may explain the difference in findings.

Many of our survey indicators of neighborhood quality and neighborhood satisfaction show that Back of the Yards resembles the high-crime neighborhoods more than it does the low-crime areas. Some of our white informants, however, do not regard the community this way. As we will discuss in chapter 3, many of the area's ethnic whites still cling to the older view of the community.

Hyde Park–Kenwood also changes its rank in victimization statistics. This neighborhood is at the high end when police-reported crime rates are used, but survey-based estimates place it in the middle. Hyde Park–Kenwood is a community well mobilized against crime. Police reporting of any sort of crime may be extremely efficient in Hyde Park–Kenwood, compared to other neighborhoods; thus, the extent of "hidden" crime

Table 2.3 Household Victimizations[a] (per 1,000 respondents by community)

Community	Personal Victimization	Property Victimization	All Victimization[b]
1. Beverly	53.98	160.71	258.97
2. Portage Park	40.82	183.67	270.41
3. East Side	39.41	198.53	289.60
4. Hyde Park–Kenwood	92.23	230.58	402.91
5. Back of the Yards	110.57	235.87	406.40
6. Lincoln Park	72.94	253.52	424.17
7. Austin	143.96	246.79	437.02
8. South Shore	94.69	243.12	451.39

[a]These figures are for a period of more than one year (15 to 18 months), whereas the figures in table 2.2 are annual crime rates. In addition, these figures represent whether or not a household experienced any type of victimization, rather than the actual number of victimizations, divided by population size.
[b]Includes personal victimization, property victimization, or vandalism.

uncovered with the sample survey may be comparatively low here. In spite of its middle ranking in table 2.3, we maintain our classification of Hyde Park–Kenwood as a high-crime area. The police-reported crime rates are among the highest for the eight communities, and the survey-based victimization rates are substantially higher than in the unambiguously low-crime neighborhoods.

Property values. As our data collection became more complete, we also found a need for revision in the property-value-appreciation rankings. To ascertain levels of property-value appreciation, we used the *Realty Sales Guide*, a listing of a nonsystematic sample of property sales throughout the city. We recorded sales of all structures for the years 1973 through 1978 and determined the type of structure by means of Sanborn maps and visits to the sale sites.

We and other scholars (see Molotch 1972) have tried to determine the merits of various sources of property-value information. Our findings all more or less agree that, despite the fact that the number of sales is seriously underestimated in the *Realty Sales Guide*, there does not seem to be any systematic bias concerning what is included or dropped. In addition, we have discussed our rates with knowledgeable observers and have compared asking prices as they appear in newspapers.

When we selected the neighborhoods for study, we had listings available for only the first six months of 1978. On the basis of these data, we ranked the neighborhoods as shown in table 2.1. When the complete listings for 1978 became available, there was an unanticipated change in the rankings. Table 2.4 shows the estimated rates of appreciation for each of the eight neighborhoods, listing them in rank order.[2] South Shore, initially classified as slowly appreciating, and Portage Park, initially clas-

Table 2.4 Median Sale Price of Detached Single-family Homes (number of sales in parentheses)

Community	1973	1978	Percent of Increase
1. Lincoln Park	$23,000 (37)	$107,250 (36)	366
2. Hyde Park–Kenwood	$42,250 (18)	$95,000 (22)	124
3. Beverly	$27,000 (207)	$57,500 (111)	113
4. South Shore	$22,900 (129)	$45,000 (29)	96
5. Portage Park	$33,000 (249)	$64,500 (61)	95
6. East Side	$25,000 (142)	$41,000 (24)	64
7. Austin	$20,000 (236)	$31,000 (47)	55
8. Back of the Yards	$17,000 (91)	$20,250 (22)	19

sified as rapidly appreciating, in fact show virtually identical rates over the five-year period.

We note, however, that housing prices in Portage Park start at a higher level than those in two of our other three high-appreciation neighborhoods. Portage Park's basic housing stock is the small bungalow, which, when set against the grander housing of Beverly and the more diverse stock of Lincoln Park, pales indeed. Because both Beverly and Lincoln Park had depressed housing prices in the late 1960s, they have had to travel farther in order to represent something more nearly approximating the true value of the housing. It may also be true, although we suggest this with diffidence, that, given both housing size and quality and other external amenities on the one hand, and the social class of the residents who live in each place on the other, higher price ceilings are possible in those two neighborhoods than is the case in Portage Park.

Racial change. Our initial estimates of neighborhood racial change were based on a report by the Chicago Urban League entitled *Where Blacks Live* (1978). This report identified areas where blacks lived in 1970 and where they lived in 1977. On that basis, we were able to distinguish communities where change had taken place. The survey data confirmed the findings from the Urban League report. There was no need to revise the ranking of neighborhoods on this variable.

These changes in the rank orderings of the neighborhoods on crime rates and property-value appreciation have implications for the overall research design. We no longer have the tidily balanced sample envisaged in table 2.1. Changes in the neighborhoods between the time we designed the study and the time of data collection produced a research design that is more like the one shown in table 2.5. The design is not completely balanced, and there are a few empty cells. However, the overall pattern does not severely limit our ability to study the behavior and attitudes of

Table 2.5 Eight Chicago Communities Selected for Study—Modified Design

Property Values	Stable		New Black Residents	
	High Crime Rates	Low Crime Rates	High Crime Rates	Low Crime Rates
Rapidly appreciating	Hyde Park–Kenwood		Lincoln Park	Beverly
Moderately appreciating	South Shore	Portage Park		
Slowly appreciating		East Side	Austin Back of the Yards	

urban residents as a function of systematic variations in neighborhood contextual circumstances.

Types of Data Collected

Three types of data are analyzed in this book. The first is survey data from a sample survey of each of the eight Chicago neighborhoods. Second is supplementary data from the Chicago study, obtained from rating check-lists, archival materials, and participant observation. Finally, we occasionally make use of survey data from other cities to replicate and in some cases extend the generality of the findings based on the Chicago data.

The Chicago Survey Data

The National Opinion Research Center conducted a telephone survey of approximately four hundred respondents in each of the eight neighborhoods. Further details about the sample and a brief discussion of the random-digit-dialing methodology are given in appendix A.

A copy of the survey used appears below as appendix B. The instrument was designed to measure victimization experience, fear of crime, attitudes toward the quality of life in the neighborhood, attitudes toward the neighborhood as an investment, and one's extent of community involvement.

Victimization was measured with a series of questions based on previous studies by Sparks, Genn, and Dodd (1977) and analyses of questionnaire quality by the National Research Council (1976).

In addition to measures of experience with crime, the survey included a number of items to tap fear of, concern about, and reactions to crime. Because fear of crime is not necessarily a direct function of actual crime levels, it is necessary to assess these factors independently of both the community-level crime rate and individual experience with crime. Our questions measured respondents' assessments of both the amount of crime in their neighborhood and the likelihood of experiencing victimization themselves, the protective behaviors they have undertaken to avoid crime, and their perceptions of what has come to be called "incivility." Similar survey questions are analyzed in studies by Garofalo and Laub (1978), Lewis and Maxfield (1978), Stinchcombe et al. (1980), and McIntyre (1967).

The relevance of racial issues is measured several ways. The Urban League report described earlier gave us one estimate of neighborhood racial patterns. In the survey, we asked respondents whether they considered their neighborhood to be racially stable or changing. Earlier analyses of this question are reported by Pettigrew (1973) and Taylor (1979). We also asked a series of questions about the perceived effects of a few black families moving into a white neighborhood. Questions similar to these appear in several survey studies of racial prejudice (Treiman 1966; Taylor, Sheatsley, and Greeley 1978).

Attitudes toward neighborhood quality, neighborhood resources, and toward the neighborhood as an investment take up a large proportion of the survey instrument. We asked respondents how satisfied they were with the neighborhood as a whole and with a number of specific features of neighborhood life.[3] In addition, those respondents who had moved into the neighborhood within the five years preceding the survey were asked how important each of the specific factors was in their decision to move into the neighborhood. We also inquired whether each of a series of items, ranging from barking dogs to abandoned buildings, was a big problem, somewhat of a problem, or not a problem in the neighborhood. Finally, we asked respondents for an overall evaluation of the neighborhood's recent past and near future.

Although several of the specific satisfaction items ask about the investment potential of the neighborhood, one in particular—the way property values are going—is more directly economic in nature. Besides this item, we asked respondents whether a hypothetical family would be making a good financial investment if they bought a house in the respondent's neighborhood or would be better off investing elsewhere.

The last major topic of concern in our study is community involvement. Not only did we expect community participation to be related to neighborhood satisfaction (Hunter 1974; Kasarda and Janowitz 1974), but also to fear of and concern about crime and to investment decisions. Questions on this topic tapped the extent of use of local facilities and the frequency of social interaction. In addition, respondents were asked about organizational memberships.

Supplementary Data from Chicago Neighborhoods

One of the innovative aspects of our study is the use of neighborhood ratings, participant observation, and archival data to supplement the respondent survey records.

The block-level police reports described earlier were used to compute neighborhood crime rates. Because of the way these data are organized, we were also able to use these reports, along with census data, to compute police-reported crime rates for the census tract of each survey respondent.

Data on the quality and upkeep of commercial areas and residential blocks were collected by raters from our research team. The shopping-strip-quality rating instrument (see appendix C) was used to collect data about stores on more than one hundred miles of shopping strips in the eight neighborhoods. With these data, we are able to analyze the characteristics of the shopping strips closest to each respondent's home as well as the general character of the shopping strips in each neighborhood.

The housing-and-neighborhood-appearance rating instrument[4] (see appendix C) was used to rate the appearance of over seven hundred residential blocks—25 percent of the blocks in each neighborhood on which survey respondents resided. To assure proper geographical coverage, blocks were randomly selected within each census tract. With these data, we have measures of the block level of deterioration for 25 percent of the survey respondents as well as measures of levels of deterioration within census tracts and for neighborhoods more generally.

In addition to neighborhood ratings, shopping-strip ratings, and archival data, we utilized a wealth of other information over the course of the study. As participant observers, we traveled around the communities; interviewed local newspaper editors, community-organization leaders, and business proprietors; and chatted with other knowledgeable informants. We attended community events ranging from open-house tours to block-club meetings. Finally, we made use of various historical materials.

Supplementary Survey Data Sets

In two chapters of this book, we use data from other cities to lend force to our arguments. Some of the questions used in the Chicago survey were also used in survey studies of Detroit (Farley et al. 1978) and Omaha (Taylor 1981a). We will occasionally find it advantageous to present data from these surveys to replicate and, in some cases, extend the conclusions we draw from the Chicago neighborhood data.

Several months after completing the field work for the Chicago survey, we had the opportunity to design a study of community needs for the city of Waukegan, Illinois (Taylor 1981b). Several of the questions in the Chicago questionnaire are replicated in the Waukegan survey. Again, we occasionally find it advantageous to compare the results of these two surveys and to follow up certain analytic issues, using questions that were designed for this purpose in the Waukegan survey.

Neighborhood Statistical Profiles

We conclude this chapter with a series of tables showing key demographic and social characteristics of the population in each neighborhood. In the chapters that follow, we identify three patterns of neighborhood ecological development. The remainder of this chapter is a description of the statistical profiles for these three groups of neighborhoods.

Neighborhoods Experiencing Ecological Succession

Back of the Yards, Austin, and South Shore are neighborhoods that represent various stages in the "classical" pattern of ecological succession as described by Duncan and Duncan (1957) as well as by others writing in the tradition of the Chicago school of sociology.

Back of the Yards is the neighborhood of the famous Union Stockyards, the neighborhood that Upton Sinclair had in mind when he wrote *The Jungle* and that Carl Sandburg thought of when he sang of the "hog butcher for the world." Getting its start as a home for low-wage immigrant workers, its housing stock consists of simple frame houses and frame double-deckers crammed together on small lots. Although Back of the Yards has a smaller proportion of single-family dwellings than several of the other communities, 44 percent of the respondents live in one (table 2.6). In addition, because most of the multi-unit buildings are small, the overall housing density is low, even though nearly 60 percent of the respondents are renters (table 2.7).

Back of the Yards ranks low on socioeconomic characteristics: among the eight communities, it has the highest proportion of blue-collar workers (table 2.8) and of persons having less than a high-school education (table 2.9). Only Austin has comparably low income levels (table 2.10).

Back of the Yards is racially the most heterogeneous of the community areas, with Hispanics and blacks constituting 26 and 19 percent, respectively, of the population (table 2.11). People of Polish descent comprise the major ethnic group among the white residents, with approximately one-third reporting that heritage (table 2.12). The area is still

Table 2.6 Type of Dwelling Unit (percentage)

Neighborhood	House	Apartment
Back of the Yards	44.3	55.7
Austin	32.2	67.8
South Shore	19.7	80.3
East Side	75.2	24.8
Portage Park	65.3	34.7
Beverly	86.8	13.2
Hyde Park–Kenwood	9.7	90.3
Lincoln Park	14.8	85.2

Table 2.7 Ownership Status (percentage)

Neighborhood	Owner	Renter
Back of the Yards	40.9	59.1
Austin	37.3	62.7
South Shore	26.5	73.5
East Side	74.8	25.2
Portage Park	66.2	33.8
Beverly	84.2	15.8
Hyde Park–Kenwood	30.3	69.7
Lincoln Park	22.2	77.8

predominantly Roman Catholic (table 2.13), although less so now than historically.

Austin is Chicago's largest community area, with a population of 125,000 people and an area of 7.2 square miles. Its housing stock is more varied than that of Back of the Yards, and it has a larger percentage of apartment dwellers (table 2.6). The proportions of renters in the two communities, however, are quite close (table 2.7).

Although its educational levels are higher (table 2.9), Austin is similar to Back of the Yards in that it is a low-income community, with the majority of respondents in blue-collar jobs (tables 2.8 and 2.10). Austin is also similar to Back of the Yards in family composition and in age (see tables 2.14 and 2.15).

Racial transition has proceeded much further in Austin than in Back of the Yards. This is reflected in the fact that 75 percent of the Austin respondents are black (table 2.11). Among the white respondents, no single ethnic background is predominant (table 2.12). As one would expect on the basis of its racial composition, Austin is heavily Protestant (table 2.13).

South Shore, located along Chicago's lakefront, is an area made up largely of apartment dwellers and renters (tables 2.6 and 2.7). Its housing is much more diverse than that of Back of the Yards or Austin; lakefront high-rises common in Hyde Park–Kenwood and Lincoln Park, large elegant houses similar to those in Beverly, brick bungalows virtually identical to those in Portage Park, small frame houses characteristic of Back of the Yards and the older sections of East Side, and two-flats like those in the southern part of Austin can all be found.

Although similar in age (table 2.15) and family composition (table 2.14) to Back of the Yards and Austin, South Shore is socioeconomically both higher and more complicated than either of them. Compared to these communities, South Shore has more respondents with white-collar positions (table 2.8), with education beyond the high-school level (table

Table 2.8 Occupations (percentage)

Neighborhood	Professional-Technical	Managers-Administrators	Clerical-Sales	Craftsmen	Operatives	Laborers	Service Workers
Back of the Yards	10.8	4.4	27.1	13.1	17.1	15.9	11.6
Austin	15.3	7.6	25.3	10.4	14.5	8.4	18.5
South Shore	21.8	10.1	29.3	8.7	9.9	3.6	16.7
East Side	12.1	9.3	28.3	15.8	10.1	9.3	15.0
Portage Park	18.1	8.1	39.1	13.7	6.5	2.4	12.1
Beverly	43.0	13.6	25.7	5.3	2.6	1.5	8.3
Hyde Park–Kenwood	51.8	12.9	18.0	1.9	2.6	1.9	10.9
Lincoln Park	43.9	21.1	19.7	4.8	3.7	1.7	5.1

Table 2.9 Educational Attainment (percentage)

Neighborhood	Less than High School	High School	More than High School
Back of the Yards	43.1	49.4	7.5
Austin	28.0	53.7	18.3
South Shore	16.9	50.8	32.3
East Side	28.6	58.7	12.6
Portage Park	22.1	56.5	21.4
Beverly	5.7	45.0	49.3
Hyde Park–Kenwood	5.1	26.2	68.7
Lincoln Park	8.0	28.2	63.8

Table 2.10 Total Family Income during 1978 (percentage)

Neighborhood	$10,000 or Less	$10,001–$20,000	$20,001–$30,000	$30,001 or More
Back of the Yards	42.5	41.2	11.9	4.3
Austin	45.1	36.5	10.6	7.8
South Shore	32.6	38.8	18.0	10.6
East Side	26.7	35.0	27.8	10.4
Portage Park	26.2	41.7	23.5	8.6
Beverly	10.6	32.4	27.4	29.5
Hyde Park–Kenwood	29.7	33.6	15.4	21.3
Lincoln Park	19.5	37.1	20.6	22.8

Table 2.11 Racial Composition (percentage)

Neighborhood	Black	White	Hispanic	Other
Back of the Yards	19.4	52.2	26.3	2.2
Austin	75.3	18.9	3.6	2.3
South Shore	90.4	6.4	1.8	1.4
East Side	1.0	91.0	7.8	.2
Portage Park	–0–	96.7	1.3	2.0
Beverly	14.6	83.7	1.0	.8
Hyde Park–Kenwood	35.1	59.0	1.0	4.9
Lincoln Park	10.0	81.2	5.1	3.7

Table 2.12 Ethnic Backgrounds of White Respondents (percentage)

Neighborhood	Polish	Lithuanian/ Slavic	Italian	Irish	German	Other/ None	Sample Size
Back of the Yards	31.8	10.6	2.8	9.7	9.2	36.0	(217)
Austin	14.1	1.4	16.9	11.3	18.3	38.0	(71)
South Shore	3.7	-0-	-0-	22.2	7.4	66.7	(27)
East Side	15.1	11.0	8.9	9.1	12.6	43.3	(372)
Portage Park	21.8	5.6	10.1	11.2	16.5	34.8	(376)
Beverly	3.7	3.3	3.0	36.0	9.8	44.2	(328)
Hyde Park–Kenwood	3.3	6.6	.8	7.5	10.0	71.7	(241)
Lincoln Park	5.5	3.5	4.0	14.7	10.4	61.9	(346)

Table 2.13   Religion (percentage)

Neighborhood	Protestant	Catholic	Jewish	Muslim/ Other	None
Back of the Yards	26.2	68.0	0.2	2.4	3.1
Austin	70.5	21.4	–0–	2.1	6.1
South Shore	68.1	18.7	0.9	3.4	8.9
East Side	26.3	64.9	–0–	5.9	2.9
Portage Park	26.7	67.2	0.3	1.3	4.6
Beverly	31.9	61.8	0.8	0.5	5.1
Hyde Park–Kenwood	45.7	15.7	13.8	7.8	17.1
Lincoln Park	30.8	35.5	9.6	4.9	19.2

2.9), and with family incomes of $20,000 or more (table 2.10). In fact, South Shore's occupational, educational, and income proportions in the top categories (professional-technical, more than high school, and $30,000 or more, respectively) are equal to or greater than those not only of Back of the Yards and Austin, but also of Portage Park and East Side. On the other hand, the percentage of South Shore respondents reporting incomes of $10,000 or less is also larger than those of Portage Park and East Side, and the proportion of residents with less than a high-school education is sizable. We will address some of the factors that contribute to South Shore's diversity in subsequent chapters.

Neighborhoods Resisting Invasion and Succession

East Side and Portage Park stand as possible exceptions to the sequence of invasion and succession predicted in ecological models of neighborhood change. Both neighborhoods are predominantly white, working-class, ethnic communities. Although East Side has a measurable Hispanic population, there are virtually no blacks living in either community (table 2.11).

East Side is located next to the steel mills in the southeastern Calumet region. Its housing consists primarily of small single-family dwellings, most of which are of frame construction, although there are some newer, brick homes in the southern section of the community. Home ownership is much more common in East Side than in the neighborhoods discussed above, with 75 percent of the respondents owning their homes (table 2.7).

Most of the East Side respondents have a high-school education or less (table 2.9), and half are employed in blue-collar occupations (table 2.8). Thirty-four percent of East Side respondents work within the com-

Table 2.14 Family Composition (percentage)

Neighborhood	Married with Children	Married/ No Children	Female- headed Household	Male- headed Household	Single Male	Single Female
Back of the Yards	38.1	19.0	11.2	1.2	11.2	19.3
Austin	32.7	18.0	20.8	1.5	11.2	15.7
South Shore	26.8	16.3	16.5	2.3	15.4	22.7
East Side	35.6	32.4	3.4	0.7	9.1	18.7
Portage Park	29.4	38.3	4.1	1.5	7.9	18.8
Beverly	42.5	25.7	6.2	1.7	7.4	16.5
Hyde Park–Kenwood	15.9	29.5	6.3	0.5	20.5	27.3
Lincoln Park	14.7	25.6	4.7	1.2	20.9	33.0

Table 2.15 Age Composition and Median Age (percentage)

Neighborhood	17–30	31–45	46–60	61 and Over	Median Age
Back of the Yards	29.5	31.5	22.7	16.3	40
Austin	29.0	43.3	18.3	9.4	37
South Shore	33.0	33.0	23.7	10.2	37
East Side	18.8	25.5	29.8	26.0	50
Portage Park	19.4	21.8	31.9	26.9	51
Beverly	18.9	35.5	24.5	21.1	43
Hyde Park–Kenwood	36.4	29.7	17.6	16.3	36
Lincoln Park	42.8	38.2	11.0	8.0	32

munity, and informants tell us that everyone in East Side has at least one relative who works in the steel mills.

Largely Roman Catholic (table 2.13), the community imparts an eastern European flavor, with people of Polish, Lithuanian, and Slavic origins making up 26.1 percent of the white respondents (table 2.12). In addition, another 14 percent (36 percent of those in the "other" category) have some eastern European ancestry. The Hispanics are the newest arrivals in the community, although there have been sizable Mexican communities in the larger steel-making region since the 1930s.

Located on Chicago's northwest side, Portage Park is also an area of predominantly single-family, owner-occupied housing (tables 2.6 and 2.7). The houses, however, are in better physical condition than those in East Side and most are of brick construction. The trim bungalows, mostly built in the 1920s and 1930s, are well cared for, with the lawns neatly cut and edged.

Portage Park and East Side are comparable in family composition, with 68 percent of the respondents in each community living in nuclear-family households (table 2.14). Also like East Side, the median age in Portage Park is high (table 2.15). Wives still stay home in Portage Park, compared to those in our other communities. During warmer weather, it is not unusual during the week to see elderly women trimming lawns and hedges or climbing ladders to wash windows or burn off paint from window frames.

Portage Park is somewhat higher on socioeconomic characteristics than is East Side; more Portage Park respondents have education beyond the high-school level (table 2.9) and hold white-collar jobs (table 2.8). Of the white-collar workers, however, 60 percent (39 percent of the entire sample) have clerical or sales positions, and income levels are quite similar (table 2.10).

Neighborhoods Experiencing Invasion without Succession

Beverly, Hyde Park–Kenwood, and Lincoln Park are middle-class communities that appear to be stable, racially integrated neighborhoods, with
blacks constituting 15, 35, and 10 percent, respectively, of their populations (table 2.11).

Large homes on tree-lined streets and some of the few hills located
within the city differentiate Beverly from our other seven neighborhoods.
The literature that promotes Beverly calls it a "village in the city." Since
it has no industry of its own, "suburb in the city" might be a more
accurate characterization. Traveling over its placid residential streets,
one does have the feeling of being in one of the city's more prosperous
suburbs.

The demographics confirm what the appearance suggests. Eighty-
four percent of Beverly residents are homeowners (table 2.7), and it has
the largest proportion of two-adult households with children under the
age of nineteen of any of our communities (table 2.14). Nearly half of the
respondents have at least some college education (table 2.9), with 15.5
percent reporting education beyond the bachelor's degree. Beverly has
the highest family income of the eight communities, with over half the
families having annual incomes of $20,000 or more (table 2.10). More
than 80 percent of Beverly respondents are employed in white-collar
occupations (table 2.8).

Hyde Park–Kenwood and Lincoln Park stand in sharp physical contrast to Beverly. Both are lakefront communities consisting chiefly of
multi-unit, rental properties (tables 2.6 and 2.7). Although Hyde Park–
Kenwood has few of the small frame houses we have seen elsewhere, its
housing stock is nonetheless extraordinarily diverse, ranging from the
great mansions of Kenwood and the elegant lakefront high-rises to the
old subdivided apartment buildings in the northwest corner of the community. Lincoln Park also exhibits substantial variation in its housing
stock, although it has more small frame houses and fewer large single-
family houses than does Hyde Park–Kenwood.

There are additional differences between Beverly, on the one hand,
and Hyde Park–Kenwood and Lincoln Park, on the other. Residents of
the latter communities are more likely to be single (table 2.14) and are
younger, although with 34 percent of the respondents aged 46 or older,
Hyde Park–Kenwood's population is older than that of Lincoln Park
(table 2.15). In addition, Hyde Park–Kenwood and Lincoln Park are
characterized by greater diversity in religion than is Beverly (table 2.13).

On several attributes, then, Beverly more closely resembles East
Side and Portage Park than it does Hyde Park–Kenwood and Lincoln
Park. However, Beverly, Hyde Park–Kenwood, and Lincoln Park are
clearly socioeconomically distinct from the other five neighborhoods.

They have the largest proportion of respondents employed in white-collar positions in general and in professional-technical occupations in particular (table 2.8), as well as the highest educational levels of the eight communities. Hyde Park–Kenwood and Lincoln Park, however, each with over 60 percent of the respondents having more than a high-school education, are higher than Beverly in educational level (table 2.9).

These three neighborhoods also have the largest proportion of respondents with family incomes of $30,000 or more (table 2.10). Hyde Park–Kenwood's income distribution is, however, more complicated than those of Lincoln Park and Beverly. With nearly 30 percent in the $10,000 or less category, it is comparable to South Shore, East Side, and Portage Park in that category of income. Some of those in the low-income group are students and retirees; Hyde Park–Kenwood is among the highest of the communities in the percentage of persons in these groups.

Although we have already covered the basic attributes of Lincoln Park, some additional comments are in order. Lincoln Park's residents, in very large part, are well-educated young professionals. Lincoln Park ranks second only to Beverly in family income. If one considers the large proportion of incomes in Lincoln Park that are attributable to only one earner and the low median age in comparison to Beverly, one has some idea of the real income levels in this area.

The homogeneity of the area, however, can be exaggerated. While Lincoln Park obviously represents the classical case of a gentrifying community with young white professionals in profusion, there is nevertheless a range of types of residents. Ten percent of the population are employed as craftsmen, operatives, or laborers; nearly 20 percent report family incomes of $10,000 or less; and 19 percent of the respondents are nonwhite.

There is little doubt that the community used to be more heterogeneous than it is today, but "diversity" is a label that people in Lincoln Park use to describe their community, and community residents do bring an easy tolerance to diversity.

In the next three chapters, we provide more detailed descriptions of these three groups of neighborhoods. We trace the historical development of each community and discuss the attitudes and attributes of today's residents. We address differences within each neighborhood group as well as differences between the three general patterns represented by each group.

3

The "Classic" Model: Back of the Yards, Austin, and South Shore

The three communities to which we now turn are, in many respects, exemplars of the traditional theories of growth, change, and decay. Yet, although the general outlines of the process are similar in each case, distinctive variations among the three give us additional insight as to how the change takes place and the role of crime in this change.

Each community was founded because of changes in transportation patterns or because of ties to economic nodes, or for both reasons. Each in its early stages attracted ethnic workers. But in two cases the early social-class composition was more complicated; each community evolved with a different class base that was reflected in the nature of the housing stock which came to characterize the community. Patterns of black in-migration were also similar, but the original differences in the class bases of the communities and the nature of adjoining communities influenced the kinds and rates of migration. The racial change from white to black in one community has also been accompanied by the growth of a Mexican population.

In each case, there was a community organizational response to the arrival of blacks. In two cases, organizations were created to deal with real or anticipated changes. In the third case, an existing community organization worked to discourage change and, when that failed, to minimize its impact. In this final case, arriving blacks formed their own organization to deal with problems that the existing organization failed to acknowledge.

All three communities have had to deal with rising crime rates and deteriorating properties, but the means of dealing with them were distinctive to each place. At present, two communities are clearly on the road to severe deterioration and its culmination, housing abandonment. In the third, the somewhat more middle-class community, a major institutional actor has entered the scene, and the chances for rehabilitation and maintenance there are somewhat higher than in the others.

With that overview, let us turn to the communities.

Back of the Yards

Back of the Yards, one of Chicago's most famous neighborhoods, began its life as a residential area with the construction and growth of an economic node, the stockyards, after the Civil War. Built on marshy land, the stockyards made use of the south fork of the South Branch of the Chicago River as the receptacle for its wastes. The community grew rapidly in the 1870s, although there were as yet no paved streets, sewers, public utilities, or even transportation facilities to the city (Kitagawa and Taeuber 1963). The first workers were Irish and German. They were subsequently supplanted by Polish workers, who were initially brought in as strikebreakers in the late 1880s. The Poles, in turn, were followed by Lithuanians and Czechoslovakians. Beginning during World War I and continuing through the 1920s, Mexicans settled in the community. In the neighborhood's heyday in the 1920s, more than 92,000 people were crowded into the area. Its population has declined steadily since then.

BACK OF THE YARDS

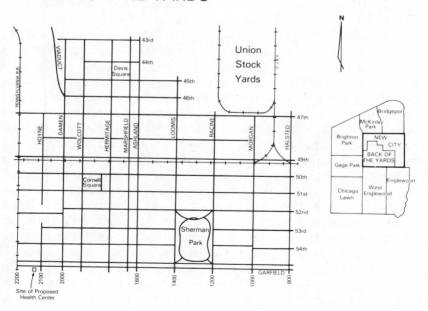

It was into this ethnic, working-class setting that Saul Alinsky and Joe Meegan came in 1939 to organize the Back of the Yards Council. The council welded together the churches and the packinghouse workers' union into a tight, cohesive organization to fight both the big meatpacking companies and the city for improved services. At the same time, it developed programs to deal with problems of youth crime. After World War II, the council continued these activities and undertook construction programs to improve local housing, much of which, having been constructed to house low-income immigrant workers, had outmoded plumbing and wiring. Alinsky left shortly after he arrived, but Meegan stayed behind. The organization he built had ties not only to the churches, but also to the political system and to groups offering city services, such as the police department, local school officials, and the department of sanitation.

In spite of these efforts, however, Back of the Yards continued to decline. The meatpackers moved away from the area in the 1950s, destroying it as a node, and the stockyards themselves closed in 1971. Back of the Yards has been following the path of deterioration that ecological theory would predict. In saying this, one must be careful not to romanticize the past, for Back of the Yards was never an affluent community. Nevertheless, under the impetus of dwindling employment opportunities and declining property values, deterioration and blight are well underway at present.

This type of neighborhood has historically been the most vulnerable to the pressures of black housing demand and, consequently, to racial change. Blacks have been moving into Back of the Yards from the south and east (see figure 3.1) and, at the time of our survey, constituted 19 percent of the area's population, a substantial increase over the 3.5-percent black population recorded in the 1970 census. Holt and Pacyga (1979) argue that racial change did not occur earlier in part because the quality of the housing was not sufficiently high to be attractive to middle-class blacks. In addition, the combination of relatively high white demand for housing and the perceived hostility toward poorer blacks kept the latter from entering the community. It wasn't until the 1970s that a sufficient housing surplus developed to enable poorer blacks to move in.

The Back of the Yards Council is still in existence and continues to maintain the kinds of ties that it has always had. The organization is still strongly rooted in the churches, and it continues to project a picture to the outside world through the press, and to its own constituency through meetings and a local newspaper, that indicates things have not changed. Although informants have told us that the council has engaged in various activities to keep blacks out of the community, one would not know from the council's public stance that blacks even existed. Nor would one

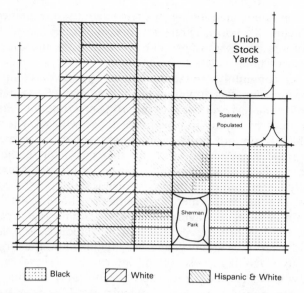

Union
Stock
Yards

Sparsely
Populated

Sherman
Park

::::: Black   //// White   \\\\ Hispanic & White

Fig. 3.1. Back of the Yards—Racial Concentrations

suspect that Back of the Yards is a rapidly deteriorating area with increasing crime and property abandonment.

The *Back of the Yards Journal*, published by the council, reflects this orientation. It does not report crime or other problems because that would disturb people. Instead, it reports news as if the world were still the tight little one of ethnic weddings and parties, churches, nuns, and priests.

A typical issue of the *Back of the Yards Journal* (2 April 1980) reported the following on its front page: A student at St. Joseph School was named junior citizen of the year by the local park district; twelve local dentists voluntarily screened the teeth of students at fifteen area Catholic grade schools; a party was being planned to honor the coach of the De Paul University basketball team; a Spanish mass will be celebrated at Sacred Heart Church; and local churches listed their Holy Week and Easter services (thirty-three churches are included). Also mentioned in this issue are: Easter-egg hunts at local parks; the injury of a young woman on the Maria High School basketball team; St. Augustine Grade School registers for fall semester; the American Legion will hold a blood drive; the archconfraternity of Our Mother of Consolation of St. Clare of Montefalco Church will hold its monthly communion (it will also have a spring card and bunco party); and St. Rita High School students have raised money to help a paralyzed alumnus. There are twenty-four more articles in the issue, mentioning in their headlines the names of nine churches or church schools. Three of its twelve pictures are of priests and nuns, two others are of the American Legion and Campfire Girls, and five are of modern China.

No other community newspaper in our sample so completely excludes news on crime, developments in housing, and related matters. The closest the *Journal* has ever come to reporting on crime was related to its own program of providing free paint for those who want to paint out graffiti (which is a major problem in the area). Nor is there ever news about the rapid rates of deterioration that characterize the area. In addition, black faces almost never appear in the *Journal*. Mexicans fare substantially better, but even their coverage is not up to the community proportion. In some sense, then, the council is a holding action of sorts for the declining number of aging whites who continue to live in the area.

Just as the Back of the Yards Council symbolizes and defines the white world for its constituency, another organization, the Organization for New City (ONC), represents and interprets the black world. The name "New City" is taken from the old University of Chicago list of names for community areas, and designates a different and somewhat larger territory than does Back of the Yards. Founded in 1976 by local black residents who were alarmed at the increasing number of abandoned houses in their area and the contribution of the Department of Housing and Urban Development (HUD) to that process, ONC meets in a local Roman Catholic church, and its black executive officer is an ex-seminarian. Like the council, ONC is a multipurpose organization devoted to upgrading its community through career days, health programs, antitruancy programs, community barbecues, and efforts to prevent housing deterioration and to reduce crime. Unlike the council, the world it portrays is a world of grim struggle and social disorganization. Where the council elicits cooperation from its old pals in city agencies, ONC fights—the difference in approach illustrates the fact that one is "on the inside" and the other is not.

ONC, in fact, has had to struggle to get cooperation from schools and from the police. Some principals will not allow ONC to organize career days at their schools. Some district police commanders will not meet with ONC officers or return their calls. The organization must at times even struggle with the Back of the Yards Council for control of the same turf. ONC efforts to build a community health center at the edge of the council area (see map), for example, were objected to by the council.

Supported at times by community anticrime funds, ONC has a vigorous anticrime program. Efforts have included a "watch dog" crisis center, busing for senior citizens, block-club organization, and youth programs—particularly the antitruancy program. ONC's blunt presentation of crime in the neighborhood stands in sharp contrast to the Back of the Yards Council's avoidance of the topic: "She said he held a gun on her, pulled her into an abandoned building and raped her. When she screamed, he beat her in the face with the gun and said he would kill her" (*New City Watch Dog*, 1979). Unlike the Back of the Yards Council, which works closely with the police, ONC believes it has to harass the agents of criminal justice in order to get them to perform their duty. ONC, however, must park its bus for transporting the elderly at the police station. When left on the street in front of the ONC offices, the vehicle was severely vandalized.

Back of the Yards, then, illustrates the process in a quintessential low-wage, working-class community that has both lost its economic function and is in the path of black expansion. In order to slow the pace of change, residents feel they have little choice but to harass the new arrivals. Younger whites with economic opportunities leave or have already left the community, and older residents sit back to await their fate. Because much of the housing stock was designed for low-income workers, it does not have broad appeal. Instead, it is an option only for those at the bottom of the income ladder—in this case, low-income blacks or relatively newly arrived Mexicans. Under the circumstances, trying to make the community attractive to more affluent newcomers is not an option. Instead, community leaders try to make life more comfortable for the older white residents during the area's seemingly inexorable decline.

By contrast, the housing stock and the social-class base of the Austin community, to which we now turn, has always been more variegated, ranging from the frame houses of the higher reaches of the working class to the Queen Anne–style Victorian housing of the solid middle class. It also contains numerous sturdy two-flats which have played a large role in the lives of the upwardly mobile as well.

Austin

Austin began as both a commuter village and as home for railway workers who were employed in the yards just east of the area. The first suburban development in the area was initiated in 1866 by Henry Austin, for whom the subdivision was named. After the Great Chicago Fire in 1871, people were encouraged to move to that area and establish their homes.

Some of the first houses in this western area were large frame houses, often constructed in the Queen Anne style, but the area also filled rapidly with small frame houses and two-flats. South Austin, with its large number of two-flats, is a product of the first quarter of the twentieth century. Most of North Austin's construction took place during the 1920s, with the predominant housing style there being the brick bungalow.

Historically, Austin has offered industrial work opportunities in profusion, although the majority of the employing corporations were located either on or just beyond the boundaries of Austin itself. Over the years, nationally known manufacturers, including Zenith Radio, Mars

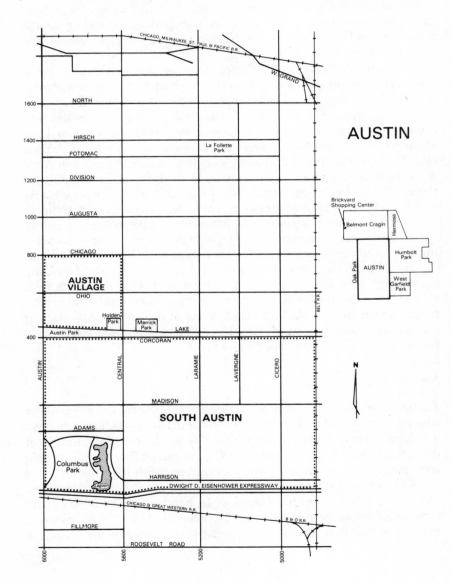

and Brachs candies, Revere Copper and Brass, and Pettibone Mulliken, have located in that region. The vast railroad yards around the area's borders also continued to be major employers.

Ethnically, the community has always been mixed. During the early part of the century, Scots, English, Germans, European Jews, Swedes, and Irish were all included in that mix. During the 1930s, large numbers of Italians began moving into Austin from the more crowded and deteriorating areas to the east, and by 1960 they were the most numerous group (Goodwin 1979, 19). However, true to Chicago's political traditions, the Irish dominated the community's political life. The Irish clergy's control of religious life was also felt in the community until the 1930s, when some of the parishes to the north became Italian. The impact of the church can even be noted in the fact, Goodwin reports, that people, whatever their religion, identified the location of their houses by parish.

It is tempting to emphasize the prosperity of Austin through the 1940s and 1950s, particularly because of the dramatic contrast it represents with the present. Goodwin's otherwise excellent analysis of Austin falls somewhat into this trap. Yet, a 1942 report on Austin identifies several large areas of severe deterioration. The area of old Austin, with its large frame houses, was beginning to show its age. In addition, the smaller frame houses interspersed among the larger dwellings and "a number of individual structures closely approach a blighted condition" (Klove 1942, 30). Some of the houses just north of that area were also reported deteriorated. In South Austin, there were areas of mixed housing use which showed similar conditions. In some sections, there were excessive proportions of vacant lots and stagnating patterns of mixed land use.

The last comments of Klove are worth quoting in detail because they help illustrate the broad ecological processes we have discussed.

> The quality of housing along most of the eastern border of Austin . . . is old and poorer. Indeed, there is a general tendency . . . for housing quality to improve from east to west. . . . In the eastern half of Austin a higher proportion of employed are in industry, while in western Austin employment in the loop is much greater.
>
> The major planning problem in Austin . . . is one of conservation and maintenance. While only a few blocks approach the blighted condition, most of the area is of older construction and needs attention to prevent it from slipping. (Klove 1942, 31)

Although there was some new construction in the southeast portion of Austin in the late 1950s, it is safe to say that Austin was an older community with signs of deterioration by the 1960s. When blacks began to enter from the south and east, that section of the community was already the most deteriorated.

If one were to pick a community in which the classic racial-change scenario was written out, one could scarcely do better (or worse) than Austin. According to Goodwin, between the years of 1966 and 1973, blocks changed over from white to black at the rate of 37½ per year. The turnover was accompanied, if not hastened, by every kind of abuse one associates with such changes: panic peddling—"blacks are moving in, you'd better get out"; racial steering; mortgage redlining; the whole panoply of problems with FHA programs—home improvements that were never made because inspectors were bribed, mortgages to unqualified applicants and subsequent building foreclosure and abandonment; and the milking of multiple-family dwellings through undermaintenance.

The situation sounds almost chaotic and it probably was. Crime rose as potential criminals were able to take advantage of ensuing social disorganization. Nobody could tell any longer, for example, who belonged on a block and who didn't. As one resident said at the time, "How can anyone know . . . if the man carrying a TV out of the house is its actual owner?" (Greenwood, A. M., "Report from a Changing Neighborhood," *Chicago Sun-Times*, April 20, 1975, p. 30).

In this setting, community organizations arose, and block clubs were organized to deal with problems around questions of social control.[1] The first important community-wide organization was the Organization for a Better Austin (OBA). Established by local clergy and organized by people trained by Alinsky, its initial focus was on racial stabilization. It attempted to discourage realtors from panic peddling—it was active in getting passed the city ordinance that prohibited For Sale signs. It worked to encourage white residents to remain in the area, to attract new whites to the community, and, with somewhat less enthusiasm, to redistribute blacks in such a way as to discourage resegregation. It encouraged more visible police patrolling and attempted to improve the schools, partly by busing students from the overcrowded schools in South Austin.

But as the area continued to change, so did the organization's priorities. Crime, deteriorating housing, and disinvestment became increasing sources of concern. OBA's approach was confrontational and hence controversial. Members picketed the homes and offices of real estate agents who seemed to be profiting from and exploiting the racial-change situation. They marched on city agencies and demanded better services. In the Alinsky tradition, they tried to get citizens angry and, through that anger, to obtain involvement.

The Town Hall Assembly arose in response to OBA, which it considered unruly, embarrassing, and unhelpful. Closely tied to the community's churches, Town Hall Assembly attempted to work with the establishment rather than against it, and usually toward goals that were

consistent with middle-class aspirations. It encouraged permissive trans-
fer programs from its overcrowded schools; got tax assessments reduced;
urged local employers to encourage their employees to live in Austin; ran
a tutoring program; and promoted holiday parades and other social
community-building events.

Over time, both groups faded away and were replaced with new
organizations that arose in response to the community's increasingly
heterogeneous needs, which resulted from the northward-moving racial
change. Spurred on by the riots after Martin Luther King's death, the
deterioration of South Austin proceeded at an increasing rate. The
number of abandoned houses rose, and shopping strips developed more
and more the "bombed-out" look distressingly familiar in such neighborhoods. In addition, South Austin had always had a larger proportion of
multiple-family dwellings, most of them two-flats, than the northern
area, thus making it a more likely candidate for undermaintenance.

The South Austin and Mid-Austin organizations, then, have devoted
more time to securing better law enforcement and to upgrading housing
quality and a whole range of related activities. The latter run the gamut
from encouraging banks to give loans and insurance companies not to
redline to taking over abandoned houses and rehabilitating them through
government programs. In fact, the organizations have been moderately
successful in fighting insurance redlining and in rehabilitating housing
units. Levels of deterioration are so serious, however, that such advances
are not immediately visible to people traveling through the neighborhood.

The North Austin community organizations are still, however, focusing on racial stabilization. Encouraging whites to move in, helping them
find mortgage money, working with businessmen to keep shopping strips
attractive, and arm twisting city departments for adequate city services
are all on their agendas.

There is one small area near the western edge of the community—the
original old Austin area—where increased efforts are being made to
attract middle-class residents, whatever their color. This is the area of
large frame houses in the Queen Anne style, with turrets, big front
porches, and the like. Following a clear "development strategy," residents have had their streets made into cul-de-sacs and have publicized the
elegant and self-conscious rehabilitation efforts of new owners. Taking its
cue from other threatened communities, the area had its first annual
house walk in the spring of 1980 as part of a major effort to market itself.

The walks were guided mainly by whites (although ownership of the
houses on the tour was more equally distributed) who emphasized the
area's distinctive architectural heritage. In front of each house selected
for the tour stood an exquisitely turned-out antique car. Radios in each
house were tuned to a local classical music station, although they did not

always drown out the rock sounds from neighboring homes. A few local residents sat on their porches offering their houses for sale to the passersby.

Most of the thousand or so people who came to look at the houses were also white. Among them were many grey-haired people who had fled the community and were coming back for their first look. They spent time with each other reminiscing about who lived where and what they did. Many of them had not returned since the time they left, although they had moved to nearby suburbs—some reported that they were literally physically afraid to come back.

Efforts to upgrade the Austin Village area have not met with universal acclaim. In fact, the local community organizations in the southern two-thirds of the area are opposed because, in their view, the deconversion (from rooming houses) of these buildings makes housing more scarce and drives up housing prices, thus forcing out the poor. In addition, they claim that most of the promotion is being done by "outsiders,"and that local people receive none of the gains. This brief discussion is a preview of some of the arguments that swirl around the questions concerning gentrification. What must be said here is that the amount of low-income housing being lost in this particular case is virtually nothing compared to the massive amounts being lost in Austin through neglect and abandonment.

Despite all the efforts of the community organizations, Austin has continued to deteriorate. Starting from a substantially higher base of housing quality, its levels of deterioration, particularly in the south, are comparable to Back of the Yards. Its level of property abandonment is high, and it cannot claim even one shopping strip up to the quality of the major one in Back of the Yards, in spite of the efforts of numerous merchants' associations to fight deterioration. Department stores in nearby Oak Park and the new Brickyard Shopping Center (discussed in the section on Portage Park) represent important counter attractions. It should be added that North Austin residents report that construction of the Brickyard has improved both the quality of their lives and their property values.

Austin, then, represents an area that historically had been a notch higher on the economic scale than Back of the Yards. In addition, it provided more diverse economic activities for its residents than did the old stockyards area. However, its large proportion of multiple-family dwellings (in this case, mainly two-flats), its aging housing stock, and the historical period in which racial change took place, produced change in the classic pattern, despite rich community organization that focused on issues related to change.

We now turn to South Shore which, historically, has been yet another notch higher on the economic ladder. Strictly a bedroom community with a valued lakefront location, its residents have worked mainly in white-collar jobs downtown rather than in industrial jobs nearby. With an enormously diverse housing stock and the social-class range that that represents, it has managed to maintain a stronger economic base than the other two communities. Consequently, its pattern of change has been somewhat different from that of the other two; this fact, coupled with the arrival on the scene of a new major institutional actor, provides it with the prospect of a somewhat better future than either Back of the Yards or Austin.

South Shore

Compared to the other two areas, South Shore got a relatively late start as a residential community. Its first burst of development came with the opening of the Illinois Central Railroad South Shore line in 1883 and was fueled by the Columbian Exposition of 1893 (located just north of South Shore), when increased railroad traffic encouraged the development of a rail yard and homes for railroad employees. Nonetheless, construction proceeded with little vigor through the 1890s. "The dawn of the twentieth century came and still nearly all of this South Shore community . . . remained vacant" (Hoyt 1942a, 42). The area's primary growth took place between 1910 and 1930, when its population grew from 7,702 to 78,755. Although there has been some decline, the population has remained more or less stable since.

South Shore never really succeeded as a wealthy lakefront community. Homer Hoyt, the developer of the sector theory of urban growth, explains the situation this way.

> High grade residential areas tend to move out from the center of the city in different sectors, and the attractiveness of the Gold Coast (north of the loop) is enhanced by the fact that there was a free open end to the north toward which the march of the socially elite could move without interruption. On the other hand, the southeastward movement of the fashionable area of the South Side . . . to the South Shore district . . . struck the barrier of the steel mills. . . . Hemmed in between Jackson Park on the north, and industrial areas to the south of 79th Street, the expansion of the South Shore district along the lake was barred. Consequently the path of growth . . . was bent to the right along the axis of 79th Street and impetus was given to the further expansion of high grade homes to the southwest in Beverly Hills. (Hoyt 1942a, 41)

South Shore did, however, enter the 1950s as a moderately prosperous, almost exclusively residential community with an incredible variety of basically well-maintained housing stock. Hoyt described South Shore as "one of the best examples of a so-called 'stable area.'" With a beautiful, wooded park with its own beach to the north; an elegant country club (excluding Jews and blacks) to the northeast; the eight-block-long Rainbow Beach Park directly to the east; excellent shopping centers, fine schools, and fast transportation to the Loop; South Shore had "advantages that cannot be duplicated in the aggregate in any other community" (p. 43).

> The South Shore is a community where the folly of the practice of migrating from older neighborhoods to new ones every generation can be strikingly demonstrated. There is no second South Shore lying along the lake front just beyond this community. A new residential area on the periphery of Chicago would be far from the cooling breezes, bathing beaches, and yachting of the lake and it would be a long way from the great parks, shopping centers, and the frequent and quick transportation to the loop. . . . Hence, conservation plans should be designed for this South Shore district far in advance of the need for their actual application, so that any idea of abandoning this choice residential location in favor of what might appear to be greener pastures in the suburbs will never be seriously entertained. (P. 43)

Hoyt was not alone in his concern—the implications of South Shore's location in the path of black residential expansion were not lost on community residents. Blacks began to move into the community from adjacent Woodlawn about the same time that blacks entered South Austin, and in the mid-1960s racial change began in earnest. The process of change in South Shore consisted of two distinct patterns which overlay one another. The first was the systematic block-by-block changes we saw in Austin, as low-income blacks fled neighboring Woodlawn. In addition, however, middle-income blacks leapfrogged some areas and began moving into regions of attractive single-family homes.

As might by now be predictable, a community organization arose prior to black entry into South Shore to deal with the issues that process would generate. The South Shore Commission was founded in 1954 by local clergymen. Whether its initial goal was the prevention of black in-migration or the promotion of orderly integration is difficult to tell. Molotch (1972) reports that factions representing both positions were present from the beginning, although the integrationists prevailed as blacks moved into the community in ever-increasing numbers.

The commission's strategy included components we have already seen. It maintained a housing referral service which attempted to widely distribute both blacks and whites in order to prevent resegregation and to screen out "undesirable" black tenants. In addition, intensive efforts were made to keep South Shore attractive to whites. These included increased pressure on the police department for more patrols so as to reduce the rising crime rate. The crime problem was complicated by the fact that the city's most famous youth gang, the Blackstone Rangers, considered part of South Shore its turf. Efforts were made to discourage the gang, particularly in the schools, and residents organized evening radio patrols to report crimes in progress.

The schools were also a focus of activity. As in Austin, the district boundaries were redrawn to increase the proportion of whites, and a new high school was constructed. Also as in Austin, the schools changed racially at a faster rate than did the community as a whole. This was partly because the resident population was older than the newcomers and hence often no longer had young children. In addition, many of the whites with children sent them to Roman Catholic and other private schools.

At a later stage in the process, a "magnet school" was constructed which required application for admission. This school was supposed to have better pupil-teacher ratios and the latest approaches to enriched education; it was also to have a 50:50 black-white ratio. Over time, this provision became a source of irritation to blacks, as their children came to form a larger and larger proportion of the applicants. Places were selected by lottery among those qualified, and a much smaller proportion of blacks than of whites was admitted.

Finally, as Austin Village has just begun to do, South Shore residents instituted an "open-house" day in which sample houses were opened to all and guided tours were conducted throughout the community. Although white residents worked very hard to keep the community attractive and had the clout to do so—the construction of a new school is one example—none of their efforts seemed to have any impact on the process of change. The things that made the community attractive to whites also made it attractive to blacks, who, because of discrimination, had fewer choices. In the late 1960s, some of the remaining white leadership invited officials of a well-known real estate consulting firm to tell them about the future of South Shore. That firm, according to one informant, had developed the technique of taking "recess photos," that is, pictures of school yards during recess. If these school yards looked predominantly black, the company would report that the community was all washed up. In the case of South Shore, the photos led to that conclusion. At this point, some of the white leadership gave up and moved away.

Racial change in South Shore was accompanied by many of the processes we have already discussed. Many of the large airy apartments were subdivided and their buildings undermaintained; the crime rate soared from less than the city-wide average to more than twice that rate. Red-lining became a real problem, and property appreciation flattened out.

It is ironic that one widely quoted article on the process of racial change (Karlen 1968), which is based on South Shore data, demonstrates that whites do not flee an area and that property values do not decline. Instead, Karlen argues, blacks replace the whites who would move away anyway, and because their own housing is in short supply, they pay a good price. That article describes South Shore in the early 1960s. In the second half of the decade, however, property sales went up dramatically, and property values, compared to those in white areas of the city, stagnated. In addition, a close look at property values suggests that prices were discounted long in advance—observers knew that racial change was coming. Whites did flee South Shore, and although some moved to Hyde Park and some moved to Beverly, most of them probably left the city for the beckoning suburbs referred to by Hoyt.[2]

Parkside, the area of two-, three-, and six-flats into which blacks from neighboring Woodlawn first moved, quickly evidenced deterioration. Overall, however, housing deterioration and abandonment did not progress as rapidly in South Shore as it did in Austin. In the Parkside case, the process was abetted by the fact that much of the area was identified as an urban-renewal area. In that situation, both landlords and homeowners lose incentive to maintain their homes because, under the eminent-domain provision associated with urban renewal, the government pays the same prices for buildings regardless of condition. Unfortunately, the renewal of Parkside was never completed—in time, the deterioration was too advanced to correct. Much of the other housing in the community, however, remained in decent shape.

Having discussed in some detail the histories of these three communities, we now turn to their present-day situations.

Stability and Social Cohesion

Reflecting the fact of racial succession and the high levels of turnover that implies, Back of the Yards, Austin, and South Shore tend to have lower levels of stability and social cohesion than the other five communities. However, although they are similar in that they are always in the bottom half of the community rankings, there is some variation among them.

For example, the proportion of respondents who consider their neighborhood to be a real home is lowest in Austin and South Shore (table 3.1). However, reflecting perhaps the impact of the University of Chicago in the community, fewer Hyde Park–Kenwood residents consider the area home than do residents of Back of the Yards. Similarly,

Table 3.1 Respondents Who Consider their Neighborhood to be a Real Home

Neighborhood	Percentage
Back of the Yards	58.6
Austin	50.4
South Shore	49.0
East Side	76.8
Portage Park	72.6
Beverly	83.4
Hyde Park–Kenwood	54.8
Lincoln Park	59.3

although Austin and South Shore, again, have the lowest proportion of residents not planning to move within the next year, Lincoln Park's young singles are more likely to plan a move than are residents of Back of the Yards (table 3.2).

Respondents in the three communities are less likely to have good friends living there than are residents of the other communities (table 3.3), and also less likely to spend social evenings with their neighbors (table 3.4). Only low-crime, all-white Portage Park reports fewer friends in the neighborhood and fewer visits with neighbors (an anomaly we will discuss in chapter 4).

A similar pattern can be seen in respondents' ability to count on their neighbors for assistance (table 3.5). South Shore and Austin rank at or near the bottom. Back of the Yards is closer to the middle, with Lincoln Park filling in the other low position. (Lincoln Park is another community with high population turnover; we shall discuss it in chapter 5).

Finally, the same pattern appears in the use of local facilities, including such matters as attending church, shopping in local stores, and getting medical care (table 3.6). While Austin and South Shore are again at the bottom, Back of the Yards residents are located around the middle, illustrating the fact that this is a community still in transition.

Table 3.2 Respondents Who Definitely Will Not Move Within the Next Year

Neighborhoods	Percentage
Back of the Yards	40.0
Austin	31.3
South Shore	31.0
East Side	66.4
Portage Park	52.4
Beverly	68.1
Hyde Park–Kenwood	43.0
Lincoln Park	38.7

Table 3.3 Respondents with Good Friends Living in the Neighborhood

Neighborhood	Percentage
Back of the Yards	70.4
Austin	70.9
South Shore	71.9
East Side	90.0
Portage Park	67.9
Beverly	83.8
Hyde Park–Kenwood	88.5
Lincoln Park	84.7

Table 3.4 Respondents Who Do Selected Activities Once a Week or More (percentage)

Neighborhood	Spend a Social Evening with Relatives	Spend a Social Evening with a Neighbor	Chat with Neighbors on the Street
Back of the Yards	41.5	29.5	84.1
Austin	44.3	24.0	74.4
South Shore	38.9	26.3	75.3
East Side	53.5	33.1	90.4
Portage Park	43.9	27.4	86.6
Beverly	41.0	29.7	90.4
Hyde Park–Kenwood	22.7	36.5	79.6
Lincoln Park	26.1	33.4	77.9

Table 3.5 Respondents Who Can Count on Their Neighbors to: (percentage)

Neighborhood	Run Errands when Respondent is Sick	Watch House when Respondent is Away	Loan Respondent $25 in an Emergency
Back of the Yards	72.7	85.3	73.6
Austin	72.5	81.9	70.0
South Shore	71.6	82.8	66.7
East Side	87.8	97.0	88.0
Portage Park	83.4	93.3	85.3
Beverly	94.3	98.0	91.6
Hyde Park–Kenwood	75.7	83.6	73.4
Lincoln Park	70.0	79.6	70.6

However, there is one index of social cohesion on which these neighborhoods rank high. These community residents are more likely to have relatives residing in the community than are residents in any other neighborhood but East Side (table 3.7). Although black family structure is somewhat different from that of working-class whites, the importance of extended kinship networks is apparent in both cases.

Overall, then, on levels of social integration, Back of the Yards is higher than Austin and South Shore, and thus more similar to some of the more cohesive communities. If we consider only the whites in Back of the Yards, this tendency is even more pronounced. Back of the Yards whites rank as high as, or higher than, Back of the Yards respondents taken as a whole, on every measure of stability and cohesion except the percentage who say they will definitely not move within the next year (table 3.8). (See appendix D for a breakdown of demographics by race for the neighborhoods whose racial compositions warrant it.)

Table 3.6 Respondents Who Use Local Facilities (percentage)

Neighborhood	Buy Groceries	Go to Restaurants	Go to Religious Services	Do Banking	Get Medical Care	Buy Clothes
Back of the Yards	73.6	39.8	72.5	72.4	43.9	48.5
Austin	63.6	35.9	55.8	41.3	41.2	17.9
South Shore	68.8	24.4	38.9	35.8	35.6	12.2
East Side	79.0	53.9	86.7	79.2	46.8	29.0
Portage Park	79.6	51.4	81.5	79.2	39.7	61.3
Beverly	74.7	49.9	82.5	64.5	33.7	45.0
Hyde Park–Kenwood	86.3	44.8	53.1	62.6	54.5	11.8
Lincoln Park	89.3	69.9	62.2	36.3	30.2	23.9

Table 3.7 Respondents with Relatives Living in the Neighborhood

Neighborhood	Percentage
Back of the Yards	54.0
Austin	57.0
South Shore	53.1
East Side	74.9
Portage Park	34.9
Beverly	43.8
Hyde Park–Kenwood	26.7
Lincoln Park	24.4

Table 3.8 Measures of Stability and Cohesion, by Race—Back of the Yards and Austin

	Back of the Yards			Austin	
Characteristic	White	Black	Hispanic	White	Black
Percentage residing in community entire life	32.1	1.2	6.4	0	0
Median length of residence for remainder (in years)	14.0	6.0	3.0	9.0	6.0
Percentage who consider neighborhood a "real home"	66.5	54.9	45.8	68.0	46.4
Percentage who will not move during next year	38.7	45.0	37.6	42.5	28.2
Percentage with relatives in the neighborhood	56.2	42.2	56.0	32.4	65.4
Percentage with good friends in the neighborhood	77.0	49.4	72.5	72.0	71.1
Percentage who do the following once a week or more:					
a. Spend a social evening with relatives	50.0	39.5	27.1	39.7	46.9
b. Spend a social evening with a neighbor	37.0	24.4	20.9	17.6	26.4
c. Chat with neighbors on the street	86.2	80.5	83.6	82.4	73.8
Percentage who can count on neighbors to:					
a. Run errands when respondent is sick	74.5	72.4	70.7	84.7	69.7
b. Watch house when respondent is away	91.0	69.1	86.4	86.3	81.8
c. Loan respondent $25 in an emergency	75.9	63.9	77.0	70.3	70.0

Thirty-two percent of the white Back of the Yards respondents have lived there all their lives, and the median length of residence for the remainder is fourteen years, making this group comparable to the most cohesive East Side respondents. Also like East Side, white Back of the Yards is somewhat ingrown. Fifty-six percent of respondents have relatives living in the neighborhood, and 77 percent have good friends there. Half of the white respondents visit their relatives once a week or more. The percentage (84.8) reporting local church attendance is comparable to those in East Side and Portage Park, as are the percentages reporting the use of local facilities more generally (table 3.9). This higher level of use no doubt reflects the fact that among our eight neighborhoods, Back of the Yards has the only really successful shopping strip outside of Portage Park, and, in addition, its white residents show patterns of behavior similar to working-class ethnics elsewhere.

There is, then, for the whites, some resemblance to the church-oriented, *gemütlich* world portrayed in the *Back of the Yards Journal*. One young white informant reported that she and her husband, both of whom had been born in Back of the Yards, had moved to neighboring Bridgeport when they were married. "But we were never really comfortable there," she said, so they moved back to Back of the Yards, which they really like—"Where you grew up is where you belong."

Although black residents have lived in Back of the Yards for a much shorter period of time than have the whites, a strikingly large proportion of them consider the neighborhood a real home, and more blacks than whites say that they will definitely not move within a year (table 3.8). However, perhaps reflecting their relative newness in the neighborhood, their ties do not run as deep as those of white residents. They are somewhat less likely to have either relatives (42.2 percent compared to 56.2 percent) or good friends (49.4 percent compared to 77 percent) in the neighborhood, and they spend fewer social evenings with relatives and with neighbors than do whites. Blacks are less likely to be able to count on their neighbors to keep watch on their house or to lend them

Table 3.9 Respondents Who Use Local Facilities, by Race—Back of the Yards and Austin (percentage)

	Back of the Yards			Austin	
	White	Black	Hispanic	White	Black
Buy groceries	75.2	57.8	81.8	68.0	63.1
Go to restaurants	44.4	17.5	44.8	31.7	39.1
Go to religious services	84.8	23.3	84.6	77.0	49.4
Do banking	82.8	26.6	79.6	45.7	38.6
Get medical care	46.0	29.5	49.5	31.1	46.3
Buy clothes	50.9	26.8	59.1	20.3	16.0

money, and they are very much more likely to do their shopping, dining out, and going to church elsewhere in the city (table 3.9).

Although 6.4 percent of the Hispanic respondents have lived in Back of the Yards all their lives, the median length of residence for the rest is only three years. Even so, the Hispanics are more similar to the longer-term white residents than to the newer black residents on other dimensions of cohesion. Fifty-six percent of the Hispanic respondents report that they have relatives in the neighborhood, and 72.5 percent report that they have good friends there. However, the frequency with which they engage in social activities is lower than that of either of the other groups. Twenty-seven percent visit relatives once a week or more, and 20.9 percent visit neighbors that often (table 3.8). The Hispanics also report spending fewer social evenings with friends outside the neighborhood than do blacks or whites (18.5 percent vs. 34.1 percent and 28.7 percent, respectively, do so once a week or more).

The fact that total visiting seems to be less for Hispanics may reflect a cultural difference that we do not fully understand, since on other measures, Hispanics display a level of integration into the community close to that of the whites. Although they are somewhat less likely to consider the neighborhood home (45.8 percent) than are the whites, they are much closer to the whites than to the blacks in being able to count on their neighbors to keep watch on their house and to lend them money (86.4 percent and 77 percent, respectively). They are also much more like the whites in that they make heavy use of neighborhood facilities, doing most of their shopping, praying, and banking within the community (table 3.9).

A comparison of Austin respondents by race does not reveal the consistently higher levels of social integration among whites that were characteristic of Back of the Yards. Austin blacks and whites have lived in the community for surprisingly similar lengths of time. The median number of years for blacks is six, for whites, nine. No respondents in either group have lived in Austin all their lives. This is quite different from Back of the Yards and suggests that the organizations in North Austin have had some success in attracting new white families into the area.

Even though blacks in Austin socialize with their neighbors a little more than whites do, they seem to be slightly less tightly integrated in other ways. A smaller proportion of blacks than whites consider the neighborhood to be a real home and say that they will definitely not move during the next year. Although equal proportions report that their neighbors watch their houses and would lend them $25.00 in an emergency, whites are more likely than blacks to be able to count on neighbors' help if they are sick (table 3.8).

The black-white differences in community-facility use are much smaller in Austin than they are in Back of the Yards, but this is partly because the white levels are so much lower than the white levels elsewhere. The only area in which there is a large discrepancy in local-facility use is in church attendance (table 3.9). Here we find a pattern typical both in our own communities and elsewhere—whites attend the local churches. This is partly a consequence of length of residence and partly a consequence of the fact that Roman Catholics usually attend church where they live. Blacks, by contrast, often attend church in the neighborhood they left behind.

Low levels of local-facility use, characteristic of Austin as well as of South Shore, present one with a chicken-and-egg problem: Do the facilities vanish first, causing people to stop using them, or do local people stop using them, for whatever reason, causing economic hardship to local shopkeepers who then go out of business or move away? We do know from other data that income-level-for-income-level, blacks in Chicago tend to support local facilities less than do whites (Wittberg 1982). This is reflected both in the quality and quantity of shopping strips within black communities and in the fact that blacks simply report using them less, no matter what the circumstances. This may result in peculiar patterns. We will see, for example, that Beverly's main shopping strip and the large shopping center adjacent to it are patronized very heavily by blacks, who from their very numbers cannot all be from the community. Informal interviews with store owners also suggest that they are not local. Neither of those shopping areas is patronized by the local whites whose residences surround them.

Our field experiences suggest that blacks often shop outside their community because they believe that better-quality goods are available in white communities. In addition, blacks are more likely to patronize heavily advertised name brands,[3] and larger varieties of these may be available in bigger stores in shopping centers and downtown. In Austin, although the strips are more deteriorated in the black areas, none of them has ever been distinguished for the quality and range of their stores. Department stores and shopping centers are quite close to Austin, so it is possible that white residents have always done much of their shopping elsewhere.

In summary, the communities that have undergone succession or are in the process of doing so reflect some of the costs of change. They are low in their levels of stability, cohesion, and community commitment. The one partial exception is Back of the Yards, where the old ethnic whites show social patterns similar to other white ethnic working-class communities.

These communities also fit the stereotype of the succession process in that they are high in crime, although, as we shall see, racial succession is not essential for high crime rates. Also, high rates of turnover accompanied by low levels of cohesion are not necessarily creators of social disorder, low levels of commitment, and high levels of deterioration.

Crime and Other Urban Problems

South Shore and Austin are clearly high-crime communities; Back of the Yards is more ambiguously so. South Shore ranks first among the eight communities both in total crime according to police reports and in total victimization according to survey responses. It ranks first on police reports of personal crime as well. Austin fares slightly better overall, ranking third on total police crime reports and second on total victimization, although it does rank first on personal victimization. Back of the Yards is lower than South Shore and Austin on both measures, ranking fifth on total crime and fourth on total victimization. It nevertheless ranks second on personal victimization, and its total rates are substantially higher than those of East Side, Portage Park, and Beverly—the three communities that are unequivocally low in crime.

Residents' assessments of the crime situation in these three communities are consistent with the levels of crime and victimization. A larger percentage of respondents than in any of the other communities say that there is a lot of crime in their neighborhood and that the likelihood they will be a victim of a crime is high (tables 3.10 and 3.11).

Residents of these communities are also among the most fearful of crime. Austin and Back of the Yards rank first and second, respectively, in the proportion of respondents who often worry that they will be the victims of a crime and that their homes will be broken into when they are away (table 3.12). Residents of these two communities are also the most fearful of strangers who ask directions at night, although the orders are reversed. South Shore respondents are somewhat less fearful, but they still express fairly high levels of fear. They rank second, behind Austin and ahead of Back of the Yards, in the percentage who feel uneasy when

Table 3.10 Respondents Who Report "a Lot" of Crime in their Neighborhood

Neighborhood	Percentage
Back of the Yards	12.7
Austin	12.8
South Shore	11.7
East Side	6.3
Portage Park	3.5
Beverly	3.5
Hyde Park–Kenwood	9.8
Lincoln Park	9.5

Table 3.11 Respondents Who Believe that the Likelihood of Experiencing Criminal Victimization during the Coming Year is High

Neighborhood	Percentage
Back of the Yards	11.5
Austin	18.1
South Shore	10.1
East Side	2.1
Portage Park	2.0
Beverly	2.7
Hyde Park–Kenwood	6.9
Lincoln Park	6.8

they hear footsteps behind them at night, and in the top half of the eight communities on the other items (table 3.12).

In Back of the Yards, blacks are somewhat more fearful than whites. Hispanics, however, are much lower than either blacks or whites in their perceptions of both the amount of crime and the probability of being victimized in the neighborhood. They are also less likely to worry about being victimized. There are no consistent racial differences on these items in Austin (table 3.13).

The crime problem in Austin is compounded by an acute sense that the police do not provide much help. Prostitution, for example, is a major problem that does not show up in our crime or victimization data. One informant (a homeowner who, in opposition to most community organizers, hopes that a contemplated city highway will slash through the community and thereby take his home, which he is unable to sell) reported that his street was daily covered by streetwalkers and their pimps. This

Table 3.12 Fear of Crime: Respondents Who Give Positive Responses to Each Item (percentage)

Neighborhood	Often Worry about Being Victimized in the Neighborhood	Would Fear a Stranger Who Asked for Directions at Night	Worry that Home Will Be Burglarized	Feel Uneasy When They Hear Footsteps behind Them at Night
Back of the Yards	39.3	68.0	51.1	73.0
Austin	44.9	63.0	57.0	79.2
South Shore	36.2	61.8	42.4	77.3
East Side	19.3	50.0	38.2	57.8
Portage Park	22.0	50.1	38.3	56.4
Beverly	15.3	50.4	24.2	53.8
Hyde Park–Kenwood	36.5	58.0	35.3	68.9
Lincoln Park	23.8	46.6	42.7	66.7

Table 3.13 Assessment and Fear of Crime, by Race—Back of the Yards and Austin

	Back of the Yards			Austin	
Characteristic	White	Black	Hispanic	White	Black
Percentage who say there is "a lot" of crime in their neighborhood	16.4	15.8	3.1	11.3	13.1
Percentage who say the likelihood of victimization in the neighborhood during the coming year is high	14.0	18.6	3.0	19.7	18.5
Percentage who:					
a. Often worry about being victimized in the neighborhood	44.9	48.1	22.4	49.3	43.7
b. Would fear a stranger who asked for directions at night	64.3	74.4	70.6	60.8	65.2
c. Worry that home will be burglarized	48.1	59.3	54.5	58.7	56.6
d. Feel uneasy when they hear footsteps behind them at night	74.0	81.3	67.0	81.1	80.5

situation was so prevalent that the neighborhood children were able to quote prices of a whole range of sexual services. A block club was formed and met with local police officials. Officials informed the club that the prostitutes could be driven out if the neighborhood and the police worked together. Much of the sexual activity, this respondent said, was covert. But one evening he looked out his window to see a couple taking off their clothes in a car and quite visibly practicing intercourse. He called the police emergency number to complain and was told that no cars were available to deal with the complaint. He was told to call his local district. There he was told the same thing. He has since given up. He would sell his house in a minute, he says, if he could find a buyer.

We anticipate our discussion of South Shore's overall position relative to that of Back of the Yards and Austin by pointing out that South Shore residents have also been plagued by prostitution. They, however, were able to get one motel and one apartment building torn down and another building closed by the city; all the buildings had been sites of prostitute activity. Some have argued that residents are simply chasing the prostitutes from building to building. Even so, the effort bespeaks the success of South Shore's organizational activity relative to that of Austin's.

Consistent with high crime and its attendant problems is the severity of other urban problems in Back of the Yards, Austin, and South Shore. We asked respondents whether each of the following items was a big problem, somewhat of a problem, or not a problem in their neighborhood:

a. Noisy neighbors; people who play loud music, have late parties, or have noisy quarrels
b. Dogs barking loudly or relieving themselves near your home
c. People not disposing of garbage properly or leaving litter around the area
d. Poor maintenance of property and lawns
e. People who say insulting things or bother people as they walk down the street
f. Landlords who don't care about what happens to the neighborhood
g. Purse snatching and other street crimes
h. Presence of drugs and drug users
i. Abandoned houses or other empty buildings
j. Vacant lots filled with trash and junk

To determine how the neighborhoods compared with each other overall in terms of the perceived severity of urban problems, we derived a composite measure from this series of items.[4] On this measure, Austin ranks first, South Shore is second, and Back of the Yards is third (table 3.14). Also indicative of their similarity is the fact that in four of the six individual items on which these neighborhoods occupy the three worst positions, the percentage differences among them are less than the differences between them and the fourth-ranking community (table 3.15). The largest disparity among the three communities is found in problems with dogs. This difference is interesting in view of the fact that the proportions of respondents who report keeping a watchdog for protection run in the opposite direction (table 3.16). It may be that in Back of the Yards and, to a lesser extent, in Austin, something such as more concern for the neighborhood or more informal social control is operating.

Our independent measures of deterioration and other evidence of neglect suggest that South Shore and Austin residents may be either somewhat fussier or more depressed than Back of the Yards residents. According to these measures, Back of the Yards is in slightly worse condition than either South Shore or Austin in both structural quality and lawn maintenance (table 3.17). If we consider only South Austin, the most deteriorated section of Austin, the ratings are closer, but even then, Back of the Yards appears to be a little more neglected.

One must be careful about this rating system. Our data indicate that lack of maintenance shows up sooner in frame buildings than it does in those of brick or stone. Back of the Yards does have a higher percentage

Table 3.14 Rank Order of Neighborhoods by Problems (1 = largest percentage who say item is a problem)

Neighborhood	Noisy Neighbors	Dog Nuisances	Garbage, Litter	Poor Care of Property, Lawns	People Who Hassle Others	Landlords Who Don't Care	Street Crimes	Drugs and Drug Users	Abandoned Buildings	Vacant Lots	Sum of Ranks	Overall Rank
Back of the Yards	1	6	2	3	2	4	4	4	3	2	31	3
Austin	3	4	1	1	1	1	3	3	1	1	19	1
South Shore	2	1	3	2	3	2	1	2	2	3	21	2
East Side	6	7	6	6	6	6	7	1	7	6	58	6
Portage Park	7	8	7	8	8	7	6	6	8	8	73	8
Beverly	8	5	8	7	7	8	8	5	4	7	67	7
Hyde Park–Kenwood	5	3	5	4	4	3	2	7	6	4	43	4
Lincoln Park	4	2	4	5	5	5	5	8	5	5	48	5

Table 3.15 Respondents Who Report Item as a Neighborhood Problem (percentage)

Neighborhood	Noisy Neighbors	Dog Nuisances	Garbage, Litter	Poor Care of Property, Lawns	People Who Hassle Others	Landlords Who Don't Care	Street Crimes	Drugs and Drug Users	Abandoned Buildings	Vacant Lots
Back of the Yards	34.3	43.0	55.8	38.7	23.7	34.8	42.9	43.1	31.8	31.0
Austin	33.7	52.2	60.7	45.2	26.6	46.4	49.7	43.9	41.5	34.7
South Shore	33.8	62.8	55.0	42.8	22.4	41.4	53.8	48.1	36.1	28.4
East Side	14.8	34.4	27.1	13.9	11.2	12.4	32.4	54.7	6.9	13.4
Portage Park	13.5	31.9	20.6	9.1	5.1	8.9	34.8	27.0	4.1	4.0
Beverly	10.2	47.6	19.5	12.7	8.7	6.6	29.8	29.3	8.7	6.0
Hyde Park–Kenwood	20.4	55.0	38.9	29.3	17.5	37.1	51.8	26.7	7.2	23.1
Lincoln Park	24.7	61.4	44.3	20.1	12.8	19.9	42.0	25.9	8.1	15.2

See Question 11 of survey instrument in Appendix B for exact wording of items.

Table 3.16 Respondents with Watchdogs and/or Dog-related Complaints—Back of the Yards, Austin, and South Shore (percentage)

	Percentage with Dogs	Percentage with Dog-related Complaints
Back of the Yards	42.7	43.0
Austin	36.1	52.2
South Shore	25.3	62.8

Table 3.17 Average Proportion per Block of Structures, Lawns, and Parkways with Flaws

Neighborhood	Structures	Lawns	Parkways
Back of the Yards	.178	.301	.209
Austin	.162	.249	.236
South Shore	.145	.260	.276
East Side	.098	.138	.102
Portage Park	.083	.070	.067
Beverly	.066	.059	.078
Hyde Park–Kenwood	.136	.206	.213
Lincoln Park	.157	.246	.168

of frame buildings than do South Shore and Austin. (For example, 69 percent of the single-family dwellings in Back of the Yards are frame compared to 53 percent in Austin.) On lawn-maintenance items, however, such variations should not show up. Even here, though, Austin and South Shore are in better shape than Back of the Yards.

Back of the Yards does fare better in the upkeep of what in Chicago are called parkways, the space between the sidewalk and the street. This difference may contribute to the observer's general gestalt that South Shore and especially Austin are in worse shape. The measurement of the appearance of neglect is a tricky business. We did our evaluations by looking with care. The average passerby, in contrast, may with a single sweep of the eye simply react generally to the scene—the components that have value in shaping his or her determination may differ from those that would be salient if he or she looked more closely. Litter on parkways may be one of those components. One urban developer with whom we discussed these matters does believe that litter, more than anything else, determines perceptions of shopping-strip quality. That littering is perceived to be a problem in Austin is illustrated by the fact that many block clubs in Austin display the following sign:

[Block club's name]
No littering

No car washing in front
No drinking or ball playing
No loud music
No speeding

Taken together, then, these three neighborhoods are the most consistently undermaintained of those in our sample. On other dimensions, however, there is more differentiation among them. One such dimension is the extent to which black in-migration is perceived to bring negative consequences to the neighborhood.

Perceived Consequences of Integration

Consistent with the discussion in chapter 1 of greater fear of and weaker tolerance for integration among the working class, Back of the Yards ranks first among the eight neighborhoods in the percentage of respondents who believe that crime goes up and property values go down when blacks move in (table 3.18). These large percentages reflect the attitudes of black residents as well as of whites. Although a greater percentage of whites than blacks agree with both statements, the black levels are nevertheless quite high (table 3.19). Compared to the other seven neighborhoods, black Back of the Yards residents rank behind only East Side residents in agreeing that crime goes up when blacks move in, and behind only East Side and Portage Park in agreeing that property values go down when blacks move in.

Austinites are less willing than Back of the Yards residents to see racial change as a source of problems. Austin ranks third, after Back of

Table 3.18 Perceived Consequences of Integration (percentage)

Neighborhood	When a few black families move into an all-white neighborhood:		
	Crime rates usually go up (mostly true)	Property values are sure to go down (mostly true)	They [black families] usually have the same income and education as the people who live there (mostly false)
Back of the Yards	57.8	75.2	38.1
Austin	40.5	52.1	40.0
South Shore	28.7	48.2	39.1
East Side	54.9	71.6	36.8
Portage Park	38.7	69.7	25.7
Beverly	24.9	27.5	14.2
Hyde Park–Kenwood	16.8	35.7	20.8
Lincoln Park	17.5	34.7	19.2

Table 3.19 Perceived Consequences of Integration, by Race—Back of the Yards and Austin (percentage)

When a few black families move into an all-white neighborhood:	Back of the Yards			Austin	
	White	Black	Hispanic	White	Black
Crime rates usually go up (mostly true)	60.0	49.3	60.5	23.8	44.4
Property values are sure to go down (mostly true)	72.4	67.1	84.8	45.6	53.5
They [black families] usually have the same income and education as the people who live there (mostly false)	37.3	47.2	34.1	26.2	44.7

the Yards and East Side, in agreeing with the statement that when blacks move in, crime goes up; Austin ranks fourth, after Back of the Yards, East Side, and Portage Park, in agreeing with the statement that when blacks move in, property values go down (table 3.18). The percentages expressing agreement with the statements are still sizable, however. Moreover, the belief that negative consequences result from black inmigration is more prevalent among blacks than among whites (table 3.19).

In line with the community's more middle-class character, South Shore residents are less ready to attribute a community's misfortunes to racial transition than are the black residents in Austin and in Back of the Yards. South Shore ranks fifth on the items concerning race, crime, and property values. Austin, Back of the Yards, Portage Park, and East Side all rank higher.

As one might expect, Back of the Yards and Austin rank first and second, respectively, in the proportion of respondents who say that their neighborhood is racially changing (table 3.20). In both neighborhoods, whites are more likely than blacks to hold this view, although the difference is larger in Back of the Yards than in Austin (table 3.21).

Nearly half of South Shore residents report that their neighborhood is changing, an initially puzzling finding for a community that is 90-percent black. That blacks in virtually all black neighborhoods are concerned about stability, however, is explicable in terms of the changing class structure of blacks discussed in chapter 1. For blacks who have achieved middle-class status, a stable neighborhood is one that is perceived as able to hold its middle-class character. An unstable neighborhood is one in which soft-market forces encourage the area to take on

Table 3.20 Respondents Who Say That Their Neighborhood is Racially Changing

Neighborhood	Percentage
Back of the Yards	67.2
Austin	55.2
South Shore	48.2
East Side	42.2
Portage Park	31.1
Beverly	26.4
Hyde Park–Kenwood	27.9
Lincoln Park	42.4

Table 3.21 Respondents Who Say That Their Neighborhood is Racially Changing, by Race—Back of the Yards and Austin (percentage)

	White	Black	Hispanic
Back of the Yards	77.3	60.8	53.3
Austin	59.5	53.7	—

increasingly the character of the black underclass. Some middle-class blacks have moved several times in order to stay one step ahead of "the element." Consequently, blacks in middle-class neighborhoods have concerns about maintaining the socioeconomic status of their community.

Overall Evaluation of the Neighborhood

In terms of residents' general assessments of their neighborhoods, Back of the Yards, Austin, and South Shore again occupy the lowest positions. Here too, however, there are differences among them.

Satisfaction levels are relatively low in Back of the Yards, with only 72 percent of the respondents reporting general satisfaction with the neighborhood, placing it just slightly ahead of the other two lowest-ranking neighborhoods, Austin and South Shore (table 3.22). Forty-five percent report that the neighborhood has declined in the past two years, and the same percentage predict that it will continue downward in the next two (tables 3.23 and 3.24). Less than half of the respondents feel that purchasing a house in the neighborhood would be a good investment (table 3.25).

Looking at the responses to these questions by race of the respondent, it can be seen that blacks and whites are quite similar and even more negative in their evaluations of the neighborhood (table 3.26). However,

Table 3.22 Respondents' Reports of Neighborhood Satisfaction (percentage)

Neighborhood	Very Satisfied	Somewhat Satisfied
Back of the Yards	26.3	45.5
Austin	23.7	44.4
South Shore	20.8	46.5
East Side	53.6	37.8
Portage Park	59.8	36.4
Beverly	71.8	22.3
Hyde Park–Kenwood	41.6	44.1
Lincoln Park	58.8	34.5

Table 3.23 Respondents' Reports of Neighborhood Conditions of Past Two Years (percentage)

Neighborhood	Better	About the Same	Worse
Back of the Yards	8.2	46.5	45.3
Austin	8.5	48.4	43.0
South Shore	16.6	44.6	38.8
East Side	14.2	68.8	17.0
Portage Park	6.8	82.6	10.6
Beverly	26.6	65.0	8.4
Hyde Park–Kenwood	22.4	65.5	12.1
Lincoln Park	43.4	50.5	6.2

Table 3.24 Respondents' Predictions of Neighborhood Conditions for Next Two Years (percentage)

Neighborhood	Better	About the Same	Worse
Back of the Yards	14.4	40.4	45.1
Austin	17.3	39.5	43.3
South Shore	35.8	35.1	29.1
East Side	10.1	73.4	16.5
Portage Park	10.0	74.1	15.9
Beverly	25.7	66.9	7.3
Hyde Park–Kenwood	30.9	57.5	11.5
Lincoln Park	51.9	40.9	7.2

Table 3.25 Respondents Who Feel That Buying a House in the Neighborhood Would be a Good Financial Investment

Neighborhood	Percentage
Back of the Yards	46.1
Austin	46.8
South Shore	59.8
East Side	82.7
Portage Park	87.5
Beverly	93.1
Hyde Park–Kenwood	81.4
Lincoln Park	85.8

the third major group, the Hispanics, stands in real contrast, showing a substantially more positive orientation toward the community. The proportions of those who are generally satisfied with the neighborhood and who think it is a good place to invest are higher for the Hispanics than for either the blacks or the whites. Only 25 percent of the Hispanics report that the neighborhood has declined during the past two years, although a substantially larger 41 percent think it will get worse within the next two (table 3.26).

The Hispanics, in their short time in the area, thus seem to have established a relatively more communal and satisfying world for themselves than either the blacks or the whites. This may reflect the fact that

Table 3.26 Measures of Overall Assessment of Neighborhood, by Race—Back of the Yards and Austin

Characteristic	Back of the Yards			Austin	
	White	Black	Hispanic	White	Black
Percentage who are very or somewhat satisfied overall with their neighborhood	67.6	62.6	85.5	70.7	66.7
Percentage who say neighborhood has gotten worse in past two years	51.9	57.5	25.0	44.6	43.8
Percentage who say neighborhood will get worse in the next two years	49.3	42.1	41.4	37.1	45.8
Percentage who say buying a house in their neighborhood would be making a good financial investment	44.4	40.3	54.3	56.3	43.8

for many of them, Back of the Yards is fulfilling its traditional function as a point of entry for groups newly coming to this country. For such new arrivals, expectations are not necessarily very high. For them, it is the first rung on a ladder, rather than a dead end or a trap. In addition, as Roman Catholics, they are able to enter into the web of relationships that has been a source of strength to the white neighborhood. The converse of this is that because they are Roman Catholic, they are also part of a social world that is very much more acceptable to the white population. Although we do not have survey data on white attitudes toward Hispanics, we do know that Hispanics live comfortably in East Side and Bridgeport, areas where black residents have not been permitted to date. In fact, Miss East Side of 1980 was Hispanic. And, as we discussed earlier, Hispanic names and faces are much more likely to appear in the *Back of the Yards Journal* than are black ones.

It would seem to be the case that through common church membership, Hispanics and whites are able to relate to each other in meaningful ways and to become part of the same world. It is also true in a more general sense that prejudice against blacks is stronger than it is against Hispanics. Nonetheless, it should be noted that in the Southwest, where the receiving culture is Protestant and anti-Catholic rather than the ethnic Catholic type of Chicago, anti-Hispanic attitudes among the whites seem to be more deeply rooted.

In general orientations toward the neighborhood, Austin residents are very similar to those in Back of the Yards. Only a few percentage points separate them on general satisfaction, evaluation of the recent past, or expectations for the near future (tables 3.22–3.25). Blacks and whites in Austin are equally likely to say the neighborhood has gotten worse in the past two years, and they express overall general satisfaction at about the same levels. However, the whites are somewhat more positive about the future of the neighborhood, with 37 percent whites compared to 46 percent blacks saying it will get worse and 56 percent whites compared to 44 percent blacks saying it is a good place for investment (table 3.26).

South Shore residents' perceptions of their community are largely negative and, in that sense, similar to those in Back of the Yards and Austin. In overall satisfaction, South Shore respondents are very close to those in the latter two neighborhoods, and the percentage who say the neighborhood has gotten worse in the past two years is not much smaller. On other indicators, however, South Shore fares better than our first two high-crime communities. Almost 60 percent of South Shore respondents, compared to about 46 percent in Back of the Yards and Austin, think that a family buying a house in the neighborhood would be making a good financial investment. Fewer respondents in South Shore than in Austin or

Back of the Yards think that the neighborhood will get worse during the next two years (29.1 percent compared to 45.1 percent and 43.3 percent, respectively).

That South Shore respondents predict a somewhat better future for their community than do those in Back of the Yards and Austin is related to the fact that property appreciation, after a period of stagnation, has begun to improve. Although South Shore was initially classified by us as a low-appreciating neighborhood, its 1973–78 rate of growth of 96 percent in unadjusted dollars puts it ahead of low-crime East Side with a rate of 64 percent, makes it comparable to low-crime Portage Park with a rate of 95 percent, and ranks it just behind low-crime Beverly with a rate of 113 percent. Its appreciation rate is nearly five times as high as Back of the Yards' and almost twice as high as Austin's.

In short, for a community so high in crime and deterioration, South Shore seems to be doing rather well in both property appreciation and optimism relative to its most comparable communities, Austin and Back of the Yards. In this difference lie several important facts. For example, there is abundant evidence that redlining continues to be a serious problem in Austin (we have no comparable information for Back of the Yards). By contrast, the flow of investment funds into the South Shore community, although almost cut off at one point, has once again been turned on, partly by virtue of community effort.

One institution sharing the general level of prosperity in South Shore during the 1950s was the South Shore National Bank. During the period of racial change, deposits began to flow out of the bank as departing residents took their money with them. Other banks began to reduce their mortgage activity, and the South Shore Bank did the same until it was no longer giving any new mortgages. Just as many of the store owners left the community or moved their stores elsewhere, the bank tried to do the same. In order to sell the bank, its owners proposed to move it downtown. In Chicago's changing communities, banks have often closed or left the area they historically served.

However, banks must secure permission from regulatory agencies to make such a move. When a public hearing was initiated to determine whether or not the bank should be permitted to leave the neighborhood, the South Shore Commission mobilized testimony against the move. It should be noted that the same well-known real estate research corporation that had informed South Shore's leaders that the community was finished also testified on the bank's behalf, explaining that the bank could not survive in South Shore. However, after much testimony and some political activity, the comptroller of the currency decided that the bank should remain in the community. The bank was judged viable, and its move would be a threat to the health of the community.

At about this time, a group that had practiced and succeeded at minority lending in nearby Hyde Park–Kenwood proposed to buy the bank with funds both of their own and of socially conscious investors. That was in 1973. Today, the bank is still doing business, its deposits substantially augmented.

The story of the bank's aggressive lending policies and its skills at attracting other investors to the area is too long to be told here. However, there has been a growing flow of both public and private investment funds into the area. Even the city, which had lost confidence in the community after racial change, in 1980 announced a program to improve conditions along one of South Shore's shopping strips. And the South Shore Bank, along with the city's second largest bank, announced in 1980 the start of a 25-million-dollar housing-rehabilitation project in the Parkside area.

South Shore community organizational activity has been noteworthy in other areas as well. The city of Chicago has a little-used law on its books that enables precincts to vote themselves dry. The organizational feat to achieve this result is substantial, partly because of the complexities involved in getting the question on the ballot and partly because tavern owners are politically well connected. In South Shore, ten precincts were able to vote themselves dry and drive away taverns.

Residents were also able to protect the elegant buildings of the old South Shore Country Club when the club was sold to the Chicago Park District. Park-district plans included replacing the building with a cement-block field house and the golf course with a pitch-and-putt course. After a prolonged conflict, the park district agreed to maintain the major structures and to make no other changes without community participation. Finally, as we discussed earlier, South Shore residents were able to close several buildings that were sites of prostitution.

South Shore's higher social-class base, changes in expectations fostered by a major institutional actor, and organizational activity have together changed the area's general direction.

Overall, then, the outlook for South Shore is more promising than that for Back of the Yards or Austin. Back of the Yards stands as a symbol of the precariousness of low-income inner-city neighborhoods. In a very short time, it has moved from a stable, low-crime, ethnic neighborhood to a deteriorating one with higher levels of crime. Austin is also an acutely depressed area. High in crime, low on most other measures of neighborhood quality, it is close to being the very model, at least in its southern two-thirds, of the deteriorated urban community. To say that South Shore has been more successful is not to say that it is no longer threatened with decline. Its problems are still of substantial proportions. Nevertheless, the experience of South Shore provides a hint that high crime and racial change do not necessarily lead to deterioration.

4

"It Won't Happen Here": East Side and Portage Park

We have looked at three neighborhoods that have been involved in the process of racial succession. We now turn to two virtually all-white, working-class neighborhoods, the residents of which are hostile to the possible arrival of blacks in their neighborhoods. One of them, East Side, is much like Back of the Yards before succession began. Working class and ethnic, its economic reason for being is weakening as the steel industry in the Midwest erodes. And low-income black families are at the neighborhood's doorstep. Portage Park, by contrast, is located further from the path of black expansion than any other neighborhood in this study. Unlike Back of the Yards and East Side, and more like South Shore, Portage Park was established primarily as a residential neighborhood, not as part of an economic node. Like East Side and Back of the Yards, its residents share the view that the arrival of blacks in a community signals its inevitable decline. In better physical condition than much of East Side, it is nevertheless feeling some of the effects of the general decline of the attractiveness of city residence generated by the macro forces we discussed in chapter 1.

Let us turn first to East Side. The growth of East Side as a residential area coincided with the growth of the Calumet region as an industrial area. Like Back of the Yards, East Side grew around an industrial node. The region has a natural port, and that attribute, coupled with the location of a rail line that was to become the New York Central, made it attractive for the production of steel. The opening of the Silicon Steel Company's rolling mills in the early 1870s heralded the beginning of the industrial era.

Improvements in the harbor and river a decade later, along with the construction of a number of rail lines, led to the further growth of the steel industry there. By the 1920s, the region had become a national industrial giant. From Gary, Indiana on the east to the United States

Steel South Works just north and west of East Side, the shore came to be dominated by the steel and, to a somewhat lesser extent, petroleum industries. In addition to United States Steel, Bethlehem Steel, Wisconsin Steel, and Republic Steel all have large plants in the area. Republic Steel's plant is located in East Side itself, and the neighborhood has seen the growth of many allied industries as well.

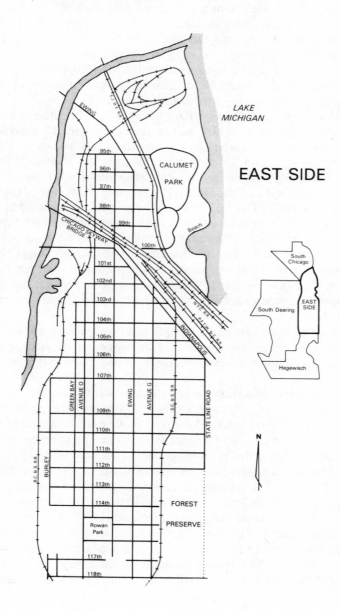

Residential construction in East Side began at the northern edge of the community, near the first steel plant, and has since moved east and south. The construction in the 1920s of Calumet Park (see map) on land fill encouraged the eastward movement of the community. The park's 194 acres with numerous athletic fields, a beach and bath house, a bandstand, and winding roads has since become the community's front yard and symbolic center. The community's teams play each other there; lovers stroll or, more likely, drive their cars in the evening on its roads; children climb on its swings; and old folks sit on its beaches. The annual Labor Day parade, an important event in the neighborhood, comes to a culmination in front of the bandstand where Miss East Side is selected. When residents are asked about East Side, they often spontaneously mention the park as one of the area's virtues.

Unlike East Side, Portage Park began as a residential community. Located at the site of an old Indian portage between the Chicago and Des Plaines rivers, the community grew up around a well-known tavern which had become a popular stopping place for travelers. Although incorporated into the city in 1889, Portage Park grew slowly until street-car lines reached it fifteen years later, and its first housing boom ensued (Kitagawa and Taeuber 1963). The park in Portage Park was constructed in 1915—its central feature then, as today, a large swimming pool (see map).

By 1924, the neighborhood was a fully established residential community. Later a small industrial area grew up on the community's eastern edge, and some housing was constructed in the section furthest from the center of the city in the late 1940s and early 1950s. However, by 1924 the community's character was firmly established and seems to have changed little since that time.

The differences between East Side and Portage Park extend beyond those of their historical growth and development. East Side is both physically more impermeable and socially more cohesive than is Portage Park.

East Side is truly distinctive in the extent of its isolation from the rest of the city of Chicago. Physically, it is tucked away between the miles of steel mills to the west and the lakefront to the east. Bounded as well on the north and west by the Calumet River, it can be reached from elsewhere in Chicago only by crossing one of its drawbridges. Residents themselves like to say that when the drawbridges are up, East Side is an inaccessible island. (Actually, it is only inaccessible from the rest of Chicago. It abuts Indiana to the southeast and another very similar community, Hegewisch, directly to the south.)

Except to conduct business, there is little reason for outsiders to pass through East Side. In fact, most of East Side lies in the shadow of the Chicago Skyway which speeds travelers on their way from Chicago to Indiana. When we were conducting this study, residents of our other

PORTAGE PARK

seven communities, even those in nearby South Shore, often refused to believe that such a community even existed. ("East side of what?" they would ask.)

Portage Park, by contrast, is relatively permeable. It has no clear boundary markers, and residents themselves are less likely to identify their neighborhood by its "official" community area name than are the residents of other areas. Ninety percent of all East Side respondents, the largest in any of the communities, identified their neighborhood by the community area name. Only 58 percent of Portage Park residents did the same (table 4.1). In addition, traveling through the area, one cannot tell where Portage Park begins and the surrounding neighborhoods end.

Portage Park's lack of differentiation from the surrounding world is illustrated in another way. Three local newspapers are published on

Table 4.1 Respondents Who Identify Their Neighborhood by the Community Area Name

Neighborhood	Percentage
Back of the Yards	50.0
Austin	79.9
South Shore	87.4
East Side	90.3
Portage Park	58.3
Beverly	77.9
Hyde Park–Kenwood	85.1
Lincoln Park	55.7

Chicago's northwest side. Each of them follows the procedure of having one basic newspaper whose logo is changed for each community area. The news, then, within each series published by a particular publisher, is almost always the same. Most of it is reported as applying to the "northwest side," and only some advertisers and sometimes one story is changed to fit the appropriate community area. Thus the *Portage Park News* and the *Irving Park News*, both products of the Peacock Publishing Company which is not located in either neighborhood, are virtually identical. By contrast, East Side, although it does not have its own paper, is regularly and thoroughly covered by the *Daily Calumet* which identifies East Side news clearly.

The permeability of the community is heightened by the fact that although Portage Park has the two most successful residential shopping areas among our communities, each is located on edges of the community rather than in the center. Consequently, in addition to the local population, the shopping areas serve a substantial segment of the city's northwest side.

Stability and Social Cohesion

Paralleling the differences between East Side and Portage Park in physical distinctiveness and identity are differences in social cohesion. With its multi-stranded, dense social relations, East Side closely resembles the ideal, typical community that has been the subject of much sociological thinking from Durkheim to the present.

Unlike the transience typical of much of modern American urban life, East Side is characterized by residential stability. According to our survey, 25 percent of its residents have lived there all their lives, and the median length of residence for the remainder is fifteen years (table 4.2). Although Portage Park is also stable relative to the other communities, it

Table 4.2 Length of Residence

Neighborhood	Percentage Living in Neighborhood All Their Lives	Median Length of Residence for Remainder (in years)
Back of the Yards	18.9	6
Austin	0	6
South Shore	2.0	7
East Side	25.4	15
Portage Park	7.6	11
Beverly	7.7	8
Hyde Park–Kenwood	2.9	6
Lincoln Park	3.7	4

is less so than East Side. Similarly, approximately three-fourths of the respondents in each community consider their neighborhood to be a real home, placing East Side and Portage Park behind only Beverly (see table 3.1), but more East Siders say that they will definitely not move from the neighborhood during the next year (table 3.2).

Modern urban life is said to attenuate family ties because of increased mobility among members, but 75 percent of East Side respondents report that they have relatives living in the community (table 3.7), and more than half report that they visit their relatives at least once a week (table 3.4). Internal social life is buttressed by the fact that 90 percent of East Side respondents report having good friends in the community (table 3.3), and one-third also report that they visit neighbors once a week or more (table 3.4). East Side respondents rank second only to those in Beverly in being able to count on their neighbors during illness, to have their neighbors keep watch on their house, and to borrow money from their neighbors in an emergency (table 3.5).

Portage Park residents, by contrast, display relatively weak social ties. Portage Park respondents rank third, after East Side, in the percentage who can count on their neighbors to run errands, watch their houses, and loan them money (table 3.5). However, with 34.9 percent of respondents reporting that they have relatives in the neighborhood, Portage Park ranks below not only East Side, but also Beverly, Austin, Back of the Yards, and South Shore (table 3.7). The 67.9 percent who report that they have good friends in the neighborhood is a smaller proportion than in any of the other communities (table 3.3): Portage Parkers also visit with their neighbors less frequently than do respondents anywhere else except in Austin and South Shore (table 3.4). Portage Park residents do make heavy use of local facilities, as do East Side residents (table 3.6).

So, although East Side and Portage Park are comparable demographically and in some dimensions of "community," on a continuum from multi-stranded to single-stranded relationships, primary to second-ary ties, and whole to limited liability, East Side is much closer to one polar type than is Portage Park. These differences will be further in evidence we as turn to issues of crime, race, and economic well-being.

Crime and Other Urban Problems

Whether measured by police-report data or self-reported victimization data, East Side and Portage Park are low-crime areas, and residents in both communities perceive this to be the case. Only 6.3 percent of East Side respondents and an even smaller 3.5 percent of Portage Park respondents report that there is a lot of crime in the neighborhood (table 3.10). In addition, only 2 percent of the respondents in either community think the probability that they will be victimized during the next year is high (table 3.11). Only Beverly has comparably low percentages on these items.

Residents of Portage Park and East Side are also generally less fearful of crime than are residents of other neighborhoods, but this fact should be placed in context. More than half of the respondents in each community feel uneasy if they hear footsteps behind them at night, and more than one-third worry that their house will be broken into when they are away. Worry, fear, and concern about crime are pervasive in the world of which we write. Nonetheless, compared to residents of the higher-crime communities, residents of East Side and Portage Park display, with those of Beverly, consistently lower levels of fear (table 3.12).

There are indications, however, that East Siders feel a greater sense of precariousness and worry about crime than do Portage Parkers, despite the fact that East Siders are confident that they do not yet have a crime problem. Residents worked to close a game arcade because it encouraged kids to hang out there. They also worked to close a particular bar where it seemed as if a disproportionate number of stabbings and other violent events took place.

In addition, East Side is physically closer to high-crime areas than is Portage Park. Responses to the question "Is there any area right around here—that is, within a mile—where you would be afraid to walk alone at night?" indicate that this difference has consequences for residents' feelings of fear. Only 38.3 percent of Portage Park respondents, the lowest percentage in any of the communities, answered yes. East Side is the next nearest community in the percentage who say yes, but 40-percent more respondents there—54.7 percent—express fear.

The seriousness of general urban problems closely tracks the crime rates for these two neighborhoods. Respondents in them (along with those in Beverly) perceive fewer problems than respondents in any of the other communities, with Portage Park residents reporting slightly better conditions for their neighborhood than East Siders do for theirs (table 3.14). The one dramatic exception concerns drug traffic and abuse which, by East-Sider-resident rankings, is worse than in any other community. Informants tell us there are lots of drugs in the steel mills; what we may have here is respondents with old-fashioned, high personal standards worried about a reality that would cause less concern in a place like Lincoln Park.

Our objective measures of deterioration also follow a similar general pattern. Both communities are objectively in better physical condition than the high-crime communities, although East Side is in a slightly worse state than Portage Park (table 3.17).

Perceived Consequences of Integration

Despite (or because of) the fact that both communities are overwhelmingly white, concern about race looms fairly large in both places. In this regard, they illustrate the pattern of working-class communities we described in chapter 1. We asked respondents whether they thought the following statements were mostly true or mostly false: "When a few black families move into an all white neighborhood, . . . crime rates usually go up. . . . Property values are sure to go down. . . . They [the black families] usually have the same income and education as the people who live there." Table 3.18 shows the percentage of respondents in each community who gave the negative response.

Portage Parkers are among those most likely to believe that negative consequences follow when blacks move into a neighborhood. What is even more astonishing is that with no blacks and a negligible number of Hispanics in the community, nearly one-third of Portage Park residents say that the neighborhood is racially changing (table 3.20). Orientals and Hispanics who have moved into nearby Albany Park do make use of Portage Park's shopping strips as well as the park itself, which perhaps accounts for the pattern of responses.

Negative feelings toward blacks are even more pronounced in East Side. Disputes between East Side neighbors seem often to include the threat that one will sell one's home to a black. East Side residents are, along with those of Back of the Yards, the most likely to believe that when a few blacks move in, crime rates go up and property values go down. And, ironically, with the exception of the communities with mostly black populations, East Side and Back of the Yards residents are the least likely to believe that the first blacks who move into a community are usually of the same economic level as the present residents.

Forty-two percent of East Side respondents say that the neighborhood is racially changing; with a population that is 8-percent Hispanic, East Side is more mixed racially than is Portage Park.

For the Hispanics, the move to East Side, probably from neighboring South Chicago, is a move upward on the social scale. They are more satisfied with their community than any other identifiable group of residents in any community, with fully 100 percent expressing overall satisfaction. They are newcomers to the community with a median length of residence of 2.5 years. As would be expected of newcomers, they are substantially less likely to consider their new neighborhood home (38.7 percent), and they are somewhat less able to count on their neighbors. Slightly more than half believe that they would count on their neighbors if they were sick, and 79.3 percent could borrow $25.00 from a neighbor. They can, however, count on their neighbors to watch their houses (93 percent). They are also more positive about the immediate past and the immediate future of the neighborhood. Only 3 percent thought the neighborhood had declined in the last two years (compared to 17 pecent for all East Side respondents), and about 11 percent expect decline in the future (compared to 16.5 percent overall).

Hispanics are less likely than other East Siders to make use of local facilities. On almost every facility-use item, they score lower than other East Side residents: shopping (66 versus 79 percent); clothing (12.5 versus 29 percent); restaurants (35.5 versus 53.9 percent); car repairs (42.9 versus 64.4 percent); banking (53.3 versus 79.2 percent); and even church attendance (48.3 versus 86.7 percent). East Side's shopping facilities are particularly paltry, and neighboring South Chicago with a wider range of shops is just across the river. It is not surprising, therefore, that newcomers would return to the familiar stores; rather it is almost more surprising that so many East Siders make such use of local facilities, given how few there are.

As in Back of the Yards, people of Hispanic background are more accepted than blacks are in East Side, although there have been tensions between Hispanics and others. Hispanics report a certain amount of abuse. According to one of our field workers, one of the uncertainties about Hispanics is the widely held belief that they would be more willing to sell their houses to blacks than would other residents.

East Siders do in general express hostility toward outsiders—perhaps the obverse of the fact that the community is such a tight one. Outsiders are always a problem for residents. A local librarian reports that people still view him suspiciously because he lives in a neighborhood five miles away and commutes to work. One of our students, herself an outsider, was told that people were reluctant to talk to her because they might get into trouble. And East Side is the neighborhood in which the most residents (79 percent) agreed: "It's pretty easy to tell a stranger from someone who lives in my immediate neighborhood."

This anxiety is most concretely expressed in open hostility toward blacks. Lacking the educational veneer of the residents of some other communities, East Siders speak out quite directly on this subject. Xenophobia in general and hostility toward blacks in particular was illustrated dramatically when one of us met with the East Side Civic Association to discuss our study.

Because the study was funded by Washington, some residents viewed us as part of a federal plot "to make us take colored." Others saw us as emissaries of the newly elected mayor. In this view, we had been sent to punish the community for voting so heavily for her opponent. Ultimately, we were expected to recommend that public housing be built in the community so that "you'll make us take that element we don't want."

Residents at that meeting were able to construct conspiracy theories about us in the way that the angry and powerless often do. At that time, the mayor's chief advisor was a professor, and we were professors, so there must be a connection. Did we know him? What had he suggested to us? Similarly, one of our research assistants had the same (fairly common) last name as the mayor's campaign manager. What was their connection? In all, there was a rather heatedly expressed consensus that we were anything but what we said we were and that we were up to no good, and, whatever it was, it was probably connected to race.[1]

Almost every plan for new nonresidential construction runs into tremendous community controversy for the same reason. At the time of the study, a group of community residents were fighting the construction of a small shopping mall on the grounds that it would bring undesirable outsiders into the community. In 1978, when a small A & P burned down, the owner of the site considered the construction of a McDonald's in its place. Residents protested on the same grounds. "They took me to court when I wanted to build the store and now they're complaining that it's not there any more," the property's owner complained (*Daily Calumet*, 12 December 1979).

In Portage Park, by contrast, a shopping center *outside* the neighborhood is a problem for residents, or at least for local merchants. There is great fear among them that this new center, the Brickyard, will draw customers away. The shop owners in the area closest to the new shopping center are now organizing themselves to strike back. The cornerstone in that effort is a new parking lot financed largely by the city. Portage Parkers may perceive that the shopping areas bring in many outsiders, but the shopkeepers at least realize that the outsiders are their bread and butter.

Overall Evaluation of the Neighborhood

The contrast in views toward new shopping facilities noted above probably reflects not only differences in the racial climates of the two communities, but also differences in their economic well-being. Portage Park has the two most successful residential shopping areas among our communities. In addition, starting with the second-highest base price of our eight communities, Portage Park showed a property-appreciation rate of 95 percent for the period 1973–78. Adequate housing appreciation coupled with the successful organization and maintenance of its shopping strips indicates that demand in Portage Park is sufficiently high, at present anyway, to forestall decline.

In East Side, on the other hand, economic uncertainty predominates. The American steel industry at the time of this study was, as it has been for many years, in a depressed condition. As one of the older steel-producing regions in the United States, the Calumet area's local plants have been left behind by forces both at home and abroad. In addition, the plants are the region's major polluters. Some have been threatening to close permanently if environmental-quality protection laws are enforced too stringently. Wisconsin Steel, one of the three major employers in the area, filed for bankruptcy during the period of our study. The others, caught in the 1979–80 recession, had laid off substantial numbers of workers.

Those layoffs ramify widely through the community. Retail business, according to some estimates, was off by 30 percent. People worried about making payments on their houses. Tensions generated by economic uncertainty can, according to informants, be felt—people are uneasy, short-tempered, and worried. When one adds to these problems East Side's lower rate of property-value appreciation, it becomes clear how much more precarious East Side is than Portage Park.

On overall satisfaction with the neighborhood, Portage Park and East Side are quite similar, with over 90 percent of the respondents in each neighborhood reporting that they are very or somewhat satisfied (table 3.22). The proportions who feel the neighborhood is a good place for investment are also quite similar, as are those who think the neighborhood has gotten better in the past two years and will get better in the next two, although East Siders' evaluations of the recent past are somewhat more negative (tables 3.21–3.25).

However, there is a sense of beleaguered feeling in East Side. It is a community which feels embattled and believes that its intransigence keeps it from disaster. This concern is not simply xenophobia. There is some evidence of undermaintenance in the northern part of the community. More importantly, the high median age of the population coupled with low levels of property appreciation and the decline of the steel industry leads us to believe that as people are increasingly unable to recover maintenance money in the market, further deterioration is around the corner.

In important respects, Portage Park represents a polar opposite when compared to East Side. Clearly, unlike East Side, Portage Park is not a defended community. People did at one time rally around efforts to prevent an expressway from being constructed through the area; but by and large, they perceive their area as unthreatened, and they have not generated community-wide organizations to deal with change, renovation, or other community problems. Not surprisingly, people in this neighborhood do not join voluntary associations to deal with community-wide problems. In East Side, where particularistic networks are very strong, 20.3 percent of respondents are members of organizations concerned with the quality of community life. The figure for Portage Park is only 11.9 percent (table 4.3). One knowledgeable informant characterized Portage Park residents as being "like so many grains of sand. . . . If they had to organize," he said, "they would have no existing basis on which to do it."

Neighborhoods that maintain levels of property appreciation through market demand and that maintain themselves physically as well do not "just happen." The maintenance of what is a more normal state of affairs in suburban housing, at least in newer suburbs, requires enormous effort of institutional actors and of residents through organizational activities as well as through strong social cohesion.

In this sense, then, Portage Park is an interesting anomaly. So far protected from the forces of decline by its distance from the central city, its residents are able to go about their business without organizing to protect themselves and without developing or maintaining the strong interpersonal social ties sometimes seen to be important in the maintenance of urban communities. By being far removed from both the poverty areas of the city and other components of deterioration, Portage Park is effectively shielded from some sources of crime.

In summary, then, these two communities add new dimensions to the discussions of the roles of racial succession and crime in neighborhood decay. Without such succession, with high levels of social cohesiveness

Table 4.3 Respondents Who Belong to an Organization Concerned with the Quality of Community Life

Neighborhood	Percentage
Back of the Yards	9.1
Austin	18.8
South Shore	17.8
East Side	20.3
Portage Park	11.9
Beverly	31.3
Hyde Park–Kenwood	20.9
Lincoln Park	15.7

and organization and low levels of crime, East Side, like some of the old New England mill communities, is deteriorating. Its economic functions have declined, making it difficult for those who want to live there and maintain their houses. In that sense, the social processes at work illustrate classical ecological theory. Reinforcing this tendency is the general trend of individuals to move away from older industrial areas and out to the suburbs—a key driving force in the older ecological theory. And the final stroke is the general move away from northern urban areas to new sections of opportunity. Hostile to and fearful of blacks, East Side residents are dug in to fight a battle that has already been lost on other dimensions.

Portage Park, with more attractive housing further away from the sources of decay, and as a residential area not too closely tied to any single set of economic activities, has a somewhat better chance for a future. Nonetheless, the age of its population and a decelerating rate of appreciation provide signals that some of the macro forces at work in East Side (the move to the suburbs and away from northern industrial cities) are being felt in Portage Park as well. The threat of the nearby shopping center to the shopping areas in Portage Park is another straw in the same wind.

We had discussed neighborhoods that followed more or less the classic pattern of racial succession, although we have seen the pattern worked out with additional levels of complexity. And we have discussed working-class white neighborhoods with low levels of crime and with differing levels of cohesion, inversely related to their levels of deterioration. To complicate, yet clarify, the picture further, let us turn to our final group of three neighborhoods. Two of these are high in crime, all have measurable minority populations, and all are economically appreciating.

5

Black and White Together: Beverly, Hyde Park–Kenwood, and Lincoln Park

Theories of racial succession attribute a certain inevitability to the process. As we discussed in chapter 1, although no time table is provided, it is assumed that once penetration has begun, a steady and cumulative sequence of events will culminate in succession. Each of the neighborhoods we now discuss has a black population. At some point in their recent history, the process of invasion and succession seemed to be well under way in two of them. However, after initial white flight and concomitant property-value decline, institutional and organizational community intervention led to stability, renewed confidence, and substantial property appreciation. The third case is more complicated—there, general decline had set in due simply to the community's age and proximity to the central core. Intervention in this case has also led to appreciation and stabilization. Poor blacks and Hispanics are being pushed out of this community, but young, middle-class blacks are replacing them.

All three of the communities are heavily middle class. Each dramatically illustrates the role creative intervention can play and demonstrates that although one cannot be complacent about crime, high crime rates are themselves not necessarily obstacles to growth.

Beverly

Although the Beverly area began its life as a farming community in the second third of the nineteenth century, it was well established as a residential community by the end of that century. Both the Rock Island Railroad and what became the Pennsylvania Railroad ran through the area, making housing necessary for railroad workers and making commuting to the city possible for the more prosperous. By the turn of the century, much of the area had been annexed to Chicago, and its distinctive topography had begun to help shape its character.

Historical experience and ecological theory suggest that higher-income groups also seek high ground. They did in Beverly—one of the few areas of the city having hills. The ridge area (the hill of Beverly Hills—see map) became the home of the wealthy businessmen of Yankee stock. The ridge overlooked the flatland areas around the railroad where both the railroad workers and white-collar workers resided. Seeking a clear identity for the area, local businessmen in 1917 petitioned the Rock Island Railroad to change the names of all the stations in the area to Beverly Hills. During the 1920s, Beverly underwent a building boom, and the pattern and diversity of housing stock already set in motion continued. The ridge area and the area nearby retained the more elaborate housing, whereas the other areas gained more modest types. Beverly grew rapidly relative to the rest of Chicago during the 1930s; the population increase for Chicago as a whole during that decade was 0.6 percent compared to 14.8 percent for Beverly. Construction, mostly of the smaller houses, continued in Beverly after the Second World War.

Beverly was described in the 1940s as "a good place to live. It has quiet tree-lined streets. . . . It has an atmosphere of peace" (Fontaine 1942, 76). Yet Beverly lay directly in the path of south-side black expansion, and a major source of worry for the community beginning in the 1950s was concern about what the future would bring. Although, or perhaps because, Beverly was the next "natural" community for blacks to move into from the east and the north, they were not well received. Their initial arrival was met with panic, and in some cases their houses were vandalized and their children beaten up. In the late 1970s, newspapers still reported stories of fire-bombings, and black Beverly respondents volunteered numerous tales of harassment by white neighbors. Three murders of white youths by blacks (all of them provoked) during the past ten years indicate how severe racial tensions have been.

Most Beverly residents disapprove of these extremist behaviors. They have, however, expended much effort to deal with the threat of neighborhood decline. In the early 1960s, many fought the development of the city's first in-city shopping center at the edge of their neighborhood for fear that such an enterprise would attract "undesirables" to the area.

In the late 1960s, Beverly residents constructed the Beverly Art Center, a theatre and art museum. The ridge was designated an historical district in the 1970s. But the major expression of Beverly-area concern is the Beverly Area Planning Association (BAPA).[1] Although it has been around since 1947, the association was revitalized in 1971 when, with substantial institutional support from a local bank and the developer of the shopping center, it became galvanized to deal with falling property values and the panoply of concerns associated with racial change. From

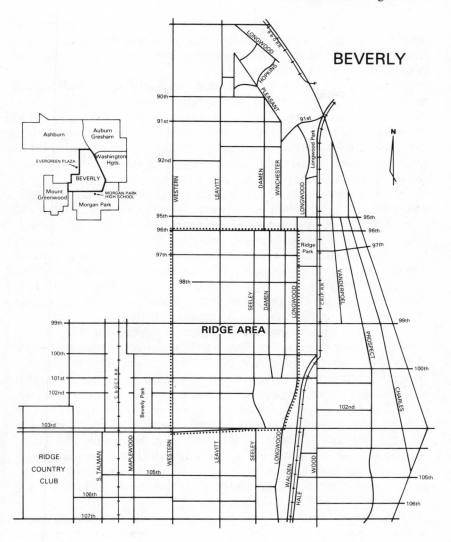

an annual budget of approximately $13,000, BAPA moved to one well in excess of $100,000 and began an aggressive multi-pronged program to "protect" the area.

Efforts by BAPA included an all-out attack on realtors who practiced "panic peddling." By persuasion and harassment (phone lines tied up continually by residents calling with nondescript questions), realtors were discouraged from employing panic peddling as well as racial steering. An information "hot line" was established to quell gossip about crimes and panic selling.

Because Beverly had become the home of many important city officials and other government employees, public efforts to maintain city services met with success. Those ties to government were also highlighted in publicity about the community.

Using tactics we have already seen in South Shore and Austin, residents devoted much effort to promoting Beverly housing to whites. Beverly house tours were established to attract people to the area and to show them the range of gracious living possible in the Beverly setting. The tours emphasize life-style quality and the village-like relations of residents to each other; in this respect they differ from the Austin tour's emphasis on architecture and housing bargains.

With the same intent, a twenty-two-page, handsomely produced brochure with little write-ups of typical families and their houses was printed. These are mailed to people from lists provided by large organizations who employ many white-collar workers. As a faculty member of the University of Chicago, one of us received such a brochure in 1976, with a cover letter from the president of BAPA along with a guarantee of mortgage money despite "accusations of redlining." Beverly-area residents have also passed out brochures at commuter railroad stations urging people to sample the neighborhood's charms.

In short, a massive part of the effort of BAPA and Beverly-area residents has been devoted to shoring up a potentially sagging real estate market. That market did, in fact, in 1976 receive support from a surprising quarter. At that time, the late Mayor Richard Daley announced that city employees would be required henceforth to live in the city. Beverly, being a neighborhood in which city employees already lived, was an attractive option, and because of increased demand, property values in the area rose shortly after that announcement. We should note, however, that Beverly has shown the least appreciation of our three high-appreciation neighborhoods. At 113 percent in unadjusted dollars for the period 1973–78, it stands below Hyde Park–Kenwood (124 percent) and well below Lincoln Park (366 percent).

Efforts were also made to bolster the area's declining shopping strips. A plan was generated to make Beverly a self-taxing area, the funds raised thereby to be utilized for commercial revitalization, but the program was never established. However, BAPA has run special promotional programs to encourage people to buy locally, and in 1978 a local development corporation was established to help funnel Small Business Administration funds into the area.

The relationship of neighborhoods to their shopping areas is a complex one. Shopping areas or strips often function the way main streets do in small towns. Not only are they places where people come together, but they also represent the area itself. A deteriorating shopping strip signals to people that the entire area is deteriorating, even if initially this is not the case. Consequently, neighborhood groups such as BAPA expend a great deal of effort trying to maintain shopping strips.

Shopping strips may be declining everywhere—they are in some respects an outmoded form. Their parking facilities are often inadequate, and the stores themselves are often too small to carry the range and variety of goods modern shoppers require. Also, because of the lower volume of sales, the store owners may have to charge higher prices than the large stores downtown or in shopping centers.

Where racial change accompanies decline, however, the problem becomes more complicated. Most Chicago neighborhoods that have undergone racial transition have subsequently deteriorated; and urban residents, both white and black, perceive this fact. Consequently, as racial change takes place, residents come to expect decline. Objective evidence that supports this interpretation of reality is played up in people's minds. Thus, in such circumstances, the decline of a strip is simply taken as further evidence of deterioration, discouraging both shoppers and merchants as well as potential housing purchasers.

An economic theory of shopping strips would suggest that as business falls off, property owners would be forced either to let their stores stand vacant or to rent them to those who will use them in less desirable ways. In addition, owners will have less money to spend on maintenance. In many of our deteriorating strips, this pattern shows up dramatically. Vacancy rates not only correlate with our measures of deterioration, but they also correlate with what might be called second-class uses of the stores. In these instances, first-class retail uses such as clothing stores, hardware stores, and furniture stores give way to second-class uses, ranging from wig shops and low-capitalized trinket shops to fortune tellers.

Beverly's main shopping strip shows the difference that adequate capital makes in the face of decline. To begin with, many of the shops were modernized or rebuilt both to appear larger and to provide additional parking. More importantly, the owners of these properties are among the largest property owners in the city. Consequently, they have been able to weather long periods of high vacancy. The vacancy rate along 95th Street is both high and of unusually long standing, yet the stores have not been rented out for second-class uses. The investors who control the properties are closely allied to the investors who own the neighboring shopping center. The blight to which second-class use would lead might discourage use of the center. BAPA, as we have indicated, has worked closely with these investors to attract new businesses.

In addition, adequate capital has made it possible to maintain vacant stores in attractive condition for long periods of time. In fact, Beverly is the only area where vacancy does not correlate with our other measures of deterioration. Adequate levels of capital flow can help a community to weather momentary set-backs caused by crime and fear of racial transition so that, ultimately, neither the fear nor the presence of other races drives whites away. In the Beverly case, unusually high capital support is available.

Both the shopping strips and the shopping center, which residents earlier fought, continue to be problems for Beverly. Both attract the majority of their clientele, who are black, from an area much larger than Beverly. In fact, very few of Beverly's residents shop there; the shoppers are more likely to be low-income renters than the Beverly population (*Chicago Sun Times* 1977). The large black presence in the shopping districts makes the whole Beverly area seem more heavily populated by blacks than it is, which is an obstacle in marketing the area to whites. We saw a similar pattern in South Shore, where whites were advised to give up trying to maintain an integrated neighborhood based on "recess photos" of a school population that had a higher proportion of blacks to whites than that found in the community's total population.

A third major focus of BAPA activity has been the control and prevention of crime. Although crime rates are low in Beverly, there are indications that racial change and fear of crime are associated in residents' minds. Although residents cite many reasons to explain the low rates of crime in the neighborhood—a high class of people live there, many police live there, the area is well patrolled—some respondents informed us that Beverly has little crime because blacks have been kept out. In addition, Beverly respondents report in disproportionate numbers that there is an area within a mile of their homes where they are afraid to walk at night. Given the fact that Beverly residents stay away from both the major shopping strip and the local shopping center which are largely black, we suspect that the area to which they are referring is the area to the north and east which is largely black.

Feelings concerning this relationship seep through in the local newspapers and in reports of the Beverly Area Planning Association. As a BAPA newsletter reported in 1976: "Sorry to disappoint the prophets of gloom, but it was a long hot summer only if you looked at the thermometer. In every other way, things were cool around Beverly Hills: the housing market grew stronger; *kids behaved themselves*; and block parties made friends out of neighbors."

To combat crime, BAPA has worked closely both with the youth in the area (who are seen as the source of the crime problem) and with the police department. In addition to encouraging heavy patrolling, BAPA has helped youth workers to keep youngsters busy, developed summer programs for youth, and given awards to police officers for distinguished service. In 1980, for example, BAPA cited the local police commander whose district had the largest crime reduction in the city.

During the summer, the police department assigns "salt and pepper" police teams to patrol parks and other areas where youth spend their time. The teams try to head off threatening situations that develop and help victims who think the crimes they have been involved in are racial. The major crime problems they report are vandalism and fights. And they report that many of the problems they deal with are intra- rather than interracial (*Beverly Review*, 18 June 1980).

The Beverly Area Planning Association's official position is that it favors integration and opposes discrimination. In the language of specialists in this particular area, the organization is fighting "resegregation." Its booklet designed to encourage families to move into the neighborhood includes one model black family among its nine vignettes, and it has worked diligently to discourage real estate agents from pursuing their customary practices of making profits by accelerating rates of change.

Although that is BAPA's official position, knowledgeable observers suggest that during some of its life, BAPA has made efforts to keep blacks out of the area. This charge is always difficult to assess because the line between preventing panic peddling and resegregation on the one hand and black exclusion on the other is often difficult to maintain. And we do not suggest that BAPA has ever encouraged the sorts of lawless behavior that lead to fire bombings and the like. BAPA has worked with the police to discourage such behavior, has supported the efforts of youth workers who have attempted to put a stop to it, and has offered rewards for information leading to the arrest of vandals. However, BAPA closed a record store where youths were congregating because officials feared it looked unsavory. Youth workers associated with BAPA objected to the closing, arguing that there was no evidence the store was, in fact, a problem. Similarly, in a kind of urban redevelopment effort, the area around one of the schools with a large black population was razed to make way for playing fields. Some observers saw this move as a way to discourage black youth from hanging around the area.

BAPA and Beverly-area youth programs are an important focus of activity. BAPA funds, among others, a youth program in the area's Morgan Park High School. This school itself figures heavily in the BAPA integration strategy. The board of education was persuaded in 1975 to maintain the school in a 50:50 black-white ratio, despite the fact that much of the area around it was changing. Although the program has come under attack from some black leaders, the ratio has been maintained. Similarly, the area around the school was torn down to create a more campus-like atmosphere, and incidentally to remove the low-income black households located there, making the school more attractive, at least in theory, to white families. Beverly residents do have other options available to them. The private Morgan Park Academy and the parochial Brother Rice and Mother Macauley are all known for their high standards.

Beverly, then, has been the site of substantial intervention to maintain racial integration and to prevent decline. Hyde Park–Kenwood, although quite different in other respects, has been the locus of many similar activities.

Hyde Park–Kenwood

Although Hyde Park and Kenwood began their lives as separate communities, developments at many points in their histories bound them together. Each, for example, owed its early growth to the extension of the Illinois Central Railroad (I.C.) south along Chicago's lakefront. The extension itself was promoted by entrepreneurs Stephen Douglas (more famous for his debates with Abraham Lincoln), who wanted to promote his own property about three miles north of Hyde Park, and Paul Cornell, who, as Hyde Park's major developer for many years, gave the I.C. land for its right-of-way in order to bring the railroad into the community.

There have been other linkages. Hyde Park residents, who always have been an independent-minded group, voted themselves and Kenwood residents out of the township of Lake and into their own separate township in 1861. When a growing population began to place a burden on local resources, the township of Hyde Park voted to join the city of Chicago in 1889. Similarly, it was Paul Cornell's efforts as a lobbyist for the development of a south parks system that led to the growth of south-side parks, parks that enhanced Kenwood's elegance by providing suitable avenues for the carriages of Kenwood residents. Finally, the location of the world's fair in Jackson Park increased enormously the traffic on the Illinois Central Line, making Kenwood as well as Hyde Park more accessible.

Kenwood got its start as an aristocratic suburb of large homes on large estates. The first suburban settler was Dr. John A. Kennicott for whom the area was named. The early residents of Kenwood included wealthy stockyard executives and other fashionable families moving southward (Holt and Pacyga 1979).

However, the sense of isolation from the city and the luxuriousness that that provided were not to last. In 1910, elevated rapid-transit lines came into the community, bringing with them much less fashionable white-collar workers from the Loop. The traditional pattern of social-class change began to appear. Wealthier families began to move away, larger lots were subdivided, and new apartment buildings were constructed, particularly along train and streetcar lines, to accommodate the new residents.

Although at that time the southern border of the Kenwood community was 51st Steet, most of the new apartment and small-house construc-

HYDE PARK - KENWOOD

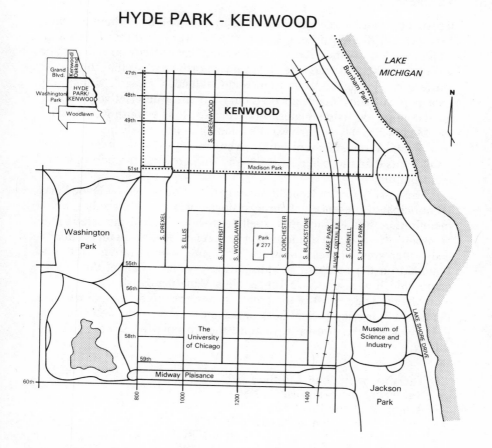

tion during this period stopped at 47th Street. Thus, 47th Street, although internal to the community, increasingly became a boundary between less intensive and more intensive uses of land. The area south of 47th Street maintained many of its big houses and, with new apartment dwellings constructed primarily along the lakefront, became the home of some of Chicago's prominent German Jews.

Population growth leveled off for all of Kenwood during the 1930s, but began again during the Second World War when it became home to a small Japanese community. After the war, blacks, whose number had grown enormously and who had been crowded into Chicago's historic "black belt," entered the community from the north and west. Racial change, accompanied by a fresh spurt of subdivision, was rapid—by 1960, the area north of 47th Street was mostly black. Although many of the large houses south of 47th Street were still standing, they too were increasingly being subdivided. However, by that time, South Kenwood's fate had become more and more linked to that of Hyde Park; in the early 1950s, South Kenwood became part of what was called the Hyde Park–Kenwood Conservation Area. The northern half of Kenwood came to be associated with Oakland, the community north of it, so that today, the entire area is referred to as Kenwood-Oakland. Chicago's community area maps still show one Kenwood, but for realistic descriptive purposes, most commentators distinguish between North and South Kenwood.

Meanwhile, Hyde Park was developing in its own distinctive direction. It evolved as a pleasant suburban community with smaller houses on smaller lots than those in Kenwood, and with growing numbers of apartment buildings.

The world's fair had a profound impact on the growth of Hyde Park. Its anticipated presence encouraged developers to build smaller apartment houses, hotels, and other dwellings to house people attracted to the community by the fair. In addition, a new, relatively low-quality commercial center grew up near the world's fair site. The community became bounded on the south by a wide parkway with a channel through its center which was supposed to become a Venetian canal.

After the fair, most of the buildings designed to be temporary were demolished, leaving behind both parks and waterways as well as Chicago's most popular tourist attraction, the Museum of Science and Industry.

> The City White had fled the earth
> But where the azure waters lie
> A nobler city had its birth
> The City Gray that ne're shall die.
> (Hoyt 1942b, 38)

Adjacent to the world's fair site the University of Chicago arose, ultimately covering about twenty-five square blocks, and bordered by single-family houses for the faculty. Its own campus "in the front rank of civic art" (Condit 1973, 14), it constituted a distinctive and attractive community.

By 1920, Hyde Park was fully built up. The Irish were the leading nationality, followed by German and Russian Jews (Kitagawa and Taeuber 1963).

Blacks began to move into Hyde Park in the 1940s, and the pace accelerated during the 1950s.[2] By 1960, blacks constituted 30 percent of the population. In the by-now familiar pattern, white residents began to flee, landlords undermaintained buildings, and crime increasingly became a problem.

Because of low rents associated with a soft housing market, economic weakness in the commercial strip, and the attraction of the university,

Hyde Park did become something of an artistic center, attracting both painters and craftsmen to the area. Its growing numbers of bars and nightclubs also became an important source of vitality and entertainment.

Between 1950 and 1956, 20,000 whites left the community and 23,000 blacks moved in (Rossi and Dentler 1961). Hyde Park had had a small number of black residents before this time, but there had also been some economic homogeneity. Now, however, the blacks moving in were mainly of substantially lower income levels.

As Hoyt had written in 1942 about Hyde Park–Kenwood, "in the next ring of growth beyond the inner core of old Chicago . . . a constant struggle is going on to preserve a community form and structure from the infiltration of blight from the broken down and disintegrated sections of the old city" (p. 37). As part of that struggle, Hyde Park–Kenwood was organized.

Led by a group of ministers, Hyde Parkers, concerned that their area would follow in the footsteps of the communities to the north and become a slum, in 1949 organized the Hyde Park–Kenwood Community Conference to deal with the issue of urban renewal. The same division of participants into hardliners and integrationists we have seen in Austin, South Shore, and Beverly also evolved in Hyde Park–Kenwood when the University of Chicago established the South East Chicago Commission in 1952.

Hardliners sound like exclusionists when the number of blacks in the community is small. Generally, at each step in the process of black in-migration, hardliners are committed to slowing the process or choking it off altogether. To the extent that blacks do enter the community, the hardliners are committed to restricting the movement as much as possible to higher income levels. The integrationists, in this case represented by the conference, were more concerned about finding adequate housing for the poor. They were, in general, less willing to take draconic measures to alter the course of events because they were concerned that some of the weaker members of the community would be harmed. One should add that many of the hardliners saw themselves as the ultimate in pragmatic integrationists (although, in fact, until recently some of Hyde Park–Kenwood's wealthy cooperatively owned buildings still excluded blacks). They argued that it was impossible to maintain an integrated community that is heterogeneous on class. If large numbers of poor blacks enter the community, the argument goes, the whites will continue to flee. A well-known comedian has characterized Hyde Park–Kenwood, in fact, as "black and white together . . . shoulder to shoulder against the poor."

At the center of everybody's agenda was the development of an urban-renewal program that would rid the area of its most deteriorated housing. Differences arose about whether new construction on the land so cleared should be subsidized in some form or should operate at market rate, with the group aligned with the South East Chicago Commission in favor of market-rate housing. (As we shall see, a similar fight took place in Lincoln Park.) Similar arguments arose as to whether the existing Hyde Park High School should be refurbished or whether, because it also served the deteriorating Woodlawn community to the south, a new high school should be built in Kenwood. The latter is what finally happened. Some version of that quarrel was replayed again and again. Although some low-income housing was built in the community, those in favor of emphasizing the middle-class orientation of the community usually won. In some cases where there had been proposals for low-income subsidized housing, nothing was built at all.

Ultimately, more than 30 million dollars of federal funds, as well as more than 30 million dollars of the university's endowment, were spent on urban renewal, following a plan developed by the university. These funds in turn generated another 90 million dollars of investment. More than forty-seven acres were cleared, including both the area's most blighted buildings and those commercial strips that housed numerous taverns. These were replaced with town houses and a shopping center. Some of the displaced businessmen organized to construct their own small shopping center. Others in the community, concerned about the displacement of craftsmen, established a shopping center with subsidized rents to house some of them.

Even today, there are vacant lots where no new use has been approved. In 1979, one large vacant area along the 47th Street border, which had originally been designated for subsidized housing, was converted into a large private tennis club. The club also closes off two through streets heading into North Kenwood, completing a pattern that included the construction of cul-de-sacs and one-way streets in order to discourage through traffic.

The university has continued to be involved in the real estate market independent of urban renewal. This has sometimes meant the purchase of marginal buildings, or buildings threatened with deterioration, and their conversion into student or faculty housing.

Simultaneously, the South East Chicago Commission has continued both to vigorously pursue code enforcement and to encourage private entrepreneurs to purchase buildings and rehabilitate them.

Other efforts have been made in this twenty-five-year period to shore up the housing market. In the 1950s, the citizens of Kenwood organized an open-house committee, which began conducting tours of the large elegant old houses that had not yet been converted to rooming houses. Also at that time, they pressured the city to begin vigorous enforcement of single-family residential zoning, forcing house owners to deconvert. In

addition, prizes were offered to private citizens who deconverted rooming houses and made them into attractive single-family houses.

During this period, much of Hyde Park–Kenwood was effectively
redlined. A federal savings and loan association was created to provide
mortgage money to new purchasers of Hyde Park and Kenwood housing.
In addition, the university encouraged faculty to live in the area—approximately 70 percent now do—and, as an incentive, provided low-cost
second mortgages.

Residents and the university have also been involved with the
schools. There have been tutorial and other specialized programs to bring
supplementary funds into the schools for educational enrichment. One
elementary school consistently scores in the top group citywide in reading
and math, and another is often not far behind. A local newspaper reports
that Kenwood High School produced more National Merit Scholarship
semifinalists in the 1980–81 academic year than any other public school in
Illinois. There is constant effort to provide enrichment in that school's
curriculum as well. Finally, the university's own private school provides
an alternative for those who wish to avoid the public ones.

It was crime and fear of crime that finally brought the university into
direct rather than passive action in the community. The robbery and
attempted rape of a faculty wife started the committee that led to the
formation of the South East Chicago Commission in 1952 (Rossi and
Dentler 1961). Prior to this time, it had become more and more difficult
for the university to attract both students and faculty because the area
was considered so unsavory; under these pressures, consideration was
given to relocating the university in a suburban location. Crime continues
to be a major concern of the South East Chicago Commission, the
University of Chicago, and the Hyde Park–Kenwood Community Conference.

To combat crime and alleviate community anxiety, the university
assembled a very large, private security force. In addition to protecting
university property, that force, consisting of eighty to ninety people
including supervisors and having a budget in excess of 2 million dollars,
actively patrols the area. One of their goals is to establish a visible
presence. Their radios communicate with the Chicago Police Department's, and extensive cooperation is involved in their efforts. The university has also installed white emergency telephones throughout the
area. Simply taking the phone off the hook leads to the dispatch of a car to
the phone location.

The university also deals with crime and the fear of it more indirectly.
It operates a fleet of buses that travel around the community both during
the day and at night. This means that people need not walk the streets
either during the day or, more importantly, at night.

Also working very closely with the police department, the South East Chicago Commission attempts to reduce crime. The commission plots crimes carefully on maps, locating problem areas which then become targets for police patrolling and intensive examination for code enforcement. The commission also offers rewards for information concerning crimes, works with witnesses to encourage them to appear in court, and provides free legal services to victims of crime. These activities are particularly important because witnesses have often been reluctant to come forward and because commission lawyers can vigorously pursue cases in the courts—they see to it that cases are not dropped, get witnesses to the trial after repeated continuances, and resist reduced sentences through plea bargaining.

The Hyde Park–Kenwood Community Conference has also been involved in anticrime activity. The activities selected by them are those suitable for an organization without much power and which, at least in principle, represents all the people. Project Whistlestop, in which citizens blow their whistles when they see a crime in progress and others call the police when they hear whistles, has been the conference's most successful effort to date. At one time, wide distribution of whistles was achieved, and some crimes were prevented and some criminals apprehended because of their use. However, given the high turnover of residents, a program like this one requires continued publicity and community-wide efforts at consciousness raising to continue to succeed. The conference has fallen on hard times and does not have the resources to maintain the necessary level of interest (although the university has in some measure picked up the support of the program). In addition, the project never fared well with the poor and black in the community. There is even some question about whether the whistles actually reduce crime. It may be that like the sodium lights the city installed to reduce crime, the whistles make people feel more secure, but do not lead to a crime reduction.

The conference also promoted Operation Identification, a program whereby an identifying number is engraved on valuables; a safe-homes program, where signs in house windows indicate to a harassed child that a concerned parent is at home; and block-club meetings to discuss what to do about crime. More Hyde Park–Kenwood residents are aware of community anticrime programs in their neighborhood than are residents in any other community.

In Hyde Park–Kenwood, as in Beverly, the fight to maintain a racial balance is unceasing and involves efforts along many lines. The role of institutions in both initiating and sustaining these efforts is clearly evidenced in Hyde Park–Kenwood. Lincoln Park represents a somewhat different pattern overall, but there too, institutional activity has been of considerable consequence.

Lincoln Park

Lincoln Park got its start midway through the nineteenth century as a truck-farming area, providing produce for the city three miles to the south. In 1860, the Presbyterian Theological Seminary was constructed in the area, and a small residential quarter grew up around it. Until the Chicago Fire in 1871, the area continued to serve predominantly as a truck-farming area. However, the fire brought refugees into the neighborhood to be housed in temporary structures, and the fact that subsequent fire-control ordinances were not enforced in the area meant that inexpensive housing could be built. Factories had also marched north after the fire, locating along the Chicago River at the western edge of the area. With the arrival of the cable-car lines in 1889, the community began to grow rapidly. Workers could be employed either in the nearby factories or by growing establishments in the central city area.

Although Germans continued to be numerically dominant, Irish, Poles, Slovaks, Serbians, Rumanians, Hungarians, and Italians moved into the neighborhood, giving it the heterogeneous character is has maintained until recently. By 1895, the area was fully developed—the more prosperous lived in its eastern (lakefront and park front) sections, the less so further westward.

During the period 1920–40, expensive new construction, including relatively high-rise apartment buildings, was under way along the lake and park fronts. Just west of this area, however, fashionable houses began to be subdivided into rooming houses. As early as the 1920s, a small group of blacks moved into the southwestern corner of the community. Among the older families in the area, growing fear of the Italian population with its "black hand" was reported. "The St. Valentine's Massacre took place in a local garage. Al Capone's girlfriend lived over a store on Halsted. John Dillinger was . . . shot down by the FBI in front of the local Biograph Theater" (Warner 1979, 21).

During the post–World War II period, Appalachians and Hispanics began to move into the area, while the earlier ethnics, now more prosperous, moved to the suburbs or to the northwest corner of the city. A separate black and Hispanic area just south of North Avenue, Lincoln Park's southern boundary, began to boil over into Lincoln Park itself. A large Japanese population also began to move into the area. Lincoln Park's overall population was declining, however, and by 1960, 23 percent of the community's housing was listed as substandard (p. 23).

Simultaneously, an area toward the southeast began attracting artists and bohemians. It was also an area where some of the old German residents had remained and, although housing prices were relatively low because of lack of demand, deterioration had not proceeded very far.

LINCOLN PARK

This area attracted, then, people who could appreciate the housing bargains and were willing to renovate to recover the aesthetic values of the area. These people were, as they often are, the first wave in the process of gentrification. Residents there formed a community association, the Old Town Triangle Association, and owners in an area further north that had resisted subdivision organized the Mid-North Association. Both organizations made efforts toward code enforcement, neighborhood clean-up, and provision of adequate city services.

The decline of Lincoln Park had become a source of concern to some of the large institutions in the neighborhood, including De Paul University, McCormick Seminary (the old Presbyterian Seminary), four large hospitals, a local bank, and local churches. In March of 1954, they and the new community organizations met to form the Lincoln Park Conservation Association (LPCA). In addition to further organizing the community and fulfilling functions similar to those of the original organizations, they took a leaf from the University of Chicago book and began to work with the Department of Urban Renewal on a renewal plan. However, the institutions did not want to become the object of controversy, as had the University of Chicago, and so maintained a low profile.

While renewal plans were being developed, housing renovation was becoming more and more popular in the eastern half of the community, and blacks and Hispanics were consolidating their position in the western half. Ultimately, the same pattern we have seen before—tensions between those who wanted to remove the poor and minorities and those who did not—developed, but with higher drama than previously. The LPCA urban-renewal plans increasingly appeared to focus on black and Hispanic removal, and earlier discussions about providing low-income housing were dropped. This process, however, was taking place during the 1960s, when the moods of minorities and students were somewhat volatile. Youth gangs, poorer residents, and students organized to fight the renewal plan, and there were demonstrations, sit-ins, and other confrontations.

Although these groups did gain some concessions, ultimately the hardliners won. A small proportion of new housing was set aside for the poor, but in the total pattern of destruction of old housing and construction of new, the poor lost substantial living space.

The period since that time has seen steady growth and renovation of the area. The middle-class areas have grown, and the remaining areas of poor residences have continued to shrink. In some sections such as the southwest corner of the community, one sees the black poor living side-by-side with newly renovated housing. But each week sees new empty houses with the trucks of contractors parked in front.

Concurrent with the urban-renewal process, both as part of it and as a separate activity, the big developers moved into Lincoln Park. The late 1960s and early 1970s saw massive new housing projects—high-rises in sections where the views over the lake and over Lincoln Park would make the apartments particularly desirable, and lower-rise buildings elsewhere. Almost every major name in the real estate industry in Chicago has been involved in that process. As one Lincoln Park investor explained, "Lincoln Park had to be the next area. The near north was already heavily built up, and the values were not there. Some of us looked south to the South Shore–Hyde Park area. But the large number of blacks in Jackson Park made such investments untenable. Once the urban-renewal process began in Lincoln Park, there was nowhere else to go."

Today, community residents fight the fights of middle-class settlements. These include a great deal of attention to the schools. The Lincoln Park School District covers the same area as Cabrini-Green, one of the city's most notorious public-housing projects. Efforts are being made to upgrade the public schools in a context where gang activity is still a threat. Nonetheless, the high school, which had gained a bad reputation, had its name changed from Waller to Lincoln Park, and more than two million dollars have been spent on renovation. Efforts have been made to enrich programs and to discourage youth from congregating in front of the school. Although families with children are not the major factor in Lincoln Park's boom, those families who wish to avoid the public schools are blessed with having two of the city's most illustrious private schools nearby. Other private schools exist, and new private elementary schools have also been started.

Residents also fight the construction of high-rise buildings which would, in their view, bring congestion to the area. Like the residents of Hyde Park–Kenwood, Beverly, and South Shore, they are also engaged in fighting the construction of subsidized housing, half-way houses, and other such institutions, and they work with the police to reduce crime.

Stability and Social Cohesion

Beverly evidences substantially more residential stability and cohesion than do Hyde Park–Kenwood and Lincoln Park. The percentage of respondents who have lived in the community all their lives is higher in Beverly than in the latter two communities as is the median length of residence for the remainder (see table 4.2). More respondents in Beverly than in any of our other communities consider their neighborhood to be a "real home," and 68 percent, also the largest among the eight communities, say they will definitely not move during the next year (tables 3.1 and 3.2). Although Hyde Park–Kenwood and Lincoln Park rank far behind Beverly on these items, the percentages are fairly large for predominantly rental areas.

Beverly residents are more likely than those in Hyde Park–Kenwood and Lincoln Park to report that they have relatives living in the neighborhood and that they visit with relatives often (tables 3.7 and 3.4). However, Beverly ranks with Lincoln Park and behind Hyde Park–Kenwood in the proportion of respondents who have good friends in the neighborhood (table 3.3), and Hyde Park–Kenwood and Lincoln Park rank first and second, respectively, in the proportion who spend a social evening with neighbors once a week or more. Beverly residents are more likely, however, to chat with their neighbors when they see them on the street as well as more likely to be able to rely on their neighbors. The proportion expressing agreement on these items is quite high in all the neighborhoods, but Beverly is the highest on all three (table 3.5). Hyde Park–Kenwood ranks in the middle of the eight communities in having residents who are able to count on neighbors; Lincoln Park is lower, residents there being the least likely to say they can count on neighbors for help if they are sick or to watch their homes when they are away. This statistic is consistent with the fact that in many respects Lincoln Park is a new community and one of renters.

In terms of overall local-facility use, residents of Beverly, Hyde Park–Kenwood, and Lincoln Park rank in the middle; they use local facilities less than residents of East Side and Portage Park do, but more than those in Austin and South Shore do (table 3.6). Yet there is substantial variation among these three in the use of particular facilities.

Crime and Other Urban Problems

Beverly is not only more cohesive than Hyde Park–Kenwood and Lincoln Park, but also less beset by crime and other urban problems. Beverly is the lowest of the eight communities in both total crime and total victimization (tables 2.2 and 2.3). Although it fares a little worse on some of the component items (ranking sixth, for example, on personal crime), Beverly is clearly a low-crime area by whatever criterion one uses. Hyde Park–Kenwood and Lincoln Park, although not the highest overall, are characterized by much higher levels of crime. Hyde Park–Kenwood ranks behind only South Shore in total crime; Lincoln Park ranks fourth, after these two and Austin. Using victimization reports, Lincoln Park ranks third overall, behind South Shore and Austin. Hyde Parkers appear to report a higher proportion of their victimizations to the police than do residents of other neighborhoods, because on total victimization they rank fifth, after South Shore, Austin, Lincoln Park, and Back of the Yards. In addition to these overall rates, Hyde Park–Kenwood has the highest rate of property crime, and Lincoln Park has the highest rate of property victimization.

Reflecting the differences in levels of crime between Beverly, on the one hand, and Hyde Park–Kenwood and Lincoln Park, on the other, are differences in respondents' evaluations of the crime situation in their neighborhood. Only 3 percent of Beverly respondents say that there is a lot of crime in the area or that their likelihood of being the victim of a crime in the neighborhood is high (tables 3.10 and 3.11). The corresponding percentages for Hyde Park–Kenwood and Lincoln Park are higher, although not dramatically so. Nearly 10 percent in each neighborhood report that there is a lot of crime in the neighborhood, and about 8 percent perceive their own probability of victimization as high. These figures are somewhat lower than those for the other high-crime neighborhoods—Austin, Back of the Yards, and South Shore.

Although residents of Hyde Park–Kenwood and Lincoln Park generally express more fear of crime than do those of Beverly, this is not uniformly true, nor are the differences as great as one might predict based on the disparity in crime rates. Fewer respondents in Beverly than in any other neighborhood report that they often worry about being the victim of a crime (table 3.12). Hyde Park–Kenwood, with just over one-third saying that they often worry about criminal victimization, similarly ranks about where one would expect; it stands behind Austin and Back of the Yards and ties with South Shore. The percentage of Lincoln Park respondents giving the fearful response on this item, however, is only marginally higher than that of Portage Park respondents. Lincoln Parkers are also the least likely to be afraid of strangers asking directions at night, although we note that fear of strangers is high in all of the neighborhoods. As members of a booming community with lots of young singles and discretionary dollars, Lincoln Park's residents tend to feel safer than the crime situation warrants. They display more worry, however, about home burglary; on that item, Lincoln Park is tied with South Shore, behind Austin and Back of the Yards. Here, it is Hyde Park–Kenwood that occupies the somewhat anomalous position; only in Beverly do residents worry less about being burglarized.

Beverly respondents are less troubled by other urban problems than are those in Hyde Park–Kenwood and Lincoln Park. Beverly ranks seventh on the neighborhood-problem measure, with only Portage Park reporting fewer serious problems in the aggregate (table 3.14). Two of the items, by their very nature, are less likely to occur in Beverly—the large-lot home sites minimize the problems of noisy neighbors, and the relative lack of multiple-family dwellings decreases the probability of undermaintenance by landlords. Nevertheless, even with these two items removed from the scale, Beverly retains its seventh-place ranking. Our independent observations there coincide closely with the low levels of concern respondents express. Beverly is the least deteriorated of the neighborhoods in terms of structural flaws and lawn neglect, and only Portage Park ranks better on parkway maintenance (table 3.17).

Hyde Park–Kenwood ranks fourth on the composite neighborhood-problem measure, behind Austin, South Shore, and Back of the Yards. On the individual items, Hyde Parkers are more likely than most to report that purse snatching and other street crimes are problems in the neighborhood and are among the least likely to be bothered by drugs and drug users. On our measures of deterioration, Hyde Park–Kenwood ranks fifth, ahead of the three low-crime neighborhoods, on maintenance of structures and lawns. Although it ranks third on levels of parkway maintenance, its major shopping strips are less littered than anywhere else.

Lincoln Park residents are a little less disturbed by urban problems than are those in Hyde Park–Kenwood, ranking fifth on the composite measure, ahead of Portage Park, Beverly, and East Side. They are less concerned about drugs and drug users than any other area in the sample despite, or perhaps because of, the fact that drug use is, we believe, fairly extensive. More of them report problems with dogs, however, than in any other neighborhood except South Shore.

Curiously, despite the boom qualities of the area, Lincoln Park ranks third in number of visible structural flaws, falling in behind Back of the Yards and Austin. On lawn maintenance, Lincoln Park ranks fourth, behind Back of the Yards, South Shore, and Austin. Litter on parkways is less of a problem; there it ranks fifth. Its shopping strips which are otherwise prosperous—Lincoln Park has become an area with trendy shops and other "boutiques" as well as the largest range of restaurants in our sample—rank high on levels of litter.

Lincoln Park, then, has some similarities to the neighorhoods that have undergone racial succession. As a gentrifying area, it too has a relatively new population and somewhat attenuated ties to its neighbors. Significantly, some areas of Lincoln Park sponsor neighborhood "walks" much like the open houses in South Shore, Beverly, Austin, and Hyde Park–Kenwood. However, the function of these events is not to attract outsiders, but to build solidarity among those who already live there. Although the area's housing stock is in transition, it is being upgraded rather than undermaintained. Deteriorated buildings in this context are understood as opportunities rather than as evidence that things are getting worse. Even the undermaintained lawns and high levels of litter are understood as evidence that good things are really happening there.

Perceived Consequences of Integration

In spite of differences in levels of crime and deterioration, residents of Beverly, Hyde Park–Kenwood, and Lincoln Park are similar in their perceptions of the consequences of black in-migration. They are the least likely of all respondents to believe that the presence of a few black families in a neighborhood leads to an increase in crime and a decrease in property values (table 3.18). All three illustrate the general levels of middle-class tolerance we discussed earlier. However, unlike Hyde Park–Kenwood and Beverly where almost three-quarters of the residents characterize their neighborhoods as racially stable (more than those in any other community), Lincoln Park residents are substantially more likely to view their neighborhood as changing, with 42.4 percent in that category (table 3.20). All of our other communities with larger proportions categorizing the neighborhood as changing (whether or not it actually is) also have larger percentages agreeing with the racial-threat statements in our instrument. In this sense, Lincoln Park is unusual.

Overall Evaluation of the Neighborhood

Beverly residents, as one might expect, express high levels of satisfaction with and optimism about their neighborhood. With 94 percent of the respondents saying that they are very or somewhat satisfied overall, Beverly is second only to Portage Park (table 3.22). When one considers only the very-satisfied category, Beverly is even more illustrative of the positive orientation—nearly 72 percent of Beverly respondents, the highest anywhere, are in that group. Ninety-three percent of Beverly respondents think that buying a house in the neighborhood would be a good investment (table 3.25), and fewer than 10 percent think that the neighborhood has gotten or will get worse (tables 3.23 and 3.24).

In spite of high crime, Lincoln Park residents are also quite satisfied with their neighborhood, with 93 percent expressing overall satisfaction. Given the neighborhood's recent history, it is not surprising that Lincoln Park has the largest percentage of respondents who think that the area is improving and will continue to do so, nor that 86 percent feel the neighborhood is a good place for investment.

Although the outlook in Hyde Park–Kenwood is less optimistic than that in Beverly and Lincoln Park, residents there are by no means gloomy. In overall satisfaction, they rank fifth after the three low-crime communities and Lincoln Park. Eighty-two percent of the respondents think that purchasing a house in Hyde Park–Kenwood would be a good financial investment, and the proportions who think the neighborhood has gotten or will get worse are small.

Attributes and Assessments—Racial Differences

In the foregoing, we have discussed the survey responses for Beverly, Hyde Park–Kenwood, and Lincoln Park as wholes. Here, we report on these findings separately for blacks and whites.

Reflecting historical differences in the timing and pattern of black in-migration in Beverly, Hyde Park–Kenwood, and Lincoln Park are current differences in length of residence by race. Nine percent of Beverly whites have lived in the community all their lives, and the median length of residence for the rest is eleven years. These figures compare to a median length of residence of only three years for blacks, none of whom have lived in the neighborhood all their lives (table 5.1).

In Hyde Park–Kenwood, just under 3 percent of both blacks and whites have lived in the neighborhood all their lives, and the median length of residence for the remainder is six years for both groups. This is not a statistical artifact of the fact that students live in the community; the median length of residence for that 25 percent who have been in the

Table 5.1 Measures of Stability and Cohesion, by Race—Beverly, Hyde Park–Kenwood, and Lincoln Park

Characteristic	Beverly		Hyde Park–Kenwood		Lincoln Park	
	White	Black	White	Black	White	Black
Percentage residing in community entire life	9.3	0	2.9	2.8	0	0
Median length of residence for remainder (years)	11.0	3.0	6.0	6.0	4.0	7.0
Percentage who consider neighborhood a "real home"	84.5	77.6	53.1	60.1	59.7	58.1
Percentage who will not move during next year	68.4	62.7	46.5	39.2	40.0	41.5
Percentage with relatives in the neighborhood	48.9	14.9	19.6	38.9	22.4	32.6
Percentage with good friends in the neighborhood	87.1	67.2	91.3	82.5	86.3	78.6
Percentage who do the following once a week or more:						
a. Spend a social evening with relatives	40.7	38.8	17.5	33.8	25.7	35.7
b. Spend a social evening with a neighbor	32.8	18.2	39.3	33.3	35.3	25.6
c. Chat with neighbors on the street	91.2	88.1	78.5	81.1	80.1	62.8
Percentage who can count on neighbors to:						
a. Run errands when respondent is sick	95.7	83.6	72.8	80.4	70.1	68.3
b. Watch house when respondent is away	98.8	92.5	83.2	83.5	81.2	74.4
c. Loan respondent $25 in an emergency	92.9	81.7	74.7	71.0	70.8	65.0

community for the longest time is 23 years for the blacks and 27 years for the whites.

In Lincoln Park, the blacks have lived in the community longer on average than have the whites—black median length of residence being seven years, compared to four for the whites. No members of either group have lived there all their lives. This finding reflects the fact that two countervailing trends are occurring simultaneously in Lincoln Park—low-income blacks are leaving the community at the same time that middle-class blacks are entering it. At the present time, the remaining long-term residents outnumber the more recent arrivals.

Consistent with a shorter average length of residence, black respondents in Beverly are less likely than whites to consider the neighborhood a real home and to say that they definitely will not move during the next year. However, the percentages of Beverly blacks responding positively on these items are higher than those for either blacks or whites in Hyde Park–Kenwood and Lincoln Park. More blacks than whites in Hyde Park–Kenwood consider the neighborhood to be a real home, but fewer say they will not move. There are no differences on these items in Lincoln Park (table 5.1).

In all three neighborhoods, fewer blacks than whites report having good friends in the neighborhood as well as visiting with their neighbors often. The differences on these items are larger in Beverly than in Hyde Park–Kenwood or Lincoln Park; only among whites in Austin is the proportion who spend a social evening with neighbors once a week or more smaller than that among blacks in Beverly.

Although fewer report having good friends in the neighborhood, more blacks than whites in Hyde Park–Kenwood and Lincoln Park have relatives living in the neighborhood and visit their relatives often. This is not the case in Beverly; although blacks and whites there report visiting relatives with about equal frequency, whites are much more likely than blacks to have relatives living in the neighborhood. Beverly blacks are also less likely than whites to be able to count on their neighbors to help in case of illness, to watch their houses when they are away, or to lend them money in an emergency. Again, however, the proportions in Beverly who can rely on their neighbors are higher than for either racial group in Hyde Park–Kenwood or Lincoln Park.

The only consistent racial difference in local-facility use across the three neighborhoods is in church attendance; as was the case in the other racially mixed neighborhoods, whites are much more likely to attend church locally than are blacks (table 5.2). Fewer blacks than whites in Hyde Park–Kenwood obtain medical care, do their banking, and buy

Table 5.2 Respondents Who Use Local Facilities, by Race—Beverly, Hyde Park–Kenwood, and Lincoln Park (percentage)

	Beverly		Hyde Park–Kenwood		Lincoln Park	
	White	Black	White	Black	White	Black
Buy groceries	73.9	77.6	90.1	81.3	91.7	79.1
Go to restaurants	51.3	50.0	41.9	47.0	71.5	62.9
Go to religious services	91.3	38.7	74.6	26.5	65.6	45.9
Do banking	64.2	67.2	67.6	52.9	34.8	35.3
Get medical care	35.3	25.8	60.5	41.8	26.0	41.5
Buy clothes	44.0	48.5	10.1	12.2	24.2	18.6

groceries in the neighborhood. In Beverly, blacks are less likely than whites to get medical care locally. Lincoln Park blacks are more likely to obtain medical care in the community than are whites, but are less likely to buy groceries or dine out there.

Racial differences in the assessment of crime and in fear of it are neither large nor consistent in Beverly, Hyde Park–Kenwood, and Lincoln Park (table 5.3). The biggest black-white differences in these items can be found in worrying about being the victim of a crime in Hyde Park–Kenwood and in feeling uneasy upon hearing footsteps at night in Hyde Park–Kenwood and Beverly; in these three cases, whites are more fearful than blacks. However, more blacks than whites worry about criminal victimization in Lincoln Park, and more Beverly blacks than whites worry about burglary. In fact, Beverly blacks are as likely as Hyde Park–Kenwood blacks to worry that their homes will be broken into when they are away.

As was true in Austin, the belief that black in-migration leads to negative consequences is more widespread among blacks than whites in Hyde Park–Kenwood and Lincoln Park (table 5.4). In both communities, the percentage of respondents who say that crime goes up and property

Table 5.3 Assessment and Fear of Crime, by Race—Beverly, Hyde Park–Kenwood, and Lincoln Park

Characteristic	Beverly		Hyde Park–Kenwood		Lincoln Park	
	White	Black	White	Black	White	Black
Percentage who say there is "a lot" of crime in their neighborhood	3.8	3.1	8.9	11.1	9.6	7.5
Percentage who say the likelihood of victimization in the neighborhood during the coming year is high	2.5	1.7	7.8	6.1	6.2	10.0
Percentage who:						
a. Often worry about being victimized in the neighborhood	14.8	19.4	39.5	31.0	23.3	31.0
b. Would fear a stranger who asked for directions at night	51.2	49.3	56.7	61.4	45.6	51.2
c. Worry that home will be burglarized	24.1	30.8	36.5	31.0	41.8	42.9
d. Feel uneasy when they hear footsteps behind them at night	55.5	47.0	71.7	63.1	66.4	65.9

Table 5.4 Perceived Consequences of Integration, by Race—Beverly, Hyde Park–Kenwood, and Lincoln Park (percentage)

When a few black families move into an all-white neighborhood	Beverly		Hyde Park–Kenwood		Lincoln Park	
	White	Black	White	Black	White	Black
Crime rates usually go up (mostly true)	26.1	22.6	14.8	18.9	12.9	38.5
Property values are sure to go down (mostly true)	28.3	26.7	32.0	39.1	30.4	43.9
They [black families] usually have the same income and education as the people who live there (mostly false)	10.7	26.6	13.6	33.9	15.2	41.0

values go down when a few black families move in is larger for blacks than for whites, and substantially larger in Lincoln Park. In all three neighborhoods, blacks are more likely than whites to say that the first black families in a neighborhood are usually of a different socioeconomic status than the whites already living there and that their own neighborhood is racially changing (tables 5.4 and 5.5).

Although the differences are not very great, white respondents in Beverly, Hyde Park–Kenwood, and Lincoln Park are in general more positive in their overall evaluation of the neighborhood than are blacks (table 5.6). Whites express somewhat higher levels of satisfaction with the neighborhood and are a little less likely to say the neighborhood will get worse in the next two years. Blacks in Hyde Park–Kenwood are much more likely than whites to say the neighborhood has gotten worse during the past two years, although somewhat more of them say the neighborhood is a good place for investment. Beverly blacks and whites are similar in their evaluation of the neighborhood's recent past and its investment potential. Lincoln Park blacks are more negative than the whites on both questions, particularly on the advisability of investing in the neighborhood.

Table 5.5 Respondents Who Say That Their Neighborhood Is Racially Changing, by Race—Beverly, Hyde Park–Kenwood, and Lincoln Park (percentage)

	White	Black
Beverly	24.5	41.8
Hyde Park–Kenwood	26.4	31.2
Lincoln Park	41.4	52.5

Table 5.6 Measures of Overall Assessment of Neighborhood, by Race—Beverly, Hyde Park–Kenwood, and Lincoln Park

Characteristic	Beverly		Hyde Park–Kenwood		Lincoln Park	
	White	Black	White	Black	White	Black
Percentage who are very or somewhat satisfied overall with their neighborhood	94.9	86.6	87.5	83.1	94.3	83.8
Percentage who say neighborhood has gotten worse in past two years	9.2	9.4	7.0	21.0	5.6	9.3
Percentage who say neighborhood will get worse in the next two years	6.6	12.5	9.1	15.7	6.5	10.3
Percentage who say buying a house in their neighborhood would be making a good financial investment	92.7	95.2	78.8	84.7	87.3	78.0

A Fragile Balance

Beverly, Hyde Park–Kenwood, and Lincoln Park give lie to the theory that racial succession must inevitably follow from the presence of a black population. The failure to change racially is partly attributable to the presence of a black middle class of increased size whose life style is similar to that of the whites. When this is coupled with the national decline in prejudice identified in surveys, we do find support for Wilson's (1979) contention that for middle-class blacks, segregation and discrimination are less problematic than they used to be. This increased tolerance is particularly evident in Lincoln Park, where a substantial proportion of the white residents believe the neighborhood is racially changing, yet hold a fairly benign view of the consequences of black in-migration.

Even with this more favorable environment, however, racial stability simply does not happen by itself; as we have seen, it requires massive intervention by community leaders and a commitment from residents to support integration. In addition, these efforts must be sustained over time, for even with stability, racial tensions and concerns persist. In Beverly, for example, residents continue to be anxious about real estate practices. When the city-of-Chicago ordinance banning For Sale signs was ruled unconstitutional in 1979, Beverly residents met to discuss how they could continue to keep the signs off their lawns. A 1980 wave of "cold-calling" by real estate agents—calling people one does not know and asking them if they want to sell—had residents alarmed that panic peddling had returned.

In Hyde Park–Kenwood, the crime issue is closely tied to race, which leads to a certain wariness among whites and a certain measure of discomfort among blacks in interracial encounters on the streets. To the extent that blacks bear the symbols of being middle class, whites feel less wary; middle-class blacks feel pressure to bear those symbols so that they are not confused with the dangerous poor. Efforts that are made to step up police patrolling make some middle-class blacks and their white friends nervous, for some of that patrolling looks like harassment of all blacks. Blacks tell wryly of taking their TV sets to be repaired and being stopped by policemen and asked to provide evidence of ownership. On the other hand, the black youth carrying a TV set over the fences and through the back yards of one of us explained to our neighbor that he was taking the set to be fixed. When she suggested she check with the police, the set was quickly left behind.

The tension is there, and both blacks and whites tread cautiously about this subject. One of the issues that continues to surface is what to do about those community activities that bring blacks into the neighborhood. Are objections to a local basketball tournament and the crowds who attend racially motivated or are they simply reactions to the inconvenience? If the latter, why does no one object to the annual art fair which brings in many more people (mainly white) and causes far more inconvenience? Should a local bar that features jazz have its lease renewed? These kinds of issues continually reappear in the community. Both Hyde Park–Kenwood and Beverly leaders have made efforts to keep black churches out of their communities.

Similarly, in all three communities, some building uses seem more threatening than others. Halfway houses for reformed juvenile delinquents and drug addicts are seen as real threats to the community. One standard community reaction is, "Why don't you put them in [some suburb]?" Each community imparts a sense of its own precariousness, and the addition of another potentially crime-related problem scares some people. The issue becomes complicated because there are those who believe it is the community's obligation to make room for the unfortunate. No decision that has an impact on the community, particularly if it involves race and class, is made without agonizing debate.

There is further, indirect evidence that vigilance continues, at least in Beverly and Hyde Park–Kenwood. Thirty-one percent of Beverly respondents report that they belong to groups "concerned with the quality of community life," a proportion higher than in any of our other neighborhoods and higher than one would expect if residents felt at ease. Hyde Park–Kenwood, with 21 percent of the respondents belonging to such organizations, ranks second. Also, more residents in these two communities than in the others belong to groups of renters and homeowners, and more of them are aware of anticrime programs and activities in their neighborhoods. Lincoln Park residents are less likely to be organizationally active, but they do rank third in both the proportion who belong to renter or homeowner groups and the proportion who are aware of community anticrime efforts.

In spite of persisting racial concerns, Beverly, Hyde Park–Kenwood, and Lincoln Park are stable, prosperous residential communities. Property appreciation in Beverly has not been as high as one would expect from its appearance, and its major shopping strip does have a vacancy rate of more than 10 percent. Nevertheless, it is a community that refused to allow falling property values and subsequent deterioration to gain a foothold. Working in groups such as BAPA, the residents of Beverly addressed themselves to a wide range of threatening community problems. Through their energies, the community has been reinforced on many fronts and continues to be a stable residential area.

Hyde Park–Kenwood was the site of massive intervention to prevent a community from deteriorating when faced with racial change and high crime rates. That intervention seems to have succeeded. The community is thriving, property values are appreciating, and properties are moderately well maintained, even though crime continues to be a major problem for its residents.

Lincoln Park represents the classic pattern of gentrification. Starting with young bohemians who saw good housing bargains for those with the time and skill to renovate, followed by the city's entry into the process through urban renewal, and then by the support of large investors, the area moved back into middle-class status. With its glorious park and lakefront beaches, and its locational advantages, it continues to prosper in the context of high crime.

Cynics may argue that the final results are not yet in, that neighborhoods have tipping points, and that Beverly and especially Lincoln Park are well below those points. Hyde Park–Kenwood is a special case because of the University of Chicago's continued active involvement and its support of the private police system. The process of change in Beverly in particular has not, they might say, been halted; rather it has merely been stalled. However, the real test of an integrated neighborhood seems to be the extent to which blacks and whites freely buy houses from each other. That pattern is well established in Hyde Park–Kenwood. It is, so far, less well established in Beverly. In Lincoln Park, whites are still buying houses from poor blacks in order to renovate. In the relatively expensive rental market, blacks and whites appear free to exchange quarters with each other, evidence that at the middle-class level, integration has been achieved.

   With these communities, we have provided alternative scenarios to both racial succession and intransigent defense. These scenarios appear to be true whether or not the areas have high crime rates. What is important for residents is that in each case the community responds to the crime problem. Even in low-crime Beverly, community activity focuses much energy on crime-related questions. With higher crime rates, Hyde Park–Kenwood residents and the University of Chicago do even more. Probably less community anticrime activity takes place in relatively high-crime Lincoln Park than in either of the other two areas; its mostly young, childless residents are too busy with other things to be seriously worried. Nonetheless, even in Lincoln Park the community-wide organization and many localized groups work closely with the police and participate in anticrime programs.

   The knowledge that an effort is being made to deal with crime and related matters and that there are other sources of gratification in their communities makes each a good investment and a satisfying place to live. Indeed, it is possible that such strategies work only because the areas themselves have so many beneficial features. Good-quality housing stock, attractive external amenities, and a solid middle-class population in areas with major, well-connected institutional actors are not broadly available. However, similar communities have in the past gone through the succession process, both in Chicago and elsewhere; had they received proper institutional support, the story might have been different in some cases.

   Until this point, we have focused on these communities in the aggregate. In fact, each community is made up of individual actors, and it is the cumulation of their decisions that ultimately determines what will happen to these areas. Individuals decide whether or not to move, what kinds of investments to make in their houses, whether or not to encourage friends and relatives to move into their area, and whether or not to join community organizations and to participate in some collective effort to maintain their area.

   It is to an analysis of these individual decisions that we now turn. Important to remember, however, is that these individual decisions are made in contexts, that how people evaluate the world they live in is related to what is happening in the world. We have provided the context. Next, we turn to efforts to understand the decision-making process of individuals. Ultimately, we must link the two components.

6
Toward A Formal Theory of Neighborhood Investment

In the last three chapters, we have shown that neighborhood aging, ethnic/racial succession, and housing deterioration are not as inescapably bound together as earlier ecological studies of "natural" areas of the city would indicate. In the next three chapters, we will study, in as general and systematic terms as possible, the individual decisions and actions that collectively bring about these altered outcomes.

This chapter analyzes individual-homeowner choices to spend or not to spend on home rehabilitation and improvement. It is almost a truism to suggest that the core problem in the prevention of neighborhood deterioration is maintaining levels of economic investment. Community organizations may help city government to provide good schools and other services such as street cleaning and garbage removal. Organizational activity or cultural traditions may generate strong social bonds that tie residents together in positive and mutually supportive interaction. Crime rates may be low, and people may feel secure. All of these things represent substantial achievements and are worthwhile indeed. And although they are often related to investment activity, the bottom line, however, is still the investment activity itself. The forces of weather and wear are relentless. Housing maintenance is a ceaseless activity, particularly when the structures are no longer new, as is the case in most urban settings.

We emphasize this point because we believe that it is often lost sight of both by scholars who write about communities and people who attempt to organize community residents for neighborhood improvement. At some point, basic economic decisions have to be made. Individuals must decide to expend resources on the maintenance and improvement of their property.

Economic models have been proposed for analyzing the investment

decisions of absentee landlords and other types of individual and corporate actors whose primary interest is the maximization of rent and returns
on capital investment (Sternlieb 1966; Stegman 1972). We noted in
chapters 3, 4, and 5 that actions of corporations and other "large"
individuals shape the climate for all types of neighborhood perceptions
and neighborhood-oriented actions among homeowners in each of the
eight Chicago communities. One of the lessons from these three chapters
is that we cannot fully explain the pattern of investment in a neighborhood without reference to the incentives and choices made by large
actors.

In this chapter, we analyze investment decisions of individual
homeowners in the context of neighborhood conditions created in part by
the actions or inactions of landlords and institutions in the community.
To do this, we consider two formal models that have been suggested in
the literature as appropriate theoretical explanations for this type of
decision making. Davis and Whinston (1961) discuss the implications of
considering rehabilitation investment as a simple prisoner's dilemma.
Granovetter (1978) presents a mathematical formalization of a diffusion
model appropriate for analyzing patterns of individual decision making in
circumstances where the benefits from acting depend partly on how many
of one's neighbors take a similar action. Home investment is, of course,
this type of decision—the value of one's investment is determined partially by value, appearance, and upkeep of the neighbors' homes.

The models we use to describe and analyze the interlocking nature of
expectations and benefits in home-investment decisions are referred to in
the literature as "formal" theories. They are formal in the sense that
there is a precise, mathematical statement of the interdependencies and
contingencies that ought to be considered by someone who wishes to act
in his or her own best interest. The purpose of this chapter is to determine
which contingencies people actually take into account in calculating the
benefits they expect from home investment.

The thrust of the literature on formal modeling and collective-action
problems is often to illustrate how decisions made by individuals on a
basis that appears rational to them result in a collective outcome that no
individual would desire for the social system as a whole. Our attempt to
construct a model of how these decisions are made is particularly
appropriate in this instance for those interested in the development of
social policy to deal with problems of urban deterioriation. Once we
understand in a precise way how individuals make investment decisions,
we may be better able to recommend policy choices that push rational
individual decisions based on perceived realities toward outcomes that
are, in fact, desirable for the entire community.

Preferences and Interdependencies Affecting Neighborhood Investment

A distinction needs to be made between two different types of investment. In the first type, obligatory home maintenance, investments are made to maintain one's house in a steady state. How one does this is constrained by the availability of resources. In the second type, nonobligatory enhancement, investments are made to increase one's pleasure and comfort in a residence; they represent investment as consumption. In general, this type of investment is limited by one's sense of the probability that an adequate economic return on the investment will be earned, should the house be sold.

The differences between the two types of investment are not always easy to identify. Improvements that may seem necessary to some individuals are seen as enhancements by others. The distinction is further obscured by the fact that it makes sense to spruce up one's house just prior to sale if one has the resources to do so. Nonetheless, as we shall see, the distinction is still a useful one.

Several authors have noted that the expected return and possibly the consumption value from an investment are affected by market interdependencies that partly determine the value of an investment in any particular neighborhood. Davis and Whinston (1961) observe that because of the way prices are established in a housing market, one person's financial investment in home improvement increases the value of his neighbor's property as well as his own. As a rule, they argue, the value of one's property is based partly on one's own investment and partly on the neighbors' actions. The kernel of this observation is contained in the familiar dictum, "The value of one property depends on the neighborhood in which it is located" (Marshal 1920, 445).

Davis and Whinston build on this observation and discuss the implications of assuming that when deciding about investment, a person will utilize the fact that, without committing any of his or her own resources, some benefit can be derived from neighbors' investments. They argue that one way to analyze neighborhood investment is to assume that people react as they would in a simple, noniterated prisoner's dilemma. The typical homeowner will most likely choose to be, in Mancur Olson's terms, a "free rider" (1965). Because of the incentives facing individual homeowners, high levels of neighborhood investment are difficult to achieve, even though that would be the desirable outcome from the point of view of the community as a whole. In the next part of this chapter, we study the extent of the free-rider problem as a determinant of neighborhood-investment levels.

The second formal model we consider proceeds from a quite different assumption about how neighbors' actions and social pressures affect the incentives for one's own investment decisions. Granovetter (1978) outlines a "threshold" model for collective action based on the assumption that the perception that others are investing may *increase* the chance that one will commit his or her own time, energy, and resources to improving things. The threshold is that point where the number of others making an investment encourages one to do so as well. Individuals are assumed to have varying threshold levels. This model is a powerful tool for analyzing investment markets because it opens up a number of different ways to study the extent of the free-rider problem. Under this model, the desirable community outcome—a high level of investment— may or may not be difficult to achieve, depending on such factors as the presence or absence of owners or institutional investors who "get the ball rolling" and whether or not, at each level of neighborhood investment, there are enough individuals who are willing to risk their own resources to "keep the ball rolling."[1]

The two models agree that investment decisions reflect personal consumption priorities and that people invest when they expect a gain from doing so. Either model can provide a frame of reference that takes account of obligatory maintenance and nonobligatory enhancement as different types of investment. Both models also agree that the net benefits from investment are affected by market interdependencies. The question separating the two models is: How do people react to their neighbors' actions? The Davis-Whinston model contemplates the possibility that each person in a prisoner's-dilemma situation will make the narrowly rational choice to act as a free rider. Granovetter's model, on the other hand, assumes that people vary in the extent to which they choose to benefit from others' actions without contributing themselves. Some may adopt the point of view of the free rider, others may act independently of the neighbors' actions, and others may be somewhere in between these extremes—choosing to act when the extent of neighborhood investment is at a sufficiently high level.

The question of which model—Davis-Whinston or Granovetter—is the more realistic depiction of the nature of interdependencies in the market for neighborhood investment can be resolved empirically. After the data were collected for the Chicago Neighborhood Survey, we had the fortunate opportunity to design a second, follow-up study that allowed a much larger section of the questionnaire to be allocated to questions analyzing the effect of neighbors' actions on homeowners' investment decisions. These data are in what we will refer to here as the Waukegan Community Survey (Taylor 1981b).[2] First we present some data from this survey, since it is more singularly focused on the theoretical analysis of collective action and home investment. We then turn to the principal data set to show how our frame of reference for analyzing home investment applies to Chicago neighborhoods.

The data in table 6.1 from the Waukegan survey are one critical test of which theoretical frame of reference—Davis-Whinston or Granovetter—explains the impact of neighbors' actions on homeowner investment behavior. The wordings for the questions are shown at the bottom of the table. The dependent variable in table 6.1 is a summary yes/no measure of whether the respondent undertook any of the home improvements listed in the question. The first column of table 6.1 presents the results for homeowners who say their neighbors are not similarly investing. Overall, 36 percent of these people report some spending on home improvement in the two years preceding the survey. The second column shows the results for homeowners who say their neighbors *are* spending money on home rehabilitation. The relative amount of investment is much higher in this group (65 percent).

These results support the threshold model and argue against the simple prisoner's dilemma as the appropriate representation of people's decision-making criteria. To lend further credibility to this conclusion, the effect of neighbors' actions on investment is shown separately for homeowners who say they did and did not consider neighbors' investment

Table 6.1 Homeowners Who Invest in Home Rehabilitation as a Function of Whether or Not Their Neighbors Have Done So

Respondent Report of Importance of Neighbors' Actions	Have Neighbors Spent Money on Rehab?	
	No	Yes
Very important	26%	63%
Less important	47%	68%
TOTAL	36%	65%

Source: Waukegan Community Survey (Taylor 1981b).
The questions were worded as follows.
INVESTMENT: "Please tell me if any of these changes or improvements were made in your home in the last two years?"
a. adding a new porch, a new room, a bathroom, a closet
b. remodeling the kitchen or bathroom
c. any other inside remodeling such as finishing the basement or anything else
d. putting on a new roof or new storm windows
e. plastering, painting, tuckpointing, or refinishing the outside
f. any other outside remodeling such as fixing a garage, a porch or anything else.
NEIGHBORS' ACTIONS: "As far as you know have any of the people who live on this block been changing their property in any of these ways?"
IMPORTANCE OF NEIGHBORS' ACTIONS: "I'm going to read a list of things some people think about when they buy a place to live in. Think back to when you bought this home. How important was each of these in your decision to buy?" . . . The likelihood that people who live around you will fix up their property or remodel it.

actions to be an important factor in their own decision to move into the neighborhood. The effect of neighbors' actions is much greater among those for whom this was a salient factor in their own investment decisions.

Table 6.2 adds further evidence for this conclusion. Respondents were asked whether they would spend more on home rehabilitation if their neighbors spent more. The wording of the question is given at the bottom of table 6.2. Those who consider neighbors' actions to have been salient are more likely than those who do not to say they will invest if the neighbors do.

The data suggest that the appropriate frame of reference for discussing the interdependence of home-investment decisions is the threshold model and not the simple prisoner's dilemma. All things equal (i.e., when the factors producing a need for obligatory maintenance or nonobligatory enhancement are held constant), there appear to be many neighborhood residents for whom the perception of others investing spurs their own level of activity. We are therefore encouraged to use Granovetter's threshold model as a guide for analyzing and interpreting the Chicago neighborhood data. We begin the discussion by explaining more fully the inner workings of Granovetter's model.

A Formal Statement of the Threshold Model

The threshold model describes: (1) how investment decisions are socially interdependent; and (2) how socially interdependent investment decisions cumulate to produce an aggregate level of neighborhood investment. The first part of the model is a mathematical representation of the assumption that the gain individuals expect from investment is usually related to the extent to which the neighbors are also investing. The

Table 6.2 Homeowners Who Say They Would Spend More on Home Rehabilitation if Their Neighbors Spent More

Respondent Report of Importance of Neighbors' Actions	Has the Respondent Spent Any Money Yet on Rehabilitation?	
	No	Yes
Very important	56%	17%
Less important	9%	8%
TOTAL	38%	13%

Source: Waukegan Community Survey (Taylor 1981b).

The questions were worded as follows.

WOULD SPEND: "Do you think you would spend more on changing your home if other people in the neighborhood were spending more on theirs?"

INVESTMENT, IMPORTANCE: See notes to table 6.1.

second part of the model is a formal statement of the dynamic principle which shows how an aggregate level of neighborhood investment is achieved, given the interdependencies.

The interdependency of decisions is defined by three assumptions:

1. People invest when they expect a positive return.
2. The exception of a positive return (sometimes discussed in terms of the subjective risk to investing) is related to the perception that other people are investing.
3. People vary in their willingness to take risks, that is, to invest. Some people might require a high level of perceived community action before investing; others might require little sign of support in the environment.

Figure 6.1 is a graphical representation of these assumptions. The dotted lines on the graph show how four different types of individuals might be affected by the extent of neighbors' actions. Line E1 shows the curve for a person who expects a positive gain when 50 percent or more of the neighbors are also seen to be investing. Line E2 is the curve for a person who expects positive gain when the proportion of neighbors investing is quite a bit lower, near 10 percent. For each of these cases, the point where the curve crosses the x axis is referred to as the person's threshold score. The threshold is the point at which the proportion of

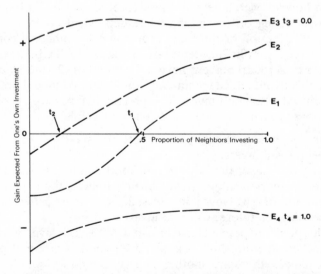

Fig. 6.1. Possible Relations between the Proportion of One's Neighbors Investing and the Gain Expected from One's Own Investment. Formal requirements of threshold models represented here: (a) E_i crosses x axis once at most; (b) E_i crosses x axis from below; (c) individuals invest at the moment the expected gain becomes positive.

neighbors acting becomes high enough to cause an individual to expect positive gain from his or her own investment.

Lines E3 and E4 show curves for people whose investment decisions are not sensitive to the proportion of neighbors acting. Line E3 is the curve for a person who will invest regardless of the level of public support (even if the proportion investing is zero). Therefore, we assign this person a threshold score of zero. It is sometimes substantively appropriate to describe such a person as a risk taker or a leader. Granovetter proposes the term "pioneer" (the same word which in common usage designates the first actors in a gentrifying area), to describe individuals with threshold values of zero.

In contrast to the pioneer, line E4 shows the curve for a person who will *not* invest even if everyone else does. The threshold value in this case is 1.0 since this person does not expect gain from investing even in situations where 100 percent of the neighbors are doing so. Granovetter proposes the term "conservative" to describe individuals with a threshold score of 1.0. Empirically, such conservatives might be old people with limited resources or others who believe that nothing can save the neighborhood. Or they may be pure free riders who recognize that they will benefit from others' investments even if they do nothing themselves. A prisoner's dilemma can be described as a situation where all individuals have a threshold score of 1.0 (Granovetter 1983).

The second part of the threshold model is the dynamic principle that explains how an overall neighborhood level of investment is attained by individuals acting on the basis of interdependent choices. Figure 6.2 shows a distribution of threshold scores in a hypothetical community. Thirty percent of the residents are assumed to be pioneers with a threshold of zero, 10 percent have a threshold of .2, and so on.

For this hypothetical community, the threshold model predicts that 60 percent will ultimately invest. This prediction is based on the following calculations, which illustrate the dynamic principle:

1. At the beginning, the 30 percent with threshold values of zero (the pioneers) will invest.
2. During this stage, the level of neighborhood investment rises to 30 percent. This percentage passes the threshold for the 10 percent of the population who will invest if at least 20 percent are active. These next 10 percent, therefore, will also invest.
3. At this point, 40 percent have invested. When this level of investment is reached, the threshold is attained for another group of people. In the example, there are another 20 percent who will join if at least 40 percent are active.
4. When step three is complete, all those with thresholds below .6 have invested and all those not investing have thresholds higher than .6.

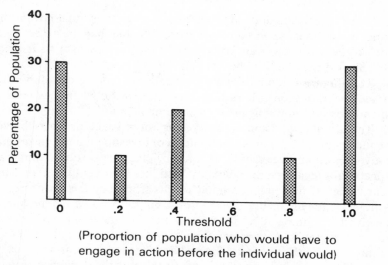

Fig. 6.2 Hypothetical Threshold Distribution

Thus, 60 percent is the equilibrium point (i.e., the level of neighborhood investment) that is predicted for a community with a threshold distribution similar to that in figure 6.2. This prediction assumes, of course, that the high levels of investment activity do not bring anyone new into the community.

The likelihood of a person investing in home rehabilitation can be thought of in terms of his or her threshold score. The need for obligatory maintenance pushes people toward lower threshold scores, provided that they have the necessary resources. Their actions occur somewhat independently from the neighbors' because of the need for property maintenance. Their actions may, however, have an effect on the overall level of neighborhood investment, depending on the distribution of threshold scores among those who are considering investment in nonobligatory enhancement.

Those who consider spending on nonobligatory enhancement are acting both as consumers and as investors. In their role as consumers, their decision making is, in some respects, insensitive to their neighbors' actions. They invest or do not invest, depending on the value to them of nonobligatory enhancement as a consumer good. However, even in this role, people's actions are not entirely independent of the social context. Part of the value of nonobligatory enhancement as a consumer good depends on the extent of neighbors' actions. Many people are socially pressured into upkeep spending because they do not want their home to be one of the worst looking on the block. Similarly, people sometimes hold back on certain kinds of investment because they do not want their home to stand out as conspicuously more valuable than the others on the block or because they want to be certain they can recover their investment should they be "forced" to sell.

The threshold model defines precisely the type of calculation that homeowners, in their role as investors, must make when they consider expenditures on nonobligatory enhancement.

The ultimate decision of whether or not to spend on nonobligatory enhancement is based on a combination of investment and consumption motives. Each motive is sensitive, in principle, to one's observations and expectations regarding the neighbors' actions. The overall level of investment achieved in a neighborhood results from a collection of people, each acting for his or her own reasons, but each possibly affecting the perceived "friendliness" of the environment for the others. Whether we are analyzing obligatory or nonobligatory expenditure, and whether we are interested in the pioneers, the middle range, or the conservatives, the threshold scores are the focal point for analyzing the dynamics of neighborhood investment. Any individual-level variable or contextual factor that affects the distribution of threshold scores in a neighborhood changes the interdependencies among the neighbors and thereby alters the level of investment that is ultimately achieved in the area. A regression analysis of threshold scores provides a guide for explaining the level of investment achieved in a neighborhood and the reasons for differences between neighborhoods in the relative levels of their upkeep.

In addition to providing a frame of reference for interpreting the statistical results, the threshold model also suggests a strategy for measuring the dependent variable, that is, willingness to invest. Individual threshold scores can be measured using survey questions like those shown in tables 6.1 and 6.2. The first measure shown in table 6.1 is a summary measure indicating whether or not people spent money on home rehabilitation. The second question asks whether or not any of the neighbors invested. With these two measures, we can determine which respondents invested even though the neighbors did not. These people are the "pioneers" and have a threshold score of zero according to the formal theory. Fourteen percent of the Waukegan sample are classified as pioneers according to this procedure.

The question analyzed in table 6.2 can be used to determine who are the conservatives with a threshold score of 1.0. Respondents who have not invested and say they will refuse to invest even if the neighbors invest more are, according to the formal model, conservatives with a threshold score of 1.0. Thirty percent of the sample are classified as conservatives by this procedure. This is the upper limit for the proportion of residents who could be considered to be acting as free riders.

The remaining respondents, those who are neither pioneers nor conservatives, fall into a middle group with threshold scores between zero and 1.0. With the data available, it is possible to further categorize the threshold scores of those in the middle. Respondents with scores between zero and 1.0 who *did* invest by the time of the survey can be assumed to have a relatively low threshold score, and those who did not invest can be assumed to have a relatively high threshold score. In the regression analysis, we convert this ordinal ranking of the middle group into an interval scale by assuming that the average threshold score for nonpioneers who did invest is .25 and that the average threshold score for nonconservatives who did not invest is .75. Forty percent of the sample are classified as having a relatively low threshold score of .25 and 13 percent are classified as relatively high with a threshold of .75.[3]

The Dynamics of Neighborhood Investment

Analysis of Threshold Scores: Waukegan Data

Since the early parts of this chapter work with data from our Waukegan survey, we will note briefly the principal substantive findings from this study before analyzing the Chicago data. The Waukegan results both introduce and replicate the Chicago findings.

Those respondents with a comparatively high income or large family tend to have lower threshold scores than others. They are more likely to invest even when few of the neighbors are doing so. Controlling for these factors, we also find that those living in the older, more deteriorated parts of the city targeted for Community Development Block Grant (CDBG) monies have much higher threshold scores. People in these areas are less willing to invest, or require a much higher level of security in the form of visible signs of others investing, before they are willing to do so themselves. They have made some sort of negative decision about the future of the neighborhood which leads them to believe that they would not be able to recover their investment if they had to sell.

What can we learn about the nature of this negative decision? Racial issues strongly affect the dynamics of investment in older, more deteriorated areas of the city. In these areas, minority concentration (black and/or Hispanic) raises the average threshold score for members of *any* racial group. This finding is displayed in table 6.3. We note that this finding is controlled for social class and income differences in two ways. First, family income appears as a control variable in the regression equation. The results in table 6.3 are predicted average threshold scores in each respondent category, standardizing for income differences between respondents (and between categories). The methodology for this adjustment is discussed in appendix E. Class and income effects are also

Table 6.3 Estimated Average Rehabilitation-Threshold Scores for Homeowners in CDBG Neighborhoods as a Function of Race and Racial Composition of Neighborhood

Perceived Racial Composition	Race of Respondent			
	White	Black	Hispanic	TOTAL
All or mostly white	.55	.33	.34	.45
More mixed	.76	.54	.55	.66
TOTAL	.71	.49	.50	.61

Source: Waukegan Community Survey (Taylor 1981b).
Estimated average scores are standardized for the effects of the other predictor variables discussed in connection with these findings (see text).

controlled by the fact that table 6.3 shows the results for a fairly homogeneous context—CDBG areas in the central city. Social class, housing quality, and income differences are much smaller within this area than in the city as a whole.

Why does minority concentration provoke such a reaction? Is it fair or helpful to call the reaction prejudice? If so, then members of all racial groups are prejudiced. The scores are higher for whites, blacks, and Hispanics living in areas of higher minority concentration. Which aspect of minority concentration is it that provides the justification to the individual homeowner for this racial encoding of neighborhoods? Is it fear of crime, expectation of economic deterioration, or some other aspect of minority presence? Is it the same aspect for whites and nonwhites? The Chicago Neighborhood Survey is a much more complete data set specifically designed to answer these questions. We now turn to an analysis of the results from that survey.

Analysis of Threshold Scores: Chicago Data

One methodological difference between the Chicago survey and the Waukegan data is the measure of the dependent variable. The Chicago survey did not contain the battery of questions for measuring the full range of threshold scores. To analyze the Chicago data, we assume that people who invested have lower threshold scores than people who did not. The analysis of threshold scores measured this way is equivalent to analyzing a dichotomous dependent variable measuring whether or not people invested in the two years preceding the survey.[4]

After preliminary tests, it became clear that further adjustment in the measure of the dependent variable had to be undertaken. The proportion of homeowners investing some amount of money in home improvement was too great (about .9) to consider this variable useful for understanding global differences in the levels of neighborhood upkeep. Because of the nature of the housing stock in Chicago, the comparatively high level of need for obligatory maintenance, and/or the market conditions in the different neighborhoods in the city, most homeowners in Chicago make some type of property investment in a two-year span. (The comparable figure in the Waukegan survey is 65 percent.) Because of this lack of variabiity we revised the dependent variable. Those who spent more than $1,000 on home improvement during the previous two years were scored "1" and the rest "0". Appropriate procedures were used to perform weighted regression analyses of this modified threshold measure (Grizzle, Starmer, and Koch 1969).

Table 6.4 shows the proportion of homeowners in each neighborhood spending more than $1,000 on home improvement in the two years preceding the survey. The results are shown separately for whites and nonwhites. The first pattern we note is that the neighborhoods that appear to be the worst maintained are not necessarily the ones with the lowest proportion of homeowner spending on upkeep. In areas where the majority of residents are renters (as is the case for all of our sample neighborhoods except Beverly, Portage Park, and East Side), the visual appearance of the neighborhood results more from the actions (or inactions) of landlords than of homeowners. Thus, we have the apparent anomaly that homeowners in some of the worst-appearing areas (e.g., Austin, South Shore) are actually above the sample average for the proportion of owners investing substantially in upkeep.

The second pattern we note is that racial encoding of neighborhoods, i.e., the depressing effect of minority concentration on upkeep spending,

Table 6.4 Proportion of Respondents Spending More than $1,000 on Home Rehabilitation in the Last Two Years, by Neighborhood and Race

Neighborhood Ordered by Percent Nonwhite Owners (lowest to highest)	Proportion Spending More than $1,000	
	White Owners	Black/Hispanic Owners
Portage Park	.62	—
Lincoln Park	.54	—
East Side	.56	.45
Beverly	.67	.59
Hyde Park–Kenwood	.52	.44
Back of the Yards	.56	.52
Austin	.61	.59
South Shore	—	.71
TOTAL	.60	.59

Source: Chicago Neighborhood Survey.
Blank cells represent too few cases to report reliably.

does not stand out as the explanation of neighborhood differences in table 6.4. The neighborhoods are arranged in the table according to the proportion of nonwhite residents. Those at the top of the list have a low nonwhite proportion; those at the bottom have a high proportion. Going down the list of neighborhoods, the proportion of white owners investing does not decline in any orderly way, which is contrary to our expectation based on the Waukegan results. The primary reason is that the absolute levels of deterioration and the age of the housing stock tend to be, on average, higher in areas of high minority concentration in Chicago. As a result, there are increased rates of investment and lower threshold scores in these areas because of the need for obligatory maintenance. When these factors are controlled, however, the pattern noted in the Waukegan data emerges more clearly. Minority concentration tends to decrease the level of investment for whites and nonwhites. Further controls and further analyses with the Chicago data will explain why this is so.

Table 6.5 shows the nonstandardized slopes for the weighted multiple-regression equation predicting investment. The first column is the set of slopes for white homeowners; the second column is the set of slopes for nonwhite homeowners.[5]

Causes of Investment: Deterioration and Obligatory Maintenance

We begin the discussion of table 6.5 by considering the relationship between the extent of investment and the level of need for obligatory maintenance. The level of need for obligatory maintenance is measured by a block-deterioration scale.[6] The relationship between deterioration and maintenance provides us with clues about the way homeowners perceive the incentives for investment in different kinds of neighborhoods markets. Tables 6.6 and 6.7 show the standardized relationships between block deterioration and investment, controlling for the homeowner's perception of the present state and the future trend of the housing market.[7] The relationships are shown separately for whites and nonwhites. These standardized relationships show the effects of the independent variable(s) on the dependent variable, controlling for the other variables in the full regression equation (shown in table 6.5). The methodology for estimating and displaying standardized effects is described in appendix E.

The general pattern for the relationship between investment, deterioration, and market evaluations is similar for whites and nonwhites. The analysis of tables 6.6 and 6.7 suggests there are two principles to be taken into account in explaining the relationship between deterioration and investment. Which principle applies to the behavior of any particular homeowner depends on how he or she perceives the strength of the local housing market.

We arrive at the first principle by looking at the behavior of those who live in the most deteriorated areas. Tables 6.6 and 6.7 show that those living both in deteriorated areas and in what is considered to be a

Table 6.5 Regression Slopes for Equation Predicting Investment

	Nonstandardized Slope	
Predictor Variable	White Owners	Nonwhite Owners
Marital/family status Dummy variables (reference category = married w/children)		
Married w/o children	−.11*	−.06
Not married	−.12*	−.22*
Log of family income	.07*	.06
Block-deterioration scale	.05*	−.03
Satisfaction w/property value	.03*	.05*
Black-white demand ratio	−.03	.03
Racial prejudice	−.02*	.01
Membership in neighborhood organizations	.06*	.02
Economic-evaluation scale	−.00	−.02*

Source: Chicago Neighborhood Survey.
$*|t| > 1.0.$

Table 6.6 Estimated Proportion of Respondents Investing as a Function of Neighborhood Economic and Block-Deterioration Levels

	Block-Deterioration-Scale Score	Score on Economic Evaluation Scale					
		0	1	2	3	4	5
White owners	0			.47	.51	.55	.59
	1			.57	.58	.58	.59
	2			.68	.64	.61	.58
	3			.78	.71	.65	.58
Nonwhite owners	0	.53	.57	.62	.67	.72	
	1	.54	.55	.57	.58	.59	
	2	.56	.53	.51	.48	.46	
	3	.57	.51	.45	.39	.33	

Source: Chicago Neighborhood Survey.
Estimated proportions are standardized for the effects of other variables shown in table 6.5.
Estimates are not shown for regions with a very small number of respondents.

Table 6.7 Estimated Proportion of Respondents Investing as a Function of Satisfaction with the Trend in Property Values and Block-Deterioration Level

	Block-Deterioration-Scale Score	Satisfaction with Property Values		
		2	3	4
White owners	0	.53	.68	.83
	1	.53	.61	.70
	2	.53	.55	.56
	3	.54	.49	.43
Nonwhite owners	0	.40	.52	.64
	1	.57	.59	.61
	2	.74	.65	.57
	3	.91	.72	.54

Source: Chicago Neighborhood Survey.
Estimated proportions are standardized for the effects of other variables shown in table 6.5. Estimates are not shown for regions with a very small number of respondents.

weak housing market have relatively high rates of investment. The pattern in the bottom row of each table shows that for those living in deteriorated areas, a strong market is apparently a sign that one can sell his or her home without improving it. A weak market is a sign that one is best off investing enough to raise the consumption value of the home to a satisfactory level to make the best of a bad situation. The first principle illustrated in tables 6.6 and 6.7 is that in already deteriorated areas, a strong market raises threshold scores.

If we look at the results for whose who live in the least deteriorated areas, we discover an opposite principle. For both whites and nonwhites living in these areas, the belief that the market is strong lowers investment-threshold values. It may be that in less deteriorated areas, a strong market signals the chance for a high economic return to rehabilitation investments. Or possibly some other aspect of the consumption value of rehabilitation expenditure is subjectively greater when the market is strong. From the point of view of the threshold model, we note that a strong market in nondeteriorated areas lowers the level of security (in the form of others acting) that is required to motivate one's own investment.

The two principles guiding investment can be summarized as: (1) making the best of a bad situation, and (2) capitalizing on a good situation. Tables 6.6 and 6.7 show that the two principles together describe the investment behavior of both whites and nonwhites. Which principle applies depends on the state of the market and the level of deterioration in the area.

One implication of our findings is that urban planners may face a vicious circle affecting the level of neighborhood investment. If public policies to promote investment have the effect of strengthening the housing market in a deteriorated area, then the effect of the policy may be to discourage investment rather than to encourage it. Strengthening the market in a deteriorated area tends to reduce the incentives for homeowner investment. The public policies with the greatest impact on deteriorated areas will be those that change the level of deterioration as well as strengthen the market. Policy makers must consider institutional investing or other building programs as keys to upgrading the physical appearance of the neighborhood to the point where homeowners see market stimulation as an incentive rather than a disincentive for investing.

As a final observation on tables 6.6 and 6.7, we note that the tendency to act on the basis of the second principle (i.e., to capitalize on a good situation) is stronger for nonwhite homeowners than for whites. For instance, in neighborhoods that are quite positively viewed—those with low deterioration and a strong market—the estimated proportion of nonwhites investing is substantially higher than the estimated proportion for whites.

Racial Encoding of Neighborhood-Investment Incentives

One of the principal observations from the Waukegan data is that threshold scores for members of any racial group are higher in the more racially mixed areas of the city. The Chicago data contain a sufficient variety of neighborhood types and a rich enough set of survey measures of the intervening variables that we can now explain why this is so. The primary reason is that both whites and nonwhites expect less favorable patterns of economic change in areas of high minority concentration. Both groups are less satisfied with the appreciation of housing values and the investment opportunities in areas of relatively high minority concentration. As the findings in tables 6.6 and 6.7 illustrate, these market evaluations are important factors promoting neighborhood investment for both whites and nonwhites. If confidence in the economic future of these neighborhoods could be improved (i.e., by policy measures such as insurance programs or institutional investments), there would be a change in willingness to invest.

Should this aspect of the racial encoding of market expectations be interpreted as prejudice? If so, members of all racial groups are at least somewhat prejudiced in this way. There are other forms of prejudice that contribute to our explanation of the racial encoding of neighborhood markets as well. Respondents in the Chicago survey were asked whether or not they believe the arrival of minorities necessarily implies: (1) an increase in crime; (2) a lowering of neighborhood socioeconomic status; and (3) a decline in property values. A scale was constructed adding together responses to these three questions. The range for this scale is −3 (disagree on all three items) to +3 (agree for all three). The average score on the scale is nearly the same for whites, blacks, and Hispanics. By this measure, we once again see that the tendency to racially encode the economic and social future of a neighborhood is not limited to any single racial group.

This finding is notable because the items in this scale were originally designed for surveys measuring trends in *white* racial prejudice after publication of *An American Dilemma* (Myrdal 1944) and after the 1954 Supreme Court decision on school desegregation (c.f. Treiman 1966; Taylor, Sheatsley, and Greeley 1978). The observation that black and Hispanic attitudes are about equally prejudiced at present is an uncomfortable finding for opinion researchers, but cannot be overlooked by those who seek to explain present-day urban phenomena.

We should note the possibility that this conclusion may apply primarily to Chicago and cities like Chicago. Schuman and Gruenberg (1970) discuss the hypothesis that structural characteristics such as demographic composition of urban areas might affect the levels of prejudice and the relationship between prejudice and other important behavioral or attitudinal measures. The race situation in Chicago and the historical patterns of neighborhood tipping there are salient factors of urban life that no resident can ignore. In this kind of situation, we might expect a greater degree of racial encoding of neighborhood markets than in other urban places where the demographic and historical facts are different.

For whites, this type of racial stereotyping, this set of negative expectations that people hold about the consequences of minority presence, also directly explains a small proportion of investment behavior. Table 6.5 shows that scores on this measure of prejudice are significantly related to investment for white homeowners. Each additional item agreed to reduces the probability of investment by .04. Whether the effects of this deeper kind of stereotyping are susceptible to change by policy measures or community-organization efforts is at this point uncertain.

The Crime Problem and Investment

The impact of crime on investment is indirect. Fear of crime and certain types of victimization (vandalism) change how positively people evaluate the economic future of and investment opportunities in the neighborhood. As we have discussed, these beliefs about the future are the primary contextual factors determining how people react to the need for rehabilitation and to the racial concentration of the area. By affecting the frame of reference for judging the future of the neighborhood, crime affects the level of investment.

To investigate the impact of crime, fear of crime, and other related factors on economic beliefs about the neighborhood, we constructed a scale of neighborhood market evaluation from measures of: (1) satisfaction with the trend in property values, and (2) willingness to recommend neighborhood investment to others. (These items are studied as separate components in Tables 6.6 and 6.7.) Scores on this scale range from −4 (negative evaluation on both) to +4 (positive on both). Neighborhood differences on average market evaluations among white, black, and Hispanic homeowners are shown in Table 6.8. The three groups are quite consistent in the relative ranking of neighborhood markets.

Market evaluations for both whites and nonwhites are affected by perceptions of the level of safety in the neighborhood, concern with the effects of racial change, and the presence of certain physical features such as parks or open spaces in the neighborhood. The effects of the crime problem on market evaluations are similar for whites and nonwhites. Based on a regression analysis of the market-evaluation scale, table 6.9 shows that among white owners, the average market evaluation is lower if the respondent: (1) is dissatisfied with the level of safety in the neighborhood; (2) avoids public transportation in order to reduce the risk of victimization; and/or (3) reports being vandalized. In short, fear of crime and vandalism reduce neighborhood investment because of the effects of these variables on market evaluations.

Both whites and nonwhites have a less favorable evaluation of the market conditions in the neighborhood if they believe that negative results necessarily follow from even small amounts of racial change.

Table 6.8 Average Scores on Market-Evaluation Scale

Neighborhood	White Owners	Black Owners	Hispanic Owners
Portage Park	2.6	—	—
Lincoln Park	3.1	—	—
East Side	2.0	—	2.2
Beverly	3.2	2.9	—
Hyde Park–Kenwood	2.1	2.5	—
Back of the Yards	−.1	−.7	.8
Austin	.3	.1	—
South Shore	—	1.1	—
TOTAL	2.3	1.0	1.1

Source: Chicago Neighborhood Survey.
The scale is based on responses to two items: satisfaction with the trend in property values and willingness to recommend investment to others. The range for this scale is −4 to +4. Blank cells represent too few cases to report reliably.

Table 6.9 Estimated Average Scores on Market-Evaluation Scale as a Function of Reactions to Crime, for White Owners

			Estimated Average
Satisfaction with safety-scale score	(low)	0	1.9
		1	2.1
		2	2.3
		3	2.4
	(high)	4	2.6
Does the respondent avoid public transportation because of crime?		no	2.4
		yes	2.1
Has the respondent's home been vandalized?		no	2.4
		yes	1.9

Source: Chicago Neighborhood Survey.
Estimated average scores are standardized for the effects of other predictor variables discussed in connection with these findings (see text).

Using the three-item prejudice scale discussed earlier, people with lower scores on this measure have, all things equal, less favorable evaluations of the neighborhood market. Once again, it is noteworthy that the racial coding of market conditions is a phenomenon that is not limited to white homeowners.

On Certain Urban Amenities

Market evaluations are also affected by certain physical aspects of the neighborhood. Whether or not a person lives on a block with a park, playground, or other open space nearby makes a difference in his or her evaluation of the market. When crime is not perceived to be a problem and when threats of racial change are low, these neighborhood features are perceived as amenities (i.e., factors that raise the value of living in the area, thus leading to more favorable market evaluations). Under these circumstances, homeowners with access to such features have more positive market evaluations. However, parks and open spaces are not always perceived as amenities.

Table 6.10 illustrates some of the typical patterns. The top part of table 6.10 shows that white owners who fear racial tipping are more *negative* about the neighborhood market if they live near open space than if they do not. By contrast, whites who do not fear racial tipping perceive open space as an amenity. The middle part of table 6.10 shows that Hispanic owners who have been victimized are more negative in their reaction to open space, whereas those who have not been victimized react

Table 6.10 Parks, Playgrounds, and Open Space as Causes of Neighborhood Market Evaluation

Market Evaluation		Open Space	
		No	Yes
White owners: Does the respondent believe the neighborhood is racially stable?	no	2.3	1.9
	yes	2.3	2.6
Hispanic owners: Has the respondent or a household member been victimized in the neighborhood in the last year?	no	1.0	1.8
	yes	1.4	−2.2
Black owners: (low) Satisfaction with safety-scale score	−1	.5	.8
	0	.9	.9
	1	1.2	1.1
	2	1.6	1.2
	3	2.0	1.4

Source: Chicago Neighborhood Survey.
Estimated average scores are standardized for the effects of other predictor variables discussed in connection with these findings (see text).

more positively. Finally, the third part of table 6.10 shows that black owners who are relatively more satisfied with the level of safety in the neighborhood have much more positive market evaluations *unless* they live near open neighborhood space, in which case the effect of satisfaction with safety on market evaluations is much less positive.

Why are parks, playgrounds, and open space a mixed blessing? One possible reason is that they are parts of the neighborhood that are especially likely to be used by children and adolescents. In situations where whites fear racial tipping, the incoming population usually has a much higher birthrate and a much younger age structure than the outgoing population (Duncan and Duncan 1957). Those members of the outgoing population who live near parks and playgrounds will observe more frequent reminders and may develop more extreme opinions about the extent of minority neighborhood penetration than those who do not live near such areas. Parks and playgrounds are also areas where problems with deterring crime are accentuated. When crime is an issue, people react to open spaces as areas where social controls are more difficult to enforce rather than as areas where the absence of confinement produces feelings of enjoyment.

To summarize this section, crime affects investment by affecting the way people evaluate the neighborhood housing market. Threshold scores do not increase directly because of victimization, absent changes in market perceptions. In fact, table 6.5 shows that those who have been victimized and/or who have experienced other aspects of the crime problem are more likely to spend money on security measures as well as other products to improve and defend their homes.

Organizational Involvement

The indirect effects of the crime problem and the direct effects of racial coding may be overcome by neighborhood organizational activity. Table 6.5 shows that controlling for other factors, those who say that they belong to a "group of renters or homeowners" or "any other group concerned with the quality of community life" are more likely to invest. The effect is especially strong for white owners, but in the positive direction for nonwhites as well.

It has been noted before that community organizations often recruit residents who are committed to maintaining and improving the positive aspects of neighborhood life in the face of problems or fears that threaten the well-being of the community (Molotch 1972). It may be that those with lower investment thresholds are a little more likely to join community organizations. Organizational activity, for these people, provides a forum for sharing one's willingness to invest in the neighborhood. It may also be the case that organizational activity provides a pulpit for emphasizing the values of neighborhood investment and a clearinghouse for obtaining information about the extent of willingness to invest among one's neighbors. Thus, to the extent that people's threshold scores are affected by the messages they receive, community organizations are a spur to higher levels of investment.

Our case studies of neighborhood change argue for the importance of all three roles—forum, pulpit, and clearinghouse—of community organizations. We cannot separate these effects with the data at hand. We hope, however, to draw attention to the theoretical and practical importance of doing so.

Other Factors

We conclude this chapter by noting that marital status, family size, and family income are strong predictors of investment thresholds in Chicago as well as in Waukegan. The importance of each of these factors is explained by the concept we have defined as the consumption value of investment. Those with larger families are more likely to be pushed by practical needs to create more liveable space in their homes. Those with a higher income are in a better position to allocate resources to nonobligatory enhancement. These effects characterize the investment decisions of white and nonwhite homeowners with magnitudes that are approximately equal regardless of market situations.

To understand whether or not particular homeowners invest, it is necessary to take account of differences in consumption values that are represented by these demographic variables. Doing so will also partly explain neighborhood differences in investment.[8] We only understand the full picture of market dynamics and neighborhood differences, however, when we examine the social factors influencing the process of neighborhood investment. Market expectations, racial encoding, community-organizational participation, and, indirectly, the crime problem affect investment-threshold values and thus affect the dynamics by which a community attains its collective level of investment.

7

A Revised Theory of Racial Tipping

The fact of racial succession and the fears associated with the process are crucially important for those who think seriously about cities and their future. Although most northern cities have declined in total population for the last two decades, the proportion of minority residents has steadily increased. In these cities, minority residents are also disproportionately poor. Consequently, as minority residence spreads, that is, as the succession process occurs over larger segments of urban territories, cities experience increasing tax burdens concurrent with decreasing tax bases.

We have already shown that the process of succession is not as simple as once was supposed and that under certain circumstances the arrival of minority residents does not mean an area must necessarily change from white to black. Social scientists have often noted, however, that there is a level of racial concentration (usually estimated between 15-percent and 30-percent black) which, once attained, very often presages complete racial turnover (Grodzins 1957; Duncan and Duncan 1957). The exact level of concentration that signals complete change is referred to in this literature as the tipping point.

In this chapter, we explore the dynamics of neighborhood tipping, as this process is understood and reacted to by individual neighborhood residents. As in chapter 6, we begin the study of this collective phenomenon with a theory that specifies the interests and decision-making processes of individual actors.

Thomas Schelling proposes a formal theory of neighborhood change that appears to explain the frequently observed patterns of tipping, even in urban areas where the resident white population is comparatively tolerant or has become so in recent decades (Schelling 1971, 1978). Schelling calls his theory the "bounded-neighborhood model."

We use the bounded-neighborhood model as the frame of reference for analyzing the role of the individual in the dynamics of neighborhood tipping for a number of reasons. First, the bounded-neighborhood model is a formal theory. As with the model analyzed in the previous chapter, there is a clear definition of the individual preferences involved and a clear statement of the dynamic principles relating individual actions to collective outcomes.

Second, this model is accepted as an important middle-range theory of neighborhood tipping by other social researchers. As Farley et al. (1978) write:

> Schelling determined through the use of mathematical models that if the residential preferences of the white residents of a neighborhood differ, the dynamics of the situation will drive the proportion black successively over each individual's maximum tolerance and the neighborhood will ultimately become a black residential area. (P. 338)

Or, as Glazer (1975) writes:

> Schelling . . . has demonstrated how difficult it is in a mobile situation to achieve any given result. . . . We can change the rules, the relative proportions: The results are the same. If the [two racial] groups are differentiable, and if they have even modest tastes affecting their behavior, a stable and even distribution is hard to achieve. (P. 156)

Finally, we are in a position to use survey data to perform detailed tests of the postulates and predictions of the bounded-neighborhood model. As it happens, we conclude that the model as discussed by Schelling, Glazer, Farley, and others does not adequately explain the causes of neighborhood racial tipping. We do not, however, reject the formal model. Instead, we use the model and the results from our empirical tests to present a revised formal theory of neighborhood tipping. The difference between our revised theory and the original formulation is the emphasis we give to housing-market variables and other sociological factors such as fear of crime as causes of neighborhood tipping. The revised theory remains consistent with the principles of Schelling's formal model, but takes into account the findings from the Chicago Neighborhood Survey as well as several additional data sets that were designed to address specific questions arising from the bounded-neighborhood model.

Following the format we developed in the last chapter, we first outline the basic principles of Schelling's formal theory. We then present results from surveys designed to test the propositions of the bounded-neighborhood model. In that section we also discuss the modifications and extensions of the model that must be undertaken to explain the patterns of racial change in American cities. Finally, we use the revised bounded-neighborhood model as the frame of reference for analyzing the patterns of racial change in the Chicago neighborhoods. Here, we weigh the relative importance of such factors as racial prejudice, fear of crime, and other market factors as causes of racial turnover.

The Bounded-Neighborhood Model

As an overview of Schelling's model, we might imagine the following scenario:

1. Begin with an all-white neighborhood in which most whites tolerate (i.e., would not move because of) at least a small amount of integration.
2. A few white families move out for reasons unrelated to race, and a few black families move into this neighborhood. This arrangement changes the percentage of blacks to a level most, but not all, whites report they can comfortably accept.
3. Further neighborhood change then results. The whites whose tolerance limit was exceeded in step 2 begin to move out, which further raises the percentage of blacks in the neighborhood. Now even more whites prepare to move out because, even though they can accept the percentage of blacks in step 2, they cannot accept the increased black percentage implied by step 2 after the whites who oppose that amount of integration have moved out.
4. Depending on the exact nature of the distribution of tolerance and the assumptions about what we will call the structural characteristics of the housing market, the cycle of neighborhood change continues to feed on itself. This can cause the neighborhood to become all black even if the pattern of white preferences appears to be extremely tolerant and there is, at first, only a small influx of black residents.

The bounded-neighborhood model assumes two racial groups. The variable systematically relating residential mobility to tipping is *racial tolerance*. Tolerance is defined as the maximum ratio of the other race to one's own (other-own ratio) that a person will abide. Table 7.1 is a histogram showing a hypothetical distribution of racial tolerance for 100 whites. The table represents a "typical" pattern—a few whites are very tolerant (i.e., have a high ratio), a few have quite low tolerance (i.e., ratios near zero), and the rest are in the middle. The bounded-neighborhood model also assumes a tolerance distribution of similar character for the black population.

The tolerance schedule for a group is based on the cumulative distribution of people ranked according to their racial tolerance. Table 7.2 is

Table 7.1 Hypothetical Distribution of Tolerance for 100 Whites

Number of Whites	Maximum-Tolerance Ratio of Blacks/Whites in a Neighborhood
10	4.5/1
20	3.5/1
20	2.5/1
20	1.5/1
20	.5/1
10	.0001/1

Table 7.2 Hypothetical Tolerance Schedule for 100 Whites

Cumulative Number of Whites	Maximum-Tolerance Ratio	Translation of Ratio into Maximum Number of Blacks Tolerated
10	4.5/1	45
30	3.5/1	105
50	2.5/1	125
70	1.5/1	105
90	.5/1	45
100	.0001/1	0

a hypothetical tolerance schedule based on the distribution in table 7.1. The first column of table 7.2 shows the cumulative number of whites; the second column shows the maximum other-own ratio that can be tolerated by the number of whites shown in the first column. The cumulative distribution, calculated this way, ranks whites from the most tolerant to the least tolerant. Again, there is a corresponding tolerance schedule for the black population.

The translated tolerance schedule shows, for each step in the cumulative distribution for whites, the maximum number of blacks that could be accepted by the number of whites specified. The translated tolerance schedule for the whites in our example is shown in the third column of table 7.2. These figures are obtained by multiplying the tolerance ratio in column two of table 7.2 by the cumulative number of whites who can abide the tolerance ratio. An alternative interpretation of the translated distribution is that each number shows the maximum number of blacks that can be tolerated by the least tolerant white at each step in the cumulative white tolerance distribution. Similarly, the translated black tolerance schedule shows the number of whites that can be tolerated at each level in the cumulative distribution for the black population.

Figure 7.1 is a graph showing hypothetical translated tolerance schedules. The white translated tolerance schedule, based on the data in

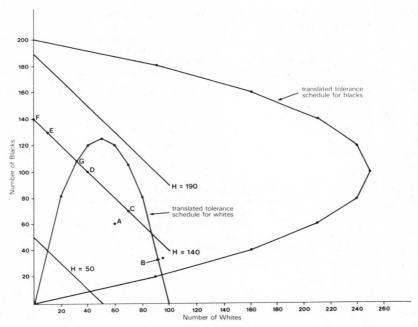

Fig. 7.1 Hypothetical Translated Tolerance Schedules for 100 Whites and 200 Blacks

table 7.2, is the parabola opening toward the *x* axis. To read the translated tolerance schedule, one determines, for any number of whites in the cumulative distribution (i.e., the *x* coordinate), the point on the parabola showing the maximum number of blacks that can be tolerated by the least tolerant white in that group. The *y*-axis coordinate of this point is the maximum number of blacks tolerated.

The larger parabola opening toward the *y* axis is a hypothetical translated tolerance schedule for a population of 200 blacks.

Market constraints in the bounded neighborhood are of two varieties. The first constraint is that any particular simulation of market dynamics must assume a particular number of blacks and a particular number of whites interested in living in the neighborhood. By assuming these numbers, the model fixes the black-white demand ratio for the population interested in housing. The black-white demand ratio for simulations based on figure 7.1 is fixed at 2:1.

The second market constraint is a supply constraint. Any particular simulation of market dynamics must also specify the number of houses that are available for occupancy. By fixing both the total number of people interested in housing (by assuming a certain number of blacks and a certain number of whites) and the total amount of housing available, any particular simulation of market dynamics fixes the level of competition for housing in the neighborhood.

The three straight, downwardly sloping lines in figure 7.1 represent different possible constraints on the amount of housing available. The bottom line shows the racial mixtures possible when there are 50 homes ($H = 50$) available, if we assume full occupancy. Given the numbers of whites and blacks assumed to be looking for housing (100 and 200, respectively), any racial mixture could potentially result if there are 50 homes to be occupied. The top line represents a market with 190 homes ($H = 190$) available. Assuming full occupancy, not all racial mixtures are theoretically possible. If all 100 whites are accommodated, there are still 90 homes available for blacks. Given the assumed black-white demand ratio, the maximum white concentration when $H = 190$ is 100/190 or 53-percent white. By assuming 190 homes for 300 potential occupants, the top line represents outcomes in a market that is weakly competitive compared to the bottom line, which assumes 50 homes for the same number of potential occupants.

Schelling's model is referred to as "bounded" because of the need to assume that both a certain number of blacks and whites are potentially interested in living in the neighborhood and a certain number of homes are available for occupancy. The model does not require the assumption of 100-percent occupancy. The model predicts what the occupancy rate will be, given the market constraints and tolerance schedules of the two populations.

The dynamic principle of the bounded-neighborhood model is used to calculate which neighborhood outcome (i.e., what degree of racial concentration) is most likely, given the assumed tolerance schedules for the racial groups and the assumed market constraints. The dynamic principle is based on a single rule for rational behavior: a person of either race will move into the neighborhood if the racial mix is tolerable; a person will move out if the racial mix is not tolerable. Beginning with a specified mix of blacks and whites, it is assumed that if someone leaves, he or she is the least tolerant among the in-resident population. If someone moves in, he or she is assumed to be the most tolerant in the non-resident population.

Neighborhood dynamics are simulated by assuming that at each step, a black family and a white family in the neighborhood decide whether or not to move out, and a black family and a white family outside the neighborhood decide whether or not to move in. For instance, if the neighborhood is assumed to be at point A in figure 7.1 (60 blacks and 60 whites), and if we assume $H = 140$, then the prediction from the dynamic principle is that both a white family and a black family will move in. If the neighborhood is at point B (96 whites and 36 blacks), the prediction is that a white family will move out (because the least tolerant white in the neighborhood will not accept 36 blacks), but a black family will move in.

Successive applications of the dynamic principle, given different starting points, lead to the discovery of theoretical equilibrium points. These are neighborhood mixtures that are acceptable to members of either indigenous racial group, points at which neither whites nor blacks will move out because of a violation of racial preferences. Given the market assumptions, points C and D in figure 7.1 are points of theoretical equilibrium. In fact, all points on the line $H = 140$ that are beneath the parabolas representing the two translated tolerance schedules are points of theoretical equilibrium.

If the neighborhood is at point E, the prediction is that a white family will exit and a black family will enter. The neighborhood is not in equilibrium. However, if point F is reached (0 whites and 140 blacks), then the neighborhood is once again in equilibrium. No blacks will leave because of racial preferences, and no whites will leave because there are no more in the neighborhood. Point F is a segregated equilibrium.

The primary heuristic use of the bounded-neighborhood model is to illustrate the propensities for segregated equilibria to emerge, given different assumptions about tolerance schedules and market constraints. The model also illustrates tipping points. A tipping point is a racial concentration that, if achieved, implies segregation as the "closest" point of theoretical equilibrium. Point G (32 whites and 108 blacks) is a tipping point. At point G, no resident is motivated to leave because of racial reasons, but if a white family should move out for other reasons, then the prediction is that a black family will be interested in moving in, but a white family will not be. Thus, the neighborhood moves a little closer to the y axis on the line $H = 140$. After this shift, whites begin to leave because of racial preferences, and blacks continue to move in until the equilibrium point of 100-percent black occupancy is reached.

The market constraints assumed for any particular analysis of neighborhood dynamics usually have a great impact on the range of theoretical equilibria and on whether or not a tipping phenomenon is likely. If we keep the same demand ratio and tolerance schedules, but examine a market with 190 homes available (weak competitiveness compared to $H = 140$), then the model predicts no point of theoretical equilibrium other than 100-percent black occupancy. Alternatively, if we keep the tolerance schedules and demand ratio the same, but take $H = 50$, then all concentrations between 20-percent white and 80-percent white are points of theoretical equilibrium in addition to the points denoting 100-percent black and 100-percent white occupancy. The importance of market constraints as a theoretical explanation of the course of neighborhood change will become even clearer as we discuss the data from surveys designed to estimate empirically the tolerance schedules for whites and blacks in American cities.

Empirical Estimates and Substantive Revisions of the Bounded-Neighborhood Model

Preference Measures

Two recently conducted surveys contain questions designed to estimate parameters for the bounded-neighborhood model. The data from these surveys will be used the same way the Waukegan Community Survey data were used in the previous chapter. Once again, we are in the fortunate position of having data from surveys that were primarily focused on theoretical issues crucially affecting our analysis of Chicago neighborhoods. The data from these companion surveys have not been published in a form that can be easily referred to in developing our argument about tipping in Chicago neighborhoods. Therefore, we briefly examine the critical results from the companion surveys before focusing the argument on the situation in Chicago.

The two companion surveys were done in Omaha and Detroit. In the summer of 1978, a telephone survey of 300 black and 300 white residents in the Omaha metropolitan area was conducted (Taylor 1981a). The purpose of this survey was to examine the importance of racial preferences in housing choice. The city of Omaha was about 12 percent black and had identifiably black neighborhoods at the time of the survey. Compared to most midwestern cities where the minority proportion is even smaller, we would have to say that the "race situation" in Omaha is somewhat salient.

In 1976, the Detroit Area Study (DAS) was designed to "better understand the nature and causes of residential segregation" (Farley et al. 1978). Personal interviews were conducted with about 1,100 residents of the Detroit metropolitan area. Detroit was about 60 percent black at the time of the 1976 study. The situation in Detroit is representative of the largest, oldest snow-belt cities with large minority populations.

In each survey, a person's tolerance ratio is measured by describing neighborhoods that vary by racial composition and asking respondents whether they would want to move out of these different neighborhoods.[1] The data from these two surveys which will be used to estimate the tolerance schedules are shown in table 7.3. In either city, the percentage of whites who are tolerant goes down as the ratio of blacks to whites increases. In either city, there is also a reasonably large segment of the white population who say they will tolerate any racial mix. It will be

Table 7.3 Empirically Estimated White and Black Tolerance Schedules

Data Source	Racial Mix	Percentage Who Would Tolerate Mix	
		White	Black
Omaha Survey	all white		95
	1 black/9 white	97	98
	3 black/7 white	87	100
	5 black/5 white	69	100
	7 black/3 white	54	98
	9 black/1 white	36	97
	all black	28	95
Detroit Area	1 black/14 white	93	
Survey	3 black/12 white	76	not
	5 black/10 white	59	asked
	9 black/6 white	36	

necessary to make some further assumptions in order to assign these whites a maximum- or preferred-tolerance ratio.[2]

Table 7.3 gives a black tolerance schedule for Omaha, but not for Detroit. The necessary questions were not asked of blacks in the Detroit survey.

Many studies of black preferences report that blacks respond to general questions about neighborhood balance by saying that they prefer integration or something near a 50:50 mix (Marx 1969; Pettigrew 1973). That whites say they prefer less integration is sometimes offered as proof of the incompatibility of black and white residential preferences. Researchers have proceeded with this conclusion even though follow-up and open-ended questions often suggest that the black response is more a statement of willingness to try to get along with whites than it is a single-peaked preference for living in a neighborhood with a particular range to the ratio of black and white inhabitants (Farley et al. 1978).

With the question wordings used in the Omaha survey, we obtain a very different picture of black preferences than that expected using the 50:50 mix as a rule of thumb. The percentage of blacks who are tolerant of all racial mixtures up to extreme minority or extreme majority status for themselves is quite high. This finding has important implications for the bounded-neighborhood model. As we work through the analysis, it will become apparent that many of the predictions of tipping that seem to follow from the bounded-neighborhood model and the white tolerance schedule shown in table 7.3 no longer hold once we take account of the actual nature of black preferences.

Table 7.3 shows that there is a small percentage of blacks who say they will leave neighborhoods that become all white or nearly so. The opinions of these blacks can be formally represented as tolerance ratios under the bounded-neighborhood model.

There is also a small percentage of blacks who say they will leave if the neighborhood becomes too black. These may be thought of as blacks who genuinely prefer integration. The preferences of these people cannot be represented as tolerance ratios in the bounded-neighborhood model, so we will work only with that part of the black tolerance schedule that measures uneasiness with increasing concentrations of whites.[3]

Deriving Tolerance Schedules and Distributions from Preferences

The tolerance schedules we will use to analyze the bounded-neighborhood model are graphed in figure 7.2.

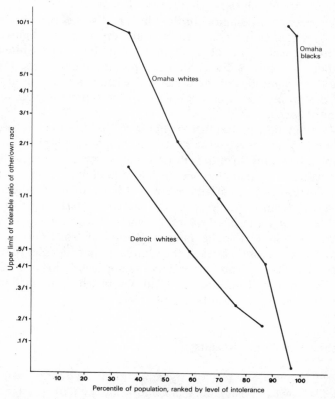

Fig. 7.2 Empirically Estimated Tolerance Schedules for Whites and Blacks

We noted above the large segment of the white population who say their housing decisions are insensitive to the racial mix of the neighborhood. This fact is reflected in figure 7.2 where the tolerance schedule for whites stops short of the y axis—the most tolerant element of the white population can accept any racial mix.

The black curve also stops far short of the y axis, indicating a large proportion who can accept high levels of black concentration. In addition, the black curve stops far short of the x axis, signifying that 100 percent of blacks are tolerant of a racial mix that is more than 2:1 white.[4] These two features reflect what we have already observed regarding black preferences—few strong preferences as to racial mix.

Following the steps in the bounded-neighborhood model, the tolerance schedules shown in table 7.3 and figure 7.2 are used to calculate translated tolerance schedules for each population. To begin, we will assume a fixed number of people ($N = 100$) in each population who are ranked according to their tolerance. The resulting translated tolerance schedules for Omaha and Detroit are displayed in figure 7.3.

In order to accommodate the black and white distributions on the same graph, it is necessary to measure the x axis in figure 7.3 on a logarithmic scale. The distance between the black and white tolerance schedules in figure 7.2 and the extreme placement of the black curve make the magnitudes of the translated schedules so different that some transformation of scale is necessary in order to portray them in the same graphical space.

Another unusual feature of figure 7.3 is that the white translated tolerance schedules cross the y axis at a comparatively high level because a number of whites (in either city) say that there is no effective limit to the black-white ratio that they would find acceptable. To most accurately represent this state of affairs, we would have to show the white curves trailing off the top of the graph. Instead, we have arbitrarily drawn in the left side of each translated tolerance schedule with a line parallel to the x axis at $y = 250$ for Omaha and $y = 240$ for Detroit. This assumes that the 37 most tolerant whites in the Omaha rank order can tolerate up to 250 blacks. The Detroit data reflect the apparently lower level of tolerance in that city. The number of indifferent whites is smaller—20. We have assumed they can tolerate 240 blacks.

Baseline Simulation Results

Several implications for the dynamics of the bounded-neighborhood model follow from using the black and white schedules in figure 7.2. We note that for the assumption of 100 blacks and 100 whites interested in

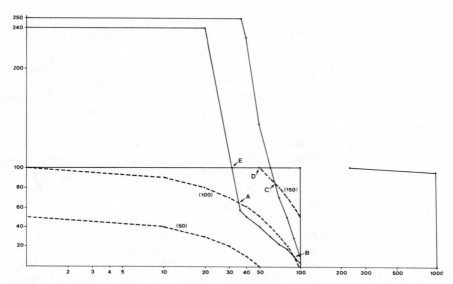

Fig. 7.3 Translated Tolerance Schedule for Whites and Blacks

housing, the black schedule is completely outside the white schedules.[5] According to the model, the nonoverlap of the black and white curves implies that blacks are always willing to move into the neighborhood, regardless of the color mix or the amount of available housing. This situation is one of the special cases analyzed by Schelling (1971, 182–83). When we use the bounded-neighborhood model as a tool for understanding reality, however, it appears that this special case is the more typical representation of an urban neighborhood.

The lines of dashes in figure 7.3 represent some of the possible constraints on the amount of available housing. The lowest line of dashes shows the racial mixes possible in a neighborhood with 50 houses (assuming 100-percent occupancy). Compared to the second and third housing constraints shown in figure 7.3, the line for 50 houses shows the outcomes in a strongly competitive market. The line of dashes showing the possible outcomes assuming 100 homes available (and 100-percent occupancy) represents the outcomes in a less competitive market. Finally, the line for 150 houses and full occupancy represents a comparatively weak competitive market.

Looking first at the most competitive market, the one with 50 houses available, we find that the curve representing the possible neighborhood outcomes is completely within both the black and the white translated tolerance schedules (using the white data from either Omaha or Detroit). According to the bounded-neighborhood model, any outcome that lies within both distributions represents a racial mixture that is a point of theoretical equilibrium. Neither whites nor blacks will move out because their tolerance ratio has been exceeded.

If we make the housing market less competitive by assuming a greater supply of housing, we begin to find some constraints on the equilibrium points, but using the preference data from either city and any of the assumptions about the level of competition, we find that the model never predicts that the neighborhood will tip to 100-percent black occupancy. Using the Detroit data, with 100 houses available, the model predicts that whites will, for racial reasons, leave a neighborhood that is between 35-percent and 90-percent white. This situation is represented by the fact that the line of dashes is outside the white tolerance distribution between points A and B in figure 7.3. However, because there are enough whites willing to live in neighborhoods that are 65 percent or more black, these neighborhoods are in equilibrium. In addition, neighborhoods more than about 90-percent white are also stable.

We find in this simulation based on the Detroit data there there is a zone of instability between 35-percent and 90-percent white, but there is no prediction of complete tipping. If we instead examine the Omaha data, we find that even with a medium level of competition for housing, there is no point along the curve representing full occupancy where the neighborhood is characterized by anything other than a theoretically stable equilibrium.

Finally, in the least competitive market (150 houses), we again find a prediction of equilibrium using either tolerance schedule for the whites. Using the Omaha data, the model predicts that whites will leave neighborhoods that become marginally integrated until such time as the neighborhood becomes about 43-percent white. This situation is represented by point C on figure 7.3. All points between 33-percent white and 43-percent white are in a theoretically stable equilibrium, that is, whites will not leave because their tolerance ratio is exceeded. Neighborhoods below 33-percent white represent a full absorption of black demand (all 100 blacks have already moved in), and there are enough tolerant whites demanding housing to fill the neighborhood to the lower end of the equilibrium range—33-percent white. This situation is shown as point D on figure 7.3.

If we use the Detroit data instead, the model predicts that all of the black demand will be absorbed and that there are up to 32 whites willing to move in, resulting in a neighborhood that is 25-percent white, with an 88-percent occupancy rate. This is shown as point E on figure 7.3.

Given the assumptions we have used so far—the empirically derived tolerance schedules, 100 members of each race interested in living in the neighborhood, and variation in the level of competition—we have not been able to find a situation where the model predicts tipping and segregation. We have found instead that because of the nature of the tolerance schedules, particularly because of the nature of black housing demand, the predicted outcome in any neighborhood is primarily sensitive to the amount of competition for housing.[6]

The results so far are a little surprising. It is obvious that neighborhoods in Detroit and Omaha have become segregated. How does this come about if, given the tolerance schedules in these cities, the bounded-neighborhood model predicts stable integration?

Practical versus Theoretical Equilibrium Points

One of the most important reasons the bounded-neighborhood model predicts an integrated equilibrium in situations where this seems implausible is that the definition of equilibrium neglects certain aspects of the housing market. To explain this problem, it is necessary to distinguish between the original definition of *theoretical* equilibrium points—based on white and black tolerance schedules—and a revised definition of *practical* equilibrium points based on tolerance schedules, black-white demand ratios, and the extent of competition for housing in the neighborhood.

A neighborhood in theoretical equilibrium is, by definition, one whose racial composition will not change because of people acting for racial reasons. This definition of equilibrium says nothing, however, about what will happen to the neighborhood should vacancies arise for nonracial reasons. If a vacancy should arise in such a neighborhood, the odds of that vacancy being filled by a black family should be proportional to the black-white mix in the interested but unmet housing demand. (The interested but unmet housing demand consists of those not currently residing in the neighborhood whose racial attitudes are such that they could tolerate living there.)

We can use the tolerance distributions in figure 7.3 to study what is likely to happen when random vacancies (i.e., those arising for nonracial reasons) occur in neighborhoods that are theoretically stable according to the original definition. Let us use the Omaha tolerance distribution and examine the case of intermediate competition (100 houses available). In this situation, all neighborhood combinations are theoretically stable. But let us examine what is likely to occur in a neighborhood that is 50-percent white and 50-percent black. If a random vacancy arises in this neighborhood, there are 50 blacks who are willing to move in. (The translated tolerance schedule shows that even the least tolerant blacks will be willing to live in a neighborhood that is 50-percent white.) How many whites are willing to move in? Some of the unmet white demand is uninterested—there are about 20 whites who will not tolerate a neighborhood that is 50-percent black. This fact can be read off the graph by tracing from the 50:50 point to the right until one comes to the line for the white tolerance distribution. The x-axis coordinate for this point shows that 80 out of 100 whites will tolerate such a neighborhood and, therefore, 20 will not.

Given the Omaha data and 100 families of each race looking for housing, the odds that a random vacancy in a 50:50 neighborhood will be filled by a black family are 5:3. Most likely the neighborhood will increase its black population, even though it is in a theoretical equilibrium as the term is defined. At what point does it become equally likely that a random vacancy will be filled by either racial group? The odds of a random vacancy being filled by a white family do not reach 50:50 until the neighborhood is about 65-percent black. Let us call this point the practical equilibrium. Given the tolerance schedules, the black-white ratio of demand, and the level of competition, the practical equilibrium is the point of theoretical equilibrium where the next random vacancy is as likely to be filled by a white family as by a black family. The practical equilibrium is the racial mix that is most likely to occur in a neighborhood when we take account of the tolerance schedules and the market constraints.

The practical equilibrium is an index of the structural position of the neighborhood with respect to the tangible factors that affect the likelihood of tipping. A neighborhood that is structurally strong is one in which the market process does not lead to segregation as the practical equilibrium. A structurally weak neighborhood is one where the market forces and the preferences of the population combine to predispose a segregated outcome in the housing market.

Simulations Varying the Neighborhood Structural Position

The effects of the amount of housing, the black-white demand ratio, and racial preferences on the structural position of a neighborhood can be illustrated by varying the parameters of the bounded-neighborhood model so as to simulate the process of racial change in different types of neighborhoods. For instance, a gentrifying neighborhood (e.g., Lincoln Park) might be thought of as one in which the white demand is high relative to the black demand, and the overall demand is high relative to the supply of housing. In terms of the parameters of the model, we would simulate this situation by: (1) leaving the white demand at 100; (2) reducing the number of blacks interested in the neighborhood to 50; and (3) setting the number of houses at 50. A neighborhood with these structural characteristics is, as we shall see, extremely unlikely to tip to 100 percent black occupancy.

As a second example, let us imagine an older white neighborhood located on the edge of an all-black area with "pent up" housing demand (e.g., Back of the Yards or Austin). In terms of the model, we can do this by setting the black demand at 200, leaving the white demand at 100, and assuming 100 available houses (weak competition with respect to white demand, strong competition with respect to black demand). This neighborhood, as we shall see, is structurally weak. Even though the tolerance schedules are assumed to be the same here as in the gentrifying neighborhood (which, in reality, they are not), the structural characteristics of the housing market predispose this neighborhood to a different outcome. The structural weakness of the older white neighborhood makes tipping and 100-percent black occupancy the most likely outcome, according to our calculation of the point of practical equilibrium.

Each of these two simulations can be compared with the "benchmark" analysis performed earlier that assumed 100 whites, 100 blacks, and 100 homes available. Compared to the benchmark analysis, the gentrifying neighborhood represents a housing market with a higher proportion of white demand and an intensification of competition. The older white neighborhood represents a higher proportion of black demand and a lower level of competition. To better understand the outcome in the gentrifying neighborhood, we also present results for a neighborhood that is similar to the benchmark neighborhood except that is has a higher level of competition (the number of houses is reduced to 50).

In these neighborhood simulations, we use the tolerance schedules estimated from the Omaha sample. The substantive findings from the analysis do not depend on which data set is used. The results from the four neighborhood simulations are summarized in table 7.4.

One thought-provoking result not shown in table 7.4 is that for all four types of areas, the bounded-neighborhood model predicts that there are no circumstances in which racial preferences will cause people to move. For all four neighborhoods, all possible racial configurations from 0-percent to 100-percent black are points of theoretical equilibrium.

Table 7.4 Simulations of Neighborhood Outcomes Given Alternative Assumptions about Market Structural Characteristics

Type of Neighborhood	Black/White Demand	Number of Houses	Practical Equilibrium
Older white	200/100	100	0% white
Benchmark	100/100	100	35% white
High competition	100/100	50	50% white
Gentrifying	50/100	50	100% white

Nevertheless, the analysis of the practical-equilibrium points shows that one neighborhood is expected to become all black, another all white, and the other two are expected to stabilize somewhere in between.

The simulation results show how the practical equilibrium is affected by the ratio of black-white housing demand, by the amount of competition for housing in the neighborhood, and by white racial attitudes (which sometimes limit white demand for housing). In older white neighborhoods where there is high black demand relative to white, the practical equilibrium indicates that it is reasonable to expect the area to become all black even though the narrow prediction from the bounded-neighborhood model is that all steps along the way are in theoretical equilibrium, and no one is moving out because of intolerance of the racial mix. Neighborhoods with a more even ratio of black-white demand are expected to stabilize at some intermediate level of racial integration. Because of the influence of white racial preferences, however, the amount of integration in these neighborhoods is related to the amount of competition for housing. A competitive market will sustain a higher percentage of whites in the neighborhood than will a noncompetitive market. In the limiting case—the gentrifying neighborhood—the demand ratio and level of competition change such that whites eventually dominate the area, even though blacks are not leaving because of racial preferences.

Expectations versus Tolerance in Neighborhood Change

Our conclusion is that the bounded-neighborhood model, as most often presented and discussed in the literature, gives an overstated impression of the significance of racial attitudes and racial tolerance in neighborhood change. Schelling's formal model does, however, contain the seeds of several ideas that are important for understanding racial turnover. The structural position of the neighborhood and the implied practical equilibrium are important concepts that raise the question of the role of expectations in the process of neighborhood racial change. In Schelling's (1971) words:

> Whites may respond not to the number or percentage of blacks currently present but to the anticipated increase in the number. They may, that is, anticipate the process. Evidently, if whites believe that the percentage of blacks will become intolerable and are prepared to leave in anticipation once they believe it, the number of blacks required to cause "out-tipping" is not the number that begins a cumulative process in our analysis but rather the number that induces this belief. (P. 185)[7]

What are the salient features of the neighborhood situation that lead individuals to anticipate such an outcome? Individuals cannot be responding merely to the presence of some specific number or ratio of members of another race. In the simulation examples, a 10-percent black neighborhood can become all black, all white, or stabilize in between depending on other circumstances. Individuals would be unwise to act on the basis of this information alone. In addition, knowledge of racial-tolerance schedules alone will not be enough. The tolerance schedule was the same for each simulation. Nevertheless, all-black (or all-white) neighborhoods are possible. Whether a neighborhood approaches this extreme as a practical equilibrium depends on the factors that define the structural position of the neighborhood. Neighborhood residents must have a sense of these factors to have some basis for speculating on whether or not the neighborhood will tip.

The factors determining the structural position of the neighborhood are combined in the index of practical equilibrium. A person's sense of whether or not the neighborhood will tip is his or her estimate of the practical equilibrium, given the perceived facts of supply and demand for the area. People may not formally calculate an index of practical equilibrium, but it seems reasonable to say that they are aware of the factors that go into this index and that they form a general opinion about the future of the neighborhood.

The bounded-neighborhood model, as extended here, suggests that people's perceptions of the structural position of the neighborhood are important intervening factors in the process of racial turnover. The model also suggests which market variables (i.e., the black-white demand ratio and the level of competitiveness) affect this perception. If we reinterpret Schelling's formal theory this way, then the implications of his model are more consistent with the findings from other case studies of tipping. Wolf, for instance, notes that people say a neighborhood is tipping even before any members of another race have actually moved in.[8] The impression of structural weakness encourages a belief in tipping as the point of practical equilibrium. The alarm about tipping and estimates of the degree of structural weakness become even more extreme once racial mixing actually begins in these types of neighborhoods.[9] It is this sense of structural position that often leads to the self-fulfilling-prophecy nature of racial change.

How do people gain their sense of the structural position of the neighborhood? What is the role of fear of crime, racial encoding of economic patterns, or other factors in the perception of the ability of a neighborhood to absorb racial change without tipping? The Chicago Neighborhood Survey was designed to answer these questions. We now turn to this analysis armed with the findings from the two companion surveys and the ensuing criticisms and modifications of Schelling's tipping model.

Racial Change in Chicago Neighborhoods

The bounded-neighborhood model, as elaborated in this analysis, points to market-structure characteristics as primary factors influencing people's expectations of racial turnover. Any analysis of additional causes of tipping such as victimization, fear of crime, or racial prejudice must first take into account the structural characteristics of the housing market in a neighborhood and the possibility that structurally weak neighborhoods may also tend to have other symptoms of social disorder, or extreme forms of racial prejudice. The first goal in this section is to study, as a baseline for subsequent analyses, the relationship between neighborhood structural weakness and the expectation of racial turnover.

Tipping and Structural Weakness

We collected data from neighborhoods displaying varying degrees of structural strength. The eight neighborhoods were chosen to represent, as best as possible, a "balanced" research design for studying the effects of the different components of neighborhood structural position on the dynamics of neighborhood change. The design variables for our sample of neighborhoods are discussed at the beginning of chapter 2. We make use of these design variables for analyzing the bounded-neighborhood model. The proportion of blacks in a neighborhood is our proxy measure of the black-white demand ratio. The average amount of appreciation in the value of single-family homes is our indicator of the level of competitiveness in the neighborhood housing markets. For purposes of analysis in this chapter, the neighborhoods were ranked from 1 (low) to 4 (high) on each of these two measures. The result is the following nearly balanced design:

1. Hyde Park–Kenwood and South Shore score high (i.e., scores of 3 or 4) on both competitiveness and the black-white demand ratio.
2. Austin and Back of the Yards score low on competitiveness (i.e., scores of 1 or 2), but high on the black-white demand ratio.
3. Portage Park, Lincoln Park, and Beverly score high on competitiveness, but low on the black-white demand ratio.
4. East Side scores low on both competitiveness and the black-white demand ratio.

We begin the analysis by examining how each component of the neighborhood structural position relates to the expectation of tipping.

Respondents were asked, "Thinking about the races of the people who live in [NEIGHBORHOOD]—that is, whether they're black, white, or hispanic—would you say the racial composition is pretty stable or would you say the racial composition is changing?" The question was asked of all respondents, but we will consider only the responses of white neighborhood residents.[10]

Table 7.5 shows the relationship between the two components of structural strength, analyzed simultaneously, and the expectation of racial change among the Chicago respondents. The cells in table 7.5 show the estimated proportion expecting racial change as a function of the two structural variables. These proportions are estimated from a weighted regression analysis. Even though we do not have data from enough neighborhoods to represent each of the sixteen cells in table 7.5, with the use of a regression model we can predict (and smooth) the proportions over the full range of variation for each of the structural variables.

As we would anticipate from our analysis of the bounded-neighborhood model, the expectation of turnover is greatest in the structurally weakest neighborhoods. What is striking about table 7.5 is the strength of the relationship. Neighborhoods in the weakest structural position (i.e., those with a score of 4 on the black-white demand ratio and a score of 1 on competitiveness) are almost unanimously expected to tip. The estimated proportion expecting change in this kind of neighborhood is .9.

On the other end of the spectrum are neighborhoods with a competitive housing market. In the simulations reported earlier, these were neighborhoods with few houses available relative to the total demand. In our study, Lincoln Park, Beverly, and Hyde Park–Kenwood rank in the top category in competitiveness. In the simulation analyses, we found that neighborhoods in which the level of competition is high are: (1) almost always in a state of theoretical equilibrium as the term is defined by Schelling; (2) unlikely to become all black; and (3) often expected to become all white. Table 7.5 shows that in neighborhoods with a competitive housing market, the proportion expecting racial change is relatively low (around .3) and is not sensitive to the black-white demand ratio.

Table 7.5 Estimated Proportion of Whites Expecting Racial Change as a Function of Neighborhood-Market Structural Characteristics

Black/White Demand Ratio	Competitiveness of Housing Market			
	1	2	3	4
1	.45	.41	.37	.32
2	.60	.50	.40	.30
3	.75	.59	.44	.29
4	.90	.69	.48	.27

Source: Chicago Neighborhood Survey.

The pattern in table 7.5 suggests an important rule relating neighbor-hood structural position to the expectation of tipping. In highly competi-tive markets where competition is defined by housing prices, there is no effect of the black-white demand ratio on people's expectations of tip-ping. In markets that are weaker, the proportion expecting tipping is higher whatever the demand ratio. But more importantly, as markets become weaker, the expectation of tipping becomes increasingly sensi-tive to the black-white demand ratio for housing. In general, then, the strength of the housing market is an important factor conditioning the way people interpret and react to racial concentration.

The results for particular neighborhoods can now be more systemati-cally understood. The estimated proportion expecting turnover in East Side (.41) is not much higher than the estimated proportion in Lincoln Park and Beverly (.30). Even though the market is much less competitive in East Side, the expectation of tipping is low because the black-white demand ratio is low.[11] As another illustration, the estimated proportion expecting tipping in Hyde Park–Kenwood (.29) is about the same as in Lincoln Park and Beverly. Even though the black-white demand ratio is higher in Hyde Park–Kenwood than in the other two neighborhoods, this does not influence people's expectations of tipping because the housing market is strongly competitive.

Our rule relating market characteristics to the expectation of tipping is an empirically informed, somewhat precise statement of how people perceive and respond to neighborhood structural weakness. As we argued earlier, it is unlikely that people calculate a formal index of practical equilibrium to guide their expectations about the neighbor-hood. On the other hand, Schelling's model specifies the demand ratio and competitiveness as principal determinants of the neighborhood prac-tical equilibrium, and table 7.5 shows that people's expectations of racial change are roughly in line with what would be calculated as the practical equilibrium in each neighborhood circumstance.

We have not yet discussed the steps by which the demand ratio and competitiveness are perceived and coded as signs of the neighborhood structural position. With further analyses, we can determine some of the characteristics of structurally weak neighborhoods that provide the basis for the expectation that the area will tip.

Market Weakness and Neighborhood Coding

In the previous chapter we noted that racial encoding of the expected patterns of economic change is one of the causes of urban-investment patterns. To study this phenomenon, we constructed a scale of market evaluations based on: (1) satisfaction with the trend in property values, and (2) willingness to recommend neighborhood investment to others. Neighborhood differences on this scale are shown in table 6.8 of chapter 6. As that table shows, market evaluations are strongly influenced by neighborhood structural characteristics. Market evaluations, in turn, determine the principles guiding investment behavior in a particular neighborhood (i.e., whether one is making the best of a bad situation or capitalizing on a good thing).

Analysis of neighborhood racial change shows that market evaluations are also a crucial link between structural characteristics and the expectation of tipping. Controlling for structural characteristics and a number of other factors to be discussed in the coming paragraphs, whites at the negative end of each component of the market-evaluation scale are 26 percent more likely to expect racial change than those at the positive end for each item.[12]

But couldn't we say that the expectation of tipping ought to be considered as a cause of economic dissatisfaction rather than vice versa? For a complete description of the dynamics of tipping, we would answer yes. The inability of structurally weak neighborhoods to resist tipping produces a vicious circle of economic dissatisfaction, expectation of tipping, and, as we shall see, plans to move that is understood—or perhaps we should say believed—by urban residents.

We have already identified some of the components of the vicious circle. The relationship between economic evaluations and the expectation of tipping, apart from structural characteristics, suggests ways the vicious circle could be modified. In the previous chapter we noted that improvements in the "physical plant" accompanied by efforts to ensure a more satisfactory market might increase the level of neighborhood investment. Here we note that institutional investors, insurance programs, or other factors affecting economic evaluations will reduce the expectation of tipping even in neighborhoods that are in other respects structurally weak.

Are there further observations we can make on the cycle of neighborhood structural weakness, economic dissatisfaction, and the expectation of tipping? Are there particular negative experiences such as victimization or particular negative features of the urban landscape such as housing neglect or abandonment that can be identified as factors reinforcing the cycle?

Crime

Crime affects the expectation of tipping, even though victimization per se does not influence people's views. Those who have been victimized are no more likely than those who have not to expect racial turnover. Fear of crime, however, strongly affects people's views on the likelihood of racial change.

In chapter 6, we noted that those who are concerned with the level of safety in the neighborhood, who avoid public transportation for fear of crime, and/or whose homes have been vandalized are less favorable in their neighborhood economic evaluations and therefore less likely to invest (see table 6.9). Apart from vandalism, victimization does not directly affect individuals' investment decisions. Victimization rates, however, indirectly affect investment because the level of fear is higher in those neighborhoods where the victimization rates are higher.

We find a similar kind of result here. Table 7.6 shows which aspects of the crime problem significantly affect individuals' expectations of tipping. The important personal factors are concern with the level of safety in the neighborhood and fear of walking in the neighborhood at night. The link between victimization and the expectation of tipping is based on the atmosphere of concern with safety and fear of crime that results from people's reactions to and interpretations of the crime problem.

This link is another example of neighborhood coding. People who view their neighborhood as unsafe are more likely than those who think it is safe to hold a lower estimate of the ability of the neighborhood to resist tipping. Fearful people may have an inflated estimate of the level of black demand for housing; they may underestimate the level of competition; they may underestimate the willingness of whites to move in; or they may have some other reason for believing that racial turnover is likely.

Table 7.6 Estimated Proportion of Whites Expecting Racial Change as a Function of Crime-Related Concerns

Concerns		Estimated Proportion
Is the respondent afraid to walk in the neighborhood at night?		
	no	.35
	yes	.43
Satisfaction with safety-scale score		
	0	.45
	1	.43
	2	.40
	3	.38
	4	.35

Source: Chicago Neighborhood Survey.
Estimated average scores are standardized for the effects of other predictor variables discussed in connection with these findings (see text).

Victimization and fear of crime are factors reinforcing the vicious circle of structural weakness, economic dissatisfaction, and tipping. The implication of the analysis is that if community responses to crime are better understood and perhaps less fearfully managed, there is reason to believe that some of the vicious circle can be controlled and hence its impact on neighborhood change reduced.

The Physical Plant

Signs of neighborhood deterioration such as abandoned buildings or lack of upkeep are visual symbols that affect how people encode the likelihood of racial change in urban neighborhoods. As with victimization, however, the effect of these environmental features on the expectation of tipping is indirect. Neighborhoods with high levels of deterioration are seen as more likely to tip primarily because deterioration aggravates one's reaction to the crime problem. Neighborhoods that are more deteriorated are more likely to be seen as unsafe; several aspects of this relationship are explored in the next chapter. As noted earlier, concern about crime affects the expectation of tipping.

Controlling for economic evaluations, reactions to crime, and market characteristics, only one measure of neighborhood deterioration or quality of the housing stock is directly related to personal expectations of tipping. Those living on blocks with a high number of frame two- or three-flats are about 10 percent more likely than those who do not to expect racial change. We suspect that the reason for this relationship has to do with both the visual appearance of frame flats and the role that this type of housing plays in the early stages of neighborhood change.

Our field researchers frequently noted that frame dwellings, and particularly multiple-unit frame dwellings, require more frequent upkeep than buildings constructed of brick or stone to maintain a similar qualitative level of appearance and tidiness. In most neighborhoods analyzed here, frame construction, compared to other kinds of housing, looks cheaper and is more likely to have visible flaws on the exterior. Because of these qualities, multi-unit frame housing might stand as an especially strong symbol of market weakness and dissatisfaction with safety and thus contribute to the expectation of tipping.

In addition, our field studies found that in some neighborhoods, particularly those where Hispanics are moving in, frame flats are the buildings first purchased for owner occupancy by an in-migrating group. Those living on blocks with multiple-unit frame dwellings are more likely than others to regard the area as racially changing because this is where racial change is most likely occurring. Our measure of the physical environment in this case, then, sorts respondents into different categories of social experience. A similar type of relationship was noted in chapter 6. Parks and playgrounds sometimes provoke uneasiness about the neighborhood among those who live near them because of the way the population or the physical appearance of these areas is perceived.

8

A Theory of Reactions to Crime and Urban Neighborhood Change

Crime is one element in a constellation of forces that affects urban neighborhoods. To understand this network of forces and the role crime plays in it, we have examined different measures of the crime problem and have analyzed data at different levels. This chapter summarizes the results of that analysis and presents a theory of crime and its relationship to the other causes of urban change.

A systematic understanding of the neighborhood crime problem requires that we simplify our approach. This chapter, therefore, addresses only a subset of the many dimensions of the crime problem. Our primary goal is to chart the regions of the problem that are most relevant for understanding neighborhood change, although there are many more issues in victimization research that are of policy relevance and worthy of study (e.g., Lewis 1981; Skogan 1976). Because we do not explore certain topics does not mean we regard them as unimportant. Rather, our substantive discussion of the crime problem is somewhat arbitrarily focused on those aspects that we can show are related to expectations of tipping, investment, and mobility intentions.

The next section of this chapter is a statement of the central propositions in our theory of the relationship between reactions to crime and urban change. The third and fourth sections introduce the evidence supporting the central propositions in the theory. Finally, the concluding section relates the discussion in this chapter to issues raised in other parts of this book and in the literature on crime, race, and urban change.

The Effect of Crime

The analysis in this chapter focuses on the individual urban resident. In the two previous chapters, we argue that most patterns of urban change can be understood as collective outcomes from individual processes of perception, calculation, and decision making. In this chapter, the focus is on crime as an explanatory variable in decision-making processes. How do individuals perceive and process information about crime? How does this information affect decisions that, taken collectively, determine the course of urban change? We expect that the level of benefit that people anticipate from their actions vis-à-vis the neighborhood is affected by the crime problem. The purpose of this chapter is to determine more precisely how and when this is so.

The links between crime and urban change are mediated by perceptions and then by evaluations. In its most succinct form, our theory of crime and neighborhood change consists of the following three propositions:

1. Crime—defined as personal victimization and/or contextual rates of victimization—affects (although it does not exclusively determine) people's fears and perceptions of risk in the environment.
2. People decide whether the level of risk and fear is acceptable, based on subjective comparisons with two standards of evaluation. The first comparison is with perceived danger levels in alternate residential areas. The second, and more important, comparison is with the value of the rewards and amenities the individual receives from living in his or her neighborhood. The result of comparing one's perception of risk with one's view of the benefits of living in the neighborhood is one's net evaluation of the seriousness of the crime problem.
3. Net evaluations of the seriousness of the crime problem are one of the causes of individual expectations regarding the future of the neighborhood and individual decisions which cumulate to produce the patterns of urban change studied in this book.

Let us examine each of these statements in more detail.

The first proposition is that people perceive crime and react to it. Social scientists have studied the accuracy of people's perceptions of crime rates (Bordley 1982), the form of the relationship between actual and perceived rates of crime (Warr 1980), and the variety of fearful reactions to crime in situations where objective rates of victimization are either especially high (Skogan and Maxfield 1981) or especially low (Taylor 1980). This chapter does not take up the analytic problems raised in these works. As with other types of social-indicator studies, we recognize that there is not necessarily a one-to-one relationship between objective and subjective measures of the environment—in this case, the crime problem (Andrews and Withey 1976; Marans and Rodgers 1974; Milbrath and Sahr 1975). Spelling out the precise nature of the relationship between actual and perceived levels of threat is an important task for criminological research. For the urban problems considered here, however, there are additional elements that must be analyzed and explained if the impact of the crime problem on urban change is to be fully understood. These elements are explained in connection with the second and third propositions.

The second proposition asserts that one's sense of the seriousness of the crime problem depends on the extent to which the level of threat in the neighborhood exceeds what one considers to be an acceptable amount. Ordinarily, people make tradeoffs in choosing and evaluating a place of residence. Evaluating the seriousness of the crime problem, we believe, involves two separate judgments. The first is a person's sense of the level of threat in the neighborhood—his or her perception of the prevailing rates of victimization. The second is a person's sense of what level of threat is acceptable, given the value of other positive and negative amenities of neighborhood life, and what alternatives are available. A person's evaluation of the seriousness of the crime problem is, then, a net judgment of comparative utility. The extent to which a person's subjective sense of the level of threat falls short of his or her standard of tolerability determines the level of dissatisfaction with the level of safety in the neighborhood.

This model of satisfaction and this step in our theory linking crime and urban change borrows heavily from Angus Campbell's (1981) theory of subjective social indicators:

> Satisfaction implies an act of judgment, a comparison of what people have to what they think they deserve, expect or may reasonably aspire to. If this discrepancy is small, the result is satisfaction; if it is large, there is dissatisfaction. (P. 22)

Campbell refers to his standards of judgment as aspiration levels because his book is primarily concerned with social indicators of economic and physical well-being and because his theoretical point of departure is grounded in reference-group theory. In our model of reactions to crime, we hypothesize, instead, that a person's standard of judgment is his or her sense of the acceptable level of risk given the other amenities of the neighborhood. Like Campbell, we argue that satisfaction with the level of safety in the neighborhood is an evaluation of one's subjective sense of threat relative to this standard:[1]

> Satisfaction-dissatisfaction is a function of the gap the individual perceives between his or her present situation and the situation or status he or she aspires to, expects or feels entitled to. Change in satisfaction level may result from a change in perceived situation or a change in aspiration level or both. (Campbell 1981, 24)

The importance of this process of judgment for the link between the crime problem and urban change is made clear in the third proposition. This proposition states that one's net judgment of seriousness—i.e., one's satisfaction level—forms the basis for a number of actions that affect patterns of urban change. The basis for this hypothesis is empirical—it summarizes the principal statistical findings discussed in later sections of this chapter. The data show that it is one's net judgment of the seriousness of the crime problem, not victimization experiences per se or even perceptions of the level of threat, that influence mobility intentions, expectations of neighborhood tipping, and willingness to invest in property maintenance.

The next section of this chapter explores in more detail the evidence for proposition two—the model of comparative judgment. The fourth section then reviews the evidence for proposition three—the importance of net comparative judgments of the seriousness of crime in explaining the patterns of urban change.

Threat and the Seriousness of the Crime Problem

Net judgments of the seriousness of the crime problem result, we argue, from comparing the perceived level of threat with a reference point denoting how much threat is tolerable. As many authors have shown, perceptions of the level of threat vary dramatically by neighborhood context. Neighborhood differences in measures of perceived threat are shown in table 8.1. Further analysis of these neighborhood differences shows that the level of perceived threat is affected by victimization, contextual rates of victimization, vandalism, avoidance of the public transportation system, and reports of disorderly or "uncivil" conduct on the streets in the area (Taub, Taylor, and Dunham 1981).

Less is known about the standards of judgment people use to evaluate the seriousness of the crime problem. There are no models in the literature showing which amenities of neighborhood life might compensate to make living with crime a tolerable or satisfactory state of affairs. Campbell's work is based on more than twenty years of research in subjective social indicators, but almost none of these studies addresses the crime problem.

Our data strongly support the argument that people tolerate high levels of threat if they find other aspects of the community to be a sufficiently gratifying compensation. We find that in certain circumstances, neighborhood amenities raise tolerance levels and thus maintain high levels of satisfaction even when the neighborhood is perceived as a comparatively threatening place to live. Evidence for this finding is shown in figure 8.1.

Table 8.1 Average Neighborhood Scores on Measures of the Perceived
Threat of Crime

Neighborhoods Classified by Police-reported Crime Rate	Perceived Quantity of Crime[a]	Perceived Risk of Victimization[b]	Scale of Perceived Threat[c]
Low			
East Side	2.42	1.25	3.67
Portage Park	2.40	1.24	3.64
Beverly	2.33	1.18	3.51
High			
Back of the Yards	2.56	1.50	4.06
Lincoln Park	2.71	1.46	4.17
Hyde Park–Kenwood	2.66	1.49	4.15
South Shore	2.71	1.58	4.29
Austin	2.68	1.68	4.36

[a]Question wording: "How much crime would you say there is in your immediate neighborhood? A lot (3), some (2), or only a little(1)."
[b]Question wording: "Would you say that the likelihood you will be a victim of crime in your neighborhood during the coming year is high (3), moderate (2), or low (1)?"
[c]Scale formed by adding responses to the previous two questions.

Average judgments of the level of threat are shown on the x axis. Average judgments of the seriousness of the crime problem in the neighborhood are shown on the y axis. The three enclosed regions show the three types of aggregate-level responses that typically occur. The points in each enclosed region show average scale scores for demographic groups in each neighborhood cluster. (Points labeled "W" represent average responses for white homeowners, etc.—see the legend for figure 8.1.)

The average responses for all demographic groups in Beverly, Portage Park, and East Side fall in the enclosed region in the upper-left quadrant of figure 8.1. These are neighborhoods in which the perceived level of threat is comparatively low and satisfaction with the crime problem is relatively high. The responses for groups in Austin and South Shore are in the enclosed region in the lower-right quadrant. All groups in these neighborhoods perceive the environment as relatively threatening and comparatively less satisfying.

The pattern in these neighborhoods shows that in many cases satisfaction levels vary systematically with perceived levels of threat. The third region of figure 8.1, however, shows a marked deviation from this pattern.

The enclosed area in the upper-right quadrant shows the average group responses in Lincoln Park and Hyde Park–Kenwood. All demographic groups perceive these neighborhoods as relatively risky, but as places where the seriousness of the crime problem is comparatively low.

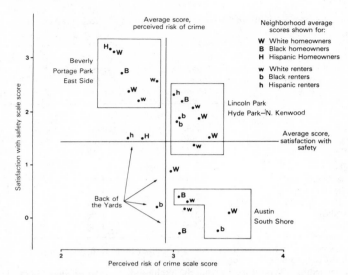

Fig. 8.1 Satisfaction with Safety and Perceived Risk of Crime for Three Racial/Ethnic Groups

Even though the level of threat is perceived to be high in these areas, the standard by which this level is judged is also high because of other neighborhood amenities, resulting in relatively few people experiencing serious dissatisfaction. We cannot be certain which neighborhood amenities raise the standards against which the threat of crime is judged. In chapter 5, we noted that Lincoln Park has the park and lakefront location, an abundance of restaurants and shops, DePaul University, convenience to downtown places of work, and the feeling that the area is an exciting place to be. Hyde Park–Kenwood has the University of Chicago, a rich array of cultural activities, the lakefront, convenience to downtown (in this case, advantageous more for recreational and shopping purposes), and a distinctive community spirit. In each neighborhood, there are also highly visible signs of extra community resources being used to deal with the crime problem (such as the private police force in Hyde Park–Kenwood). The commitment of extra resources may act as a type of insurance—or perhaps a better term would be reassurance—and thereby raise the level of tolerability or satisfaction people feel with any given level of threat.

The points outside the three enclosed regions in figure 8.1 are the average responses for the demographic groups in Back of the Yards. This neighborhood does not fit any of the ideal types overall; rather, the different groups see the crime problem differently. Blacks and whites see the area as one with high risk and low satisfaction, similar to the pattern for South Shore and Austin. Compared to the blacks and whites, Hispanics see the area as one with low risk and high satisfaction—more like the pattern in Beverly, Portage Park, and East Side.

This pattern illustrates the role expectations play in people's judgments of the value of neighborhood amenities. As discussed in chapter 3, the white residents of Back of the Yards, who are on average much older and longer-term residents than the rest, see themselves as trapped. They believe they are unable to leave a comparatively threatening situation. Blacks, living in the most deteriorated parts of the neighborhood, see themselves as caught in a dead end. But for Mexicans, who make up almost all of the Hispanic population in this community, there is the standard of comparison with what they left behind and the more general expectation that their present residence is a way station up a ladder of well-being.

The patterns in table 8.1 and figure 8.1, interpreted from the point of view of Campbell's argument, are the bulk of the evidence for the model of net comparative judgment outlined in proposition two. Next, we document the overriding importance of these judgments for explaining the effect of the crime problem on neighborhood change.

The Crime Problem and Urban Change: Empirical Patterns

Statistical analyses of expectations of racial tipping, willingness to invest in property maintenance, and intentions to move out of the neighborhood show that the crime problem significantly shapes the course of neighborhood change.

Satisfaction with the level of safety in the neighborhood, our measure of one's net judgment of the seriousness of the crime problem, is a consistently stronger predictor of the dependent measures considered here than are levels of victimization in the area, perceptions of the level of threat or riskiness of the neighborhood, or even whether or not the individual or a household member has recently been victimized. In this section, we review these results and discuss some of the implications of these findings for understanding urban-neighborhood change.

The Crime Problem and Neighborhood Investment

The statistical analysis in chapter 6 shows that the crime problem affects patterns of neighborhood investment because crime affects how people evaluate the economic opportunities in the housing market. Neighborhood market evaluations are measured by a two-item scale asking how people evaluate the trend in property values in the area and whether or not they would recommend investment to others. This measure is strongly related to investment behavior and determines, in combination with other factors, the approach one takes to the market for rehabilitation—capitalizing on an opportunity as compared to making the best of a bad situation.

The relationship between crime and neighborhood-housing-market evaluations is shown in table 6.9. Satisfaction with the level of safety is the critical intervening variable explaining the relationship between the crime problem and neighborhood investment. Most other measures of fear and victimization do not affect housing-market evaluations except for their impact on satisfaction.

These results support the third proposition in our theory of reactions to crime and urban change. Net judgments of the seriousness of the crime problem explain most of the relationship between crime and individual reactions that contribute to urban change. This general finding also holds for the analysis of moving intentions and the expectation of tipping.

Each dependent variable does show some exception to this general rule. For instance, avoidance of the public transportation system and having had one's home vandalized affect willingness to invest, but not expectations of tipping or plans to change one's place of residence. These exceptions do not, we believe, detract from the general result. The statistical findings support the thoery insofar as the measure of satisfaction with the level of safety in the neighborhood is consistently and strongly related to the dependent measures. Fear is a complex and subtle motivation. Its antecedents and consequences have components we are not yet prepared to explain.

The Crime Problem and Plans for Moving

Intentions to move are measured by asking people "How likely is it that you might move out of [NEIGHBORHOOD] within the next year? Will you definitely move (5), probably move (4), is there a fifty-fifty chance of moving (3), will you probably not move (2), or will you definitely not move (1)?" This type of survey measure is as close as we can come to assessing a person's current judgment of the net value of remaining in the neighborhood as opposed to the expected value of moving somewhere else. Measuring net value is, of course, different from analyzing actual mobility. Diverse factors intervene between deciding it would be worthwhile to move and actually doing so. For the issues analyzed in this book, it would be valuable to study both intended and actual moves. Without panel data, however, we can study only part of the decision to move—the factors affecting one's judgment of the net value of remaining in the neighborhood as opposed to moving somewhere else.[2]

Average scores for the white respondents in each neighborhood are shown in table 8.2. In most neighborhoods, residents plan to stay. The neighborhood averages range from about 2.0 (probably will not move in the next year) to about 3.0 (fifty-fifty chance of moving in the next year). Further analysis shows, however, that there are certain types of concern about the neighborhood that greatly reduce the expected value of staying and that crime is prominent on this list.

We observed in another publication based on the Omaha survey analyzed in chapter 7 that mobility intentions often appear to be racially motivated (Taylor 1981a). The net value whites attach to staying in the neighborhood is lower where there is high black-white demand ratio or where racial change is expected. The Chicago data are consistent with this pattern. When racial issues are considered apart from other urban problems, predicted average scores on the measure of moving intentions are higher by .22 for those who expect tipping as opposed to stability; higher by .19 for each unit increase in the 1-to-4 measure of the black-white demand ratio; and higher by .04 for each unit decrease in the three-item racial-tolerance scale described in chapter 7. The first column of figures in table 8.3 shows the parameter estimates for this regression equation (standardized slopes are shown in parentheses).[3]

These results echo other findings that link minority concentration with rates of residential mobility in the white population. The central propositions in what we term "classic" ecological models for invasion and

Table 8.2 Average Neighborhood Scores for White Respondents' Likelihood of Moving in the Coming Year

	Neighborhoods Ranked by Satisfaction with the Crime Problem	Average[a] Score
High	Beverly	1.55
	Portage Park	1.93
	East Side	1.56
	Lincoln Park	2.17
	Hyde Park–Kenwood	2.23
	Back of the Yards	2.43
	South Shore	2.78
Low	Austin	2.38
	TOTAL	1.96

[a]Question wording: "How likely is it that you might move out of [neighborhood] within the next year? Will you definitely move (5), probably move (4), is there a fifty-fifty chance of moving (3), will you probably not move (2), or will you definitely not move (1)?"

Table 8.3 Regression Results for the Analysis of Moving Intentions among White Residents of Chicago Neighborhoods

Predictor Variables	Equation (1) Demographic and Race Effects Only		Equation (2) All Significant Predictors and Race Effects	
	B	(β)	B	(β)
Age (dummy categories)				
Over 55 years	−.60*	(−.22)	−.56*	(−.20)
40–54 years	−.40*	(−.15)	−.40*	(−.16)
Owner vs. renter	−.50*	(−.19)	−.41*	(−.16)
Presence of abandoned dwellings on block			.96*	(.10)
Block-Deterioration-scale score			.08*	(.07)
Satisfaction with crime problem			−.10*	(−.16)
Census-tract crime rate (per thousand)			.0014*	(.06)
View on neighborhood investment (favor vs. oppose)			−.28*	(−.09)
Expect tipping	.22*	(.09)	.08	(.03)
Black-white demand ratio	.19*	(.13)	.04	(.03)
Racial-tolerance-scale score	−.04*	(.07)	−.01	(−.02)
INTERCEPT	2.40		2.60	
R^2	.13		.19	

*$p < .05$.

succession are based on this correlation (e.g., Duncan and Duncan 1957). More recently published economic theories of prejudice and urban social structure also depend for their validity on a prominent effect of racial issues on individuals' net judgments of the value of staying in the neighborhood (e.g., Courant and Yinger 1977).

The aggregate data collected and statistical procedures used in both the classic ecological studies and the more recent economic analyses often do not allow much exploration of why people racially encode the value of remaining in the neighborhood as opposed to moving somewhere else. The correlation between racial mix and white mobility is usually accepted as the primary social fact around which the theories are built. Some formal models even adopt the convention of *defining* a correlation between racial mix and white mobility as revealed racial prejudice. Only rarely do ecological or formal analyses focus on the constellation of factors people take into account in determining the value of staying in their neighborhood.

With the data from the Chicago Neighborhood Survey, we can open the question of whether the correlation between racial issues and mobility intentions results from racial prejudice or from other neighborhood concerns, correlated with racial mix, which affect people in such a way as to produce cumulative patterns of invasion and succession. Adding further explanatory variables to the analysis of moving intentions is a way of asking whether or not there are other issues that influence people's judgments of the value of staying in the neighborhood that supplement or possibly account for the racial effects shown in equation (1) of table 8.3.

From a formal point of view, table 8.3 shows that the apparent effects of racial issues on moving intentions are negligible once we take account of other factors that more directly explain moving intentions. Racial factors *do* covary with the direct explanatory variables—i.e., where there is more deterioration, more crime, and less satisfaction with the crime problem, there is also a greater tendency to fear racial transition. The analysis in table 8.3 shows, however, that fear of racial change and intentions to move are both products of neighborhood deterioration, crime, and dissatisfaction.[4]

Lack of property maintenance and rehabilitation reduces the value a person attaches to remaining in the neighborhood. Having one or more abandoned dwellings on the block increases one's score on the moving-intentions question by almost one full point. Each unit increase on the 0-to-3 scale of visible signs of property deterioration (described in chapter 6) increases scores on the moving-intention measure by .08 units. Finally, having a sense that the economic future of the neighborhood is in decline decreases the attractiveness of staying.

The effects of the crime problem are even stronger. The eight neighborhoods are ranked in table 8.2 according to the average judgment of the seriousness of the crime problem. The pattern in the table shows a strong aggregate-level relationship. Neighborhoods in which the amenities are not judged compensatory for the level of threat also have much higher average scores on the measure of likelihood of moving. When the data are analyzed at the individual level and many indicators of the crime problem tested, this relationship remains. In fact, apart from the demographic predictors, table 8.3 shows that satisfaction with the safety of the neighborhood is the strongest single predictor of intentions to move.

As with the previous analysis, satisfaction with safety explains most of the effects of crime, but there is an exception. People living in areas where police-reported crime rates are comparatively high are more likely to say that they intend to move. This finding gives some support to models relating to contextual rates of crime to aggregate mobility patterns (e.g., Hakim forthcoming).

In short, explanations of succession that focus exclusively on racial issues simplify the matter in ways that distort what actually takes place. The presence of deteriorating housing and increased crime rates gives meaning to other contextual forces that increase one's desire to move.

The Crime Problem and Expectations of Tipping

We argued in chapter 7 that whether or not someone expects tipping is a measure of his or her impression of the structural position of the neighborhood housing market. We doubt that people formally calculate the index of practical equilibrium used in the simulation studies in chapter 7. However, people do acquire some sense of the strength of black demand for housing in the neighborhood, the weakness of white demand, and the tolerance of their neighborhoods for racial integration.

Negative features of the neighborhood can affect how one perceives the demand characteristics and tolerance schedules that determine the structural position of the neighborhood. Table 7.6 shows that for whites, one's net judgment of the seriousness of the crime problem is one such feature. Those who are dissatisfied with the level of safety in the neighborhood are more likely to expect racial change than those who are satisfied.

Satisfaction with safety is the principal variable explaining the impact of crime. As with the other analyses, however, there is an additional crime effect. Those who are afraid of walking in the neighborhood at night are also more likely to believe the neighborhood is racially unstable. Detailed discussions of reasons for the link between this measure of fear of crime and the neighborhood black-white demand ratio appear in other works by one of the authors (Taylor, Scheppele, and Stinchcombe 1979; Stinchcombe et al. 1980).

A Summary of Empirical Patterns

Crime, deterioration, and dissatisfaction create the conditions of neighborhood change and neighborhood tipping. In neighborhoods where crime, deterioration, and dissatisfaction are great, the probability that residents will move soon is higher. In these areas, the fear and expectation of racial change and prejudice against incoming black families is also greater. However, fear of and prejudice against racial change is not the cause of racial change. In fact, once account is taken of the factors directly influencing people's plans to move and people's perceptions of neighborhood stability, fear of and prejudice against racial change do not, in any scientific sense, "explain" what is going on.

Rather, crime, deterioration, and dissatisfaction create circumstances in Chicago and in other American cities where the likelihood of an increase in the black-white demand ratio for neighborhood housing increases. Residents of these neighborhoods want to leave, and it is mainly blacks who are interested in moving in. Similarly, crime, deterioration, and dissatisfaction create circumstances where the competitiveness of the housing market is likely to decrease. These are the two factors explaining neighborhood tipping. People living in neighborhoods unfavorably situated with respect to these two variables are (and ought to be) more aware of the possibility of neighborhood change.

Understanding the connections between crime, deterioration, and neighborhood change (and the epiphenomenal role of racial attitudes and racial preferences) leads to a number of concrete suggestions for appropriate policy changes that might make the situation in American urban neighborhoods less turbulent and less costly. Some of these recommendations are discussed in the concluding chapter of this book.

Conclusions

On Reactions to Crime

Our theory of satisfaction and net judgments of the seriousness of crime gives us a reasonably good handle for charting the constellation of forces relating crime and urban change.

Crime affects willingness to invest in neighborhood upkeep. Lack of neighborhood upkeep, along with crime, affects perceptions that the neighborhood is in a structurally weak position and expectations that the neighborhood will tip. Crime and lack of upkeep also affect one's own judgment about moving out of the neighborhood. Deciding to absorb the expenses of moving is, of course, one of the alternatives people weigh when they evaluate the expected return from investing in upkeep. The belief that it would be better to live in some other neighborhood may be a sign that one accepts the judgment he or she believes outsiders have made—that the neighborhood is of low value and therefore structurally weak. The interdependency between these judgments inspires our use of the term "vicious circle" to describe neighborhood problems.

The full impact of the crime problem is that it affects one's thinking about both sides of each of these interdependent issues. Reactions to crime create the circumstances and sometimes increase the momentum linking deterioration and moving, deterioration and tipping, and tipping and moving.

On Victimization

The crime problem begins but does not end with victimization. Those who attempt to measure the impact of crime on the city by looking only at victimization rates and measures will not succeed in their task. Our data, as well as many other surveys, show that victimization rates are very nearly even over many demographic categories in the city. Variations in victimization rates are usually not great enough or in the right pattern to explain the urban-neighborhood outcomes analyzed here (Taylor forthcoming).

The data show that personal experiences of victimization are not necessarily consequential for the dependent variables analyzed in this book. The critical issue is whether victimization is thought to be a low-probability random event or whether it is seen as one element in a class of threatening events thought to occur commonly in an area.

The level of threat of crime is then judged against one's standard—the amount of inconvenience one is willing to tolerate given the other amenities in the neighborhood. A multiplicity of factors enters into one's evaluation of the seriousness of the crime problem. The positive factors appear to be the amenities of the neighborhood and possibly the availability of particular neighborhood resources such as private police patrols for protection. The negative factors are the perceived levels of threat and expected chances of victimization.

The need to balance the positive aspects of neighborhood life against the threat of crime leads some researchers to describe crime as an endemic problem in American cities. Everyone must judge whether or not the level of threat of crime exceeds some tolerable level—whether it is "worth it" to live in the neighborhood, or in the city for that matter. The outcomes from these judgments vary greatly, much more than actual crime rates.

On Race and Urban Problems

The impact of racial issues on urban change cannot be clearly stated without reference to the crime problem and the deterioration problem. In most cases, we find that what we call racial issues—i.e., expectations of tipping, minority concentration, and racial prejudice—do not exert a strong independent effect on the calculations people make when they determine the utility of investing, the utility of moving, or their assessment of neighborhood structural weakness.

This conclusion does not mean that race is unrelated to the individual decisions that cumulatively produce the patterns of deterioration and tipping described in chapter 1. Problems of disinvestment and abandonment are clearly greater in areas of high minority concentration. In addition, our data show that expectations of tipping and the black-white demand ratio affect the standards by which one judges the seriousness of the crime problem (Taub, Taylor, and Dunham 1981).

Perhaps the clearest statement we can make about the impact of race on the urban resident is that decisions contributing to neighborhood change are made largely on the basis of the crime problem and the deterioration problem, but that the resident, whether black or white, is aware that these problems tend to be more severe in areas of high minority concentration. In people's generalizations about urban-neighborhood patterns, racial stereotypes may substitute as symbols representing, and perhaps for some explaining, deterioration and crime. Insofar as we can measure the thought process of the urban resident, however, racial stereotypes do not control the reactions that contribute to the cumulative patterns of urban change discussed in chapter 1. Most of the models analyzing the returns people expect from actions that cumulatively contribute to urban change show that racial stereotypes do not affect these calculations with the same force as the more concrete realities of crime and deterioration.

9

A Revised Approach to Neighborhood Change

This book suggests several revisions and expansions of some of the standard models of urban neighborhood change that have been developed by both ecological theorists and economic geographers. In previous chapters, we have proposed that some components be added to these models. Chapters 4 and 5 document the most frequently occurring neighborhood departures from the ideal-typical invasion-deterioration-succession sequence. Chapters 6, 7, and 8 are formal approaches to understanding these neighborhood departures.

We are now in a position to make a more general statement about the nature of the forces affecting urban neighborhood change. By revising the theory, we hope to provide a more general set of tools for understanding, anticipating, and possibly influencing the direction of urban development in the coming years as our cities grow and age.

Neighborhood Context and Neighborhood Change: A Theoretical Statement

Variables in the Theory

There are three types of social and ecological pressures that interactively determine the pattern of change in urban neighborhoods: (1) ecological facts; (2) corporate and institutional decisions; and (3) decisions of individual neighborhood residents.

Ecological facts. The ecological facts define the social and economic context for a neighborhood. The ecological facts that particularly concern us are: *a*) the potential employment base for neighborhood residents as determined by the economics of location and transportation; *b*) demographic pressures on the neighborhood housing market; *c*) the age and original quality of the housing stock; *d*) external amenities such as attractive physical locations (hills, views, etc.)

Ecological facts place general limits on what patterns of neighborhood change are possible and what directions of change are most likely. Neighborhood ecological facts are like the genetic, family, and socialization variables in theories of individual development and achievement. The resources individuals begin with tend to be carried forward and converted to advantages in markets for education, employment, and marriage. Ecological facts similarly influence patterns of neighborhood change. Neighborhoods that are ecologically disadvantaged will not, other things equal, be viewed as desirable sites for either corporate or individual investment. But, as we have seen, the supposed bedrock of ecological fact is spongier than it might initially seem. The aging and nondistinctive housing stock of western Lincoln Park, for example, suddenly took on value when other forces became newly arrayed. Similarly, parks in some settings are indeed amenities, while in others they are defined as negative features.

Corporate decisions. Corporate decisions are the decisions of corporate actors such as banks, universities, insurance companies, or manufacturing firms to buttress or abandon a neighborhood. Corporate decisions can be treated as any of the three types of variables included in this theoretical sketch. First, institutions can be seen as individual actors, deciding whether to remain in the neighborhood or move away. It is true that because institutions are larger and control more resources than individual actors, their decisions have more profound consequences. Nonetheless, they can be viewed as merely big property owners.

At a second level, corporate actors can be considered part of the underlying ecological framework. The stockyards in Back of the Yards or the steel mills in East Side represent part of the economic structure of opportunity that helps to shape their regions. But corporate actors are not simply other neighbors, no matter how large, nor are they passive background since they enjoy disproportionate normative, economic, and influence resources.

As potential campaign contributors, as major area employers, and as organizations that can staff lobbying and related activities, corporate actors possess substantial influence resources. These resources can be used to mobilize city government to provide services and to utilize components of federal and state programs. Secondly, because of their size and position in American society, corporate actors are able to marshal opinion and to create the proper normative climate for the promotion of the area. Finally, their economic resources, combined with their preferential tax status, are so great that even a very small proportion of those resources devoted to the appropriate strategies can notably affect neighborhood stability. Corporate actors are able to have an impact on the real estate market and to deploy their personnel at a level that individuals cannot. We have seen these forces at work in Hyde Park–Kenwood, Beverly, and Lincoln Park.

An important component of that resource deployment involves the creation and support of community voluntary organizations. As we have pointed out elsewhere (Taub et al. 1977), these organizations are often not quite what they seem. In the present case, the South East Chicago Commission in Hyde Park–Kenwood, the Beverly Area Planning Association, and the Lincoln Park Conservation Association all receive their economic underpinning from such actors.

This underpinning, then, has a multiplicative effect. The investment corporate actors make serves as an incentive to bring new members into the organization. This impact is important to understand. The evidence in chapters 6 and 7 underscores the fact that there is little individuals can do to change the course of direction of their neighborhood. Because they know this, their inclination is to withdraw participation and investment. But by providing baseline support at a level that individuals cannot, corporate actors encourage individual participation because individuals feel new levels of efficacy in such a situation.

In effect what corporate participants do is lower the threshold level at which groups of residents enter the process. Unlike the actors in the prisoner's dilemma model, individuals in neighborhoods where corporate actors support community organizations come to realize that the organization is not about to be abandoned, that resources will be available to them at a level substantially beyond what individuals can contribute, and that their investment has a reasonable probability of bearing fruit. Consequently, new levels of involvement are elicited.

Our analysis shows several common features of the life cycle and the chances of success of these organizations, or emergent corporate actors, when they are confronted by the various neighborhood circumstances analyzed in this book.

There is substantial evidence that community organizations created solely to fight crime have neither long lives nor much success recruiting members. Fear of crime per se is not much motivation for long-term collective action. Our findings suggest that community organizations that have multiple goals, one of which may be crime control, are more likely to be successful.

Most of the strong community organizations considered in this book arose in response to impending or actual racial change. In this situation, successful community organizations usually develop three agenda items. The first is to maintain a stable real estate market. This is done by discouraging panic peddling, steering, and related real estate practices; by implementing programs to market the neighborhood and maintain a flow of investment funds; and by working with the city through urban-renewal and related federal subsidy programs to clarify neighborhood boundaries, using demolition or renovation of older deteriorated housing along the borders, construction of new, usually subsidized housing, and the insertion of cul-de-sacs and one-way streets which discourage through traffic.

The second agenda item is usually to maintain the quality of neighborhood schools and to make concern and activity about them visible. This item is especially important in parts of the city that contain many nuclear-family residences.

The third agenda item is customarily an anticrime package that includes establishing youth programs and promoting citizen crime-prevention activities such as safe houses, beat representatives, and "whistle stop." As we have suggested earlier, there is little evidence that such programs reduce crime. Instead, the programs give residents a feeling of security because they believe their crime problem is being confronted.

Overarching these three agenda items in those neighborhoods that are able to sustain market demand from whites in the face of black in-migration is the self-conscious promotion of the virtues of racial integration. This item is important because the presence of minorities must be talked about openly and in an appropriate normative climate. Without this effort, whispers and gossip may contribute to individual decisions which are likely to speed the process of change.

One crucial lesson from our research is that the importance of full-time paid professional staff in these organizations cannot be overestimated. Because of the limited commitment of individual neighborhood residents (including a lack of time), paid staff in these organizations provide the scaffolding around which individuals build their own participation. This is not to minimize the importance of others kinds of groups. Churches, for example, are instrumental in most communities in generating organizational activity, and Hyde Park–Kenwood and Beverly have a base of active citizens as well. But the job of maintaining community morale in the face of an array of erosive forces is full time and requires professional skills.

A second critical lesson is that full-time organizations without substantial resources and "clout" are not very effective. South Shore during its period of decline, Back of the Yards, and Austin had a great deal of organizational activity without resources. South Shore's efforts at stabilization began to show success only after its bank made the commitment to participate.

Individual decision making. The third force determining the pattern of change in urban neighborhoods is individual decision making. By this term we mean the cumulative effects of the actions of individual homeowners and renters, each acting in a way that seems reasonable and efficient, but collectively contributing to the overall patterns of deterioration, housing-market decline, and community anxiety about the crime problem. The task in chapters 6, 7, and 8 was to advance and test theories of individual perception and individual decision making as these actions are relevant for determining the course of change in a given neighborhood setting.

The working out of our models demonstrates that once forces are set in motion for the withdrawal of white residents, there is little individuals acting alone can do to reverse the pattern, nor are there likely to be many who would be willing to try. The irony here is that the maintenance of high market prices in a middle-class neighborhood will keep the process of change under control, yet individual actors are in no position to create the conditions that will maintain the prices. Even with higher levels of tolerance and a substantial black middle class, some sort of firm undergirding is necessary to allow citizens to take hold.

Corporate actors play an important role in determing how individuals will make their decisions in this situation. Under proper circumstances, the corporate actors reduce the thresholds at which individuals will decide to invest in property maintenance. They also reduce anxiety that individuals will be abandoned—that is, stuck with their depreciated property—as, in the prisoner's dilemma model, their neighbors jump the sinking ship. Finally, through the promotion of the ideology of integration, they provide the normative underpinning for those who are willing to try to stay.

Explanations of Change

Most theories of neighborhood change concentrate on the ecological facts as the main explanatory variable. This emphasis gives, we believe, the wrong impression about the internal dynamics of neighborhood change. Individual residents and local corporate actors are, after all, the ones whose day-to-day decisions define the texture and quality of urban life. If ecological facts are overwhelming, it is because of the effect of these facts on the perceptions and actions of individual and corporate actors. In a neighborhood that goes up or down, it is ultimately the actions of these residents that make the outcomes real.

Because early sociological theories do not make a place for the decision rules of individual and corporate actors, the theories lead to the too-simple view that the neighborhoods in a city are somewhat interchangeable parts of a single, integrated urban system that operates according to univariate rules of evolution.[1] The neighborhood case studies in chapters 3, 4, and 5 show that ecological facts do not, in fact, unidirectionally determine neighborhood outcomes. Corporate and individual decisions always intervene and sometimes modify the connection between ecological circumstances and neighborhood outcomes. Sometimes the corporate and individual decisions reaffirm what might have been expected on the basis of the ecological facts. Chapter 3 discusses three neighborhoods in various stages of the tipping process and the individual and corporate decisions (such as redlining and blockbusting) that guide this process. Chapters 4 and 5, however, show that there are exceptions to the ecological "rules" and that individual and corporate decision making must be analyzed to explain these exceptions.

We see from these three chapters that none of the factors influencing urban neighborhoods can be considered independently from the other two. Corporate decisions take into account the ecological facts; individual decisions take into account the ecological facts as well as corporate decisions; community organizations depend on corporate and individual contributions for survival; and so on.

The interlocking nature of the pressures on neighborhood change does not make all statements about causal ordering hopeless, however. Corporate investments are necessary but not sufficient for achieving desirable neighborhood outcomes. When corporate investment is at a high enough level, then the market for individual investment becomes secure enough that individuals choose to spend on rehabilitaiton, to withstand the fears of crime or impending racial change, and to take part in other actions that collectively determine the quality of neighborhood life. Corporate investment is necessary to achieve these goals because individuals acting alone are too strongly affected by urban fears and too strongly inclined to protect their self-interests to act to achieve them otherwise. But corporate investment is not sufficient to achieve desirable neighborhood outcomes. The market dynamics of individual decisions determine whether high aggregate levels of neighborhood investment will be reached.

The models in chapters 6, 7, and 8 suggest how ecological facts, corporate decisions, and individual choice might be combined in a descriptive analysis of neighborhood change. In chapter 6 it is apparent that not so much the level of deterioration as one's sense of the ecological facts and the strength of corporate contributions to the market guide individual home-rehabilitation decisions. In chapter 7 we argue that ecological facts determine the structural position of a neighborhood. Individual and corporate expectations of tipping proceed from impressions of the neighborhood structural position. The ability to achieve a desirable outcome depends on the extent to which the structural position of the neighborhood can be controlled and the extent to which expectations of change can be shaped. Chapters 3, 4, and 5 suggest how this shaping and control might be attempted.

Lincoln Park, Hyde Park–Kenwood, and Beverly all look as if they will remain stable, integrated communities. However, because of structural characteristics of the housing market, each neighborhood requires massive efforts by concerned corporate actors with substantial resources and close ties to government. It is true that there is a sizable number of urban middle-class residents who no longer believe that decline is inevitable with racial change. But the structural characteristics of the housing market, coincident with high crime rates, stack the deck against these residents acting on their beliefs. The forces generating soft markets in such settings are so wide spread that there is more to do than individuals alone can handle. The potential cost for a white or black middle-class homeowner taking a chance that the neighbors will act in concert and agree not to move and that outsiders looking for housing will not be deterred by the presence of minorities in the neighborhood is high.

Under these circumstances, few homeowners or realtors are necessary to begin the actions that lead to soft markets. The difference in the consequences of five houses for ten purchasers and ten houses for five purchasers is dramatic. In these settings, it is only the corporate actors with capital investments and full-time employees who can take the lead. The University of Chicago in Hyde Park–Kenwood, DePaul University and several banks and hospitals in Lincoln Park, and the developers of Evergreen Shopping Plaza in Beverly have all played substantial roles in the lives of their communities both directly and by creating and working through community organizations. In Lincoln Park and Hyde Park–Kenwood, corporate actors were able to provide large investments of their own as well as to generate urban-renewal projects through contacts with government agencies. Community organizations in all three neighborhoods promoted high-quality services, discouraged shoddy real estate practices, and organized close ties to the police and community anticrime programs.

In a less dramatic way, we have shown that this scenario works even in more deteriorated areas—areas that now exhibit some evidence of making a comeback. The commitment and efforts of the South Shore Bank have generated vast investments from outsiders, including government agencies that provided subsidies and substantial funds for infrastructural improvements. Similarly, the gentrification of the Austin Village area has been supported by agencies in neighboring Oak Park.

In chapter 8, we discuss the interlocking relationship between the ability to achieve desirable outcomes and the impact of crime. At the theoretical level, we note that people's willingness to contribute to desirable community outcomes is based partly on net judgments of the seriousness of crime. Net judgments of seriousness take into account the neighborhood level of risk, but also consider whether the level of desirability of the community is such that the prevailing level of risk is worth enduring. Corporate actions contribute to desirable outcomes over and above the levels that can be generated by the collectivity of neighborhood residents; thus corporate actions increase the chance that individuals will contribute despite the level of risk.

Our findings have several practical implications for understanding the effect of crime on neighborhood change. First, crime, by itself, is not a deterrent to community economic growth. Lincoln Park and Hyde Park–Kenwood have each demonstrated economic growth in spite of both high crime rates and the perception of relatively high risk among their residents. South Shore and Austin Village, both with even higher crime rates, may be on the same path.

One explanation for the limited impact of crime on individuals' collective responses is that it is a statistically rare event (Skogan and Maxfield 1981). This fact by itself does not seem to be a satisfactory explanation because of the high general levels of concern in society as evinced in social surveys (Taylor, Scheppele, and Stinchcombe 1979), the debilitating effects of crime on victims as described by Silberman (1978), and the fact that one-third of the households in the Chicago Neighborhood Survey report a victimization experience during the year preceding the interview. We offer the alternative explanation that satisfaction with neighborhood safety is a global concept linked to general satisfaction with community life. One can perceive high crime in the community and be fearful of it, but still discount it because of other compensatory aspects of the neighborhood.

Our second practical observation on the nature of the crime problem is that despite reams of literature to the contrary, dense internal community organization is not, by itself, protection for the community against those consequences of crime that lead to reduced demand for housing and subsequent deterioration. Back of the Yards has been densely organized by the Back of the Yards Council and by rich networks of church-related activity. Yet the neighborhood deteriorates rapidly. Conversely, Lincoln Park residents are optimistic about their community and its future in the face of little community-based social organization and the lowest amount of neighborly social activity of any of our communities.

Theories of neighborhood change should focus on the forces affecting both corporate *and* individual decisions in the neighborhood ecological context. Maintaining the local economic base, maintaining the housing stock, maintaining orderly neighborhood life, and maintaining an orderly housing market are all highly desirable neighborhood outcomes. Achieving these outcomes is not a simple collective-action problem. There are brute ecological realities. For certain neighborhood situations, there is almost nothing that can be done to preserve amenities in the face of overwhelming demographic pressures and a declining economic base. In other situations, however, where neighborhood maintenance is desired and there are resources to be mobilized, it is frequently the case that corporate and individual actors will find it advantageous to contribute to achieving the desired end. We now turn to a consideration of some of the policy recommendations that, given our understanding of the dynamics of individual and corporate decision making in urban neighborhoods, can make this outcome likely.

Policy Recommendations

Even if there were little urban crime, and racial succession were not an issue, there would be serious problems in maintaining neighborhoods in a city like Chicago because overall demand for housing has declined as the city has lost population. The effects of this phenomenon are exacerbated by the fact that the population loss lies most heavily with those who can afford to pay for good-quality housing.

The population losses can be conceived of as two distinct streams. The first is the middle-class loss which has been under way since the 1950s and coincides with the move to the suburbs with their newer houses and, in some instances, higher levels of other amenities. This loss was followed by the movement of industry and retail functions to the suburbs, and with that, the increased movement of the white working class as well.

The second stream is related to the large-scale transformations of American society which have moved industries to the South and West as well as to Asia, taking large numbers of jobs with them. The consequences of the collapse of the older heavy industries in the North are clear in East Side—a community that is declining without the types of severe urban problems we have been discussing.

It is now in vogue to recommend programs for reindustrialization for the urban North. But it is hard to imagine how macro social forces can be combatted by local interventions. Enterprise zones have been proposed as one kind of solution. It is certainly possible that an urban policy that concerned itself with jobs as well as housing would try to develop an environment more favorable to industry than the present one. Programs that provide a subsidy for land acquisition and preparation and, perhaps, concessions on taxes for industries might lead in that direction. Such a policy would have the consequence of slowing the process of decline and reducing the hardships of dislocation.

A second set of problems seems also not to lend itself to simple policy recommendations. That a large minority underclass increases fear of crime among both whites and middle-class blacks is not surprising. Recommendations, which we support, to reduce its size by providing training and jobs for the poor along with a full-employment policy have been made (Wilson forthcoming). However, here too the magnitude of the problem seems to preclude dramatic local-level solutions.

Efforts to maintain stable real estate markets in the face of these declines in demand often go unrewarded. Sometimes to the extent that they succeed, the participants are accused of gentrifying, and, consequently, of unhousing the poor. Even in Austin, which is so deteriorated that one would think any effort to upgrade housing stock would meet with approval, the six-square-block area undergoing gentrification is being bitterly attacked by the community organizations in the surrounding area for that very reason. The gentrifiers comprise in this instance an interracial—about 50-50—middle-class group. An effective government policy would encourage rather than discourage such gentrification activity.

The gentrification of Austin Village points to one set of perturbations in the general pattern which may provide some guidelines for policy. The gentrification of Lincoln Park, for example, continues strong as the baby-boom professionals put pressure on the housing market in order both to be near their places of work—the service sector in the city remains strong—and to be near each other. Their anticipation of a bright future leads to investment and maintenance in such a setting despite high crime.

Under such circumstances, one policy recommendation might be to reduce the supply of housing. A middle-class neighborhood that has appeal to young professionals can thrive partly because its housing is in short supply. The boundaries of the area in demand expand as appreciation prices new young professionals out of the housing market at its core. Under these circumstances, investment thresholds are low. People gobble up housing and quickly decide to make improvements no matter what their immediate neighbors are doing. What is truly amazing is the level of housing stock that attracts such investments. Simple frame cottages of no distinction, located far from the developed core areas that have appeal because of their parks or their views, are lavished with levels of attention similar to those in some of the more attractive older areas. Most gentrification literature emphasizes that gentrifying areas contain housing that has some inherent and previously unnoticed virtue—fine old Victorian houses with porches, high ceilings, the presence of details that emphasize craftsmanship; row houses with oak, maple, and marble as construction materials. While this quality is certainly true for the initial gentrification impulse, demand spreads and carries rather diverse properties with it. If one were to generalize from this kind of experience, one might want ruthlessly to destroy deteriorated older housing stock far removed from developing nodes in order to generate housing shortages.

The opposite situation now more nearly obtains in working-class neighborhoods threatened with either succession or more general economic decline. In those areas, there is an excess of housing which becomes the locale of the poor as working-class neighborhoods without inherent sources of buoyancy are abandoned. The fear of being swamped by the minority underclass haunts both whites and blacks, raising the thresholds at which they will make investments and encouraging the process of tipping.

Given the goal of maintaining solid working-class neighborhoods, a policy that emphasized the rapid removal of declining housing from the market accompanied by visible policing might indeed prove successful. However, it is precisely such housing that provides homes for those in the large and growing urban poverty class.

Unfortunately, housing questions and poverty questions often become confused. The provision of housing for the poor is a different problem from either the improvement of the plight of poor people or the promotion of solid urban neighborhoods and the improved quality of life that goes with them. But the artificially induced construction of such housing has the effect of weakening the market for existing housing by reducing demand in an already declining population. Our observations in this regard lead us to support the recommendations of others for some type of voucher system that, by putting resources in the hands of the house hunter, encourages maintenance of the more desirable older housing and abandonment of the rest.[2]

Similarly, our observations point toward the kind of urban-triage recommendations made by Downs (1978), supplemented with programs to minimize the negative consequences to the poor of dislocation. Under this system, those neighborhoods that are doing well would be left alone. Those neighborhoods that can succeed would be the focus of various rehabilitation efforts that would encourage investment; the others would be left to decline. Perhaps a triage approach coupled with vouchers would be the most humane as well as the most successful. Such an approach would not drive low-income people out of the market or force them to double or triple up in ways that hasten deterioration.

All of these recommendations fit within the framework of what we have considered as ecological theory. Much of our research, however, points to the tremendous potential of corporate actors in helping to maintain neighborhoods, particularly those that have a middle-class base. A sophisticated urban policy would substitute participation in such activities for more general forms of taxation.

Our observations point very much in this direction. As we have discussed, corporate actors play a large role in three of the settings and something of a role in a fourth (South Shore). The corporate actors, in this case, are not ones who can easily move away. Hospitals and universities in Hyde Park–Kenwood and Lincoln Park have vast quantities of invested capital, highly restricted markets for their properties, and little aspiration to maximize profits. The owners of real estate under a shopping center do not have the flexibility of movement that large industrial producers do. Even banks in Illinois, because they are not permitted to branch, have some inherent constriction of their movement.

These actors, with increasing sophistication and substantial investments, were able to have profound impacts on their neighborhoods, generating community-resident participation at the same time. Their role in maintaining full-time paid staff both to generate resident involvement and to pursue vigorously the policies we have outlined above is crucial. Dissemination of knowledge of this model is one important step in neighborhood maintenance. Indeed, that is one of the reasons this book was written. There are many large not-for-profit institutions, caught in similar situations, which would benefit from this kind of activity. In addition, there ought to be ways to encourage large profit-seeking institutions to do the same. Some corporations have enough resources to do the job without community involvement at all. General Motors has attempted this sort of activity in the area around its downtown Detroit office buildings. However, the social costs in that setting may be excessively high,[3] and most corporations do not have General Motors' resources. Still, the encouragement of corporate actors helping to fund community organizations and working together to intervene in the ways we have described holds out the most promise of success on a limited basis.

There is a further recommendation, made within a more limited framework, which will have an impact on individual decisions. This recommendation concerns visible crime-prevention activity. At present, policing efforts are determined primarily by levels of demand, usually defined as either calls or crimes. Similarly, efforts at para-policing, beat-representative programs, safe homes, Whistle Stop, and organized youth activity are called into play only when a community is threatened by crime (or racial change). Our data suggest that this array of activity may be most important in low-crime areas in which movement of minorities is likely to occur. It is precisely at this time that residents' sense of security must be developed if crime is not to become linked with racial fears, driving individuals away and softening the housing market. At the same time, efforts that are racially sensitive, such as salt-and-pepper police teams, interracial sporting activities for youth, and community-based organizations for adults become of primary importance. Now is not the time to pretend that one is color blind. It is the self-conscious attempt to link the stable elements of both races that will help to reduce the fears associated with race and crime. In high-crime gentrifying areas, a sense that the police and the community are working together to do something about crime may also contribute to stability.

Extra policing is designed to illustrate that the world is still under control and that the dreaded negative consequences of change are being forestalled. In a similar spirit, control of litter, open spaces, vacant structures, and activities in parks all take on new significance. The litter in a secure neighborhood, for example, is just "one of those things." In a neighborhood in the path of change, it is evidence that things are out of control.

What we have done through a multi-level, multi-method approach to the theory of neighborhood change is both alter the theory and clarify the processes that lead to the rise and fall of urban neighborhoods. As the problems can be seen at many levels, so can the solutions. What is clear is that interventions can and do work, and that they sometimes do so in situations that might be considered unpromising on the basis of historical understandings. The issues we raise and the problems they generate will not go away by themselves. And they threaten us with substantial social and economic cost. By dispelling some of the old myths and tentatively proposing courses of action, we suggest that something can be done. Whether the political and economic resources are available to do them is another matter.

Appendix A

The Chicago Survey Data

Our survey sample was chosen by means of the National Opinion Research Center's random-digit-dialing (RDD) selection program. A telephone survey has several advantages over in-person interviews, especially in a study such as ours.

In particular, the use of cluster samples in a study of crime and fear of crime in urban neighborhoods is suspect. Although clustering decreases costs considerably, the power of the sample to estimate population characteristics is reduced in proportion to the number and size of the clusters and the degree of within-cluster homogeneity. Thus, to the extent that clusters within neighborhoods are homogeneous in terms of factors such as socioeconomic status or race, which are likely to be related to crime and fear of crime, the cluster method substantially decreases the sample's power to estimate accurately the characteristics of the neighborhood. Telephone sampling is not subject to this constraint.

On a more practical level, a random telephone survey offers other advantages. It is often difficult to gain access to the residences of potential respondents in an urban setting. Additionally, because some of the neighborhoods are high in crime, the safety of the interviewers was a major consideration. Centralized calling increases the probability that interviews in unsafe neighborhoods will be completed and helps with quality control.

Telephone-survey methodology has been criticized in the past because of the bias resulting from the fact that not all families could afford a telephone. However, present-day saturation of the telephone market has become so great that the exclusion of nontelephone households is no longer a liability for telephone-survey sampling (see Lucas and Adams 1977). Further, random digit dialing has the advantage over sampling from telephone directories in that unlisted numbers are included.[1] Telephone numbers are assigned by three-digit exchanges, and within these exchanges they are assigned consecutively within blocks of a thousand. Assuming that unlisted numbers are distributed throughout all exchanges and blocks, we can assume that the RDD technique yields an unbiased probability sample of all residential telephones and, hence, households. Lucas and Adams (1977) found that listed and unlisted numbers were indeed evenly distributed throughout the Pittsburgh area.

We originally estimated that approximately 16,750 telephone numbers would be necessary in order to reach our goal of 400 interviews in each neighborhood. However, with our need to interview respondents located within a well-defined area—the neighborhood—the number of telephone numbers required ran much higher than initial expectations.

We were forced to screen out of the gross sample a large number of telephone numbers, ranging from 22.0 percent in Austin to fully 53.8 percent in Back of the Yards, and averaging a substantial 43.5 percent of the gross sample. This result reflects a generic problem with RDD when applied to small units of analysis such as neighborhoods—the boundaries of the sample and the telephone company's system of prefix allocation are not always in agreement. In addition, it is possible to have nonexclusive prefixes among the neighborhoods being sampled. This occurred in Hyde Park–Kenwood, South Shore, and East Side where four prefix areas fell in some combination within the three communities. To deal with this problem, a combined sample was generated in all four prefix areas, allowing the numbers to be screened for invalid, business, or ineligible numbers in all three communities simultaneously.

The final numbers of completed interviews in each neighborhood are given below:

Portage Park	395
Lincoln Park	433
Austin	395
Back of the Yards	418
Beverly	401
Hyde Park–Kenwood	417
South Shore	441
East Side	410
TOTAL	3,310

In our survey, an average of 20.4 percent of the net fielded sample broke off the interview before the screening could be completed. In addition, an average of 9.1 percent for whom eligibility could be established terminated the interview before completion. For the net fielded sample as a whole, then, we compute an approximate refusal rate of 29.5 percent. Because refusal rates are calculated in such a myriad of ways, comparisons are problematic. However, our rate compares favorably with Wiseman (1972) who reported a refusal rate of 36 percent over the telephone, and with Hauck and Cox (1974) who reported a refusal rate of 35 percent.

Completion rates are similarly calculated in different ways. We computed completion rates for our survey two ways, one more conservative than the other. The conservative method includes any case not determined to be invalid, a business, or an ineligible number, i.e., all unknown numbers, all missing questionnaires (those lost in the mail, etc.), and all unpublished numbers for whom eligibility could not be established. With this method, we obtain a completion rate of 51.8 percent. The other method involves a different computation of eligible households, one that we think is reasonable for our study. Here, eligible households include all completed cases; all missing documents; all published numbers for which either the screener or the questionnaire was broken off; and all those numbers for which there was no answer the entire field period, for which a language other than English or Spanish was spoken, and for which the respondent was too aged, senile, or hard of hearing to complete the interview. The unknowns and the unpublished eligibility-unknown numbers were allocated proportionately to each neighborhood, on the assumption that eligibility rates are identical within a neighborhood for published and unpublished numbers. Using this method, we obtain a completion rate of 62.9 percent. Both of these rates are in line with Groves's (1978) finding that response rates for telephone surveys generally lie between 59 and 70 percent.

Appendix B

Chicago Neighborhood Survey

-3- DECK 01

1. What is the name of your neighborhood? (PROBE: Some neighborhoods in Chicago have names such as Rogers Park or Englewood; what is the name of your neighborhood?)

(RECORD NAME VERBATIM; IF NAME MATCHES NAME ON COVER OF QUESTIONNAIRE, GO TO Q. 2)

16-17/

A. Some people have called your neighborhood (NAME ON COVER). Have you ever heard this name used to describe your neighborhood?

18/

Yes .... (GO TO Q. 2) 1
No .... (ASK B, p. 2) 2

2. In what year did you move into (NEIGHBORHOOD ON COVER)?

RECORD YEAR: 19 [ ]   (IF R MOVED IN BEFORE 1974, SKIP TO Q. 4)   19-20/

Lived here all my life (SKIP TO Q. 4) .. 85

3. I'm going to read a list of things some people think about when choosing a neighborhood to live in. Think back to when you first moved into (NAME ON COVER). How important was each of these in your decision to move into the neighborhood. First, the quality of public schools—was that very important, somewhat important, or not important? CIRCLE ONE CODE IN EACH LINE.

	Very important	Somewhat important	Not important	Don't know	
A. The quality of public schools	1	2	3	8	21/
B. The general appearance of the streets, grounds, and buildings in the area	1	2	3	8	22/
C. The reputation of the neighborhood	1	2	3	8	23/
D. The availability of convenient shopping	1	2	3	8	24/
E. The safety of the neighborhood	1	2	3	8	25/
F. The convenience of the neighborhood to place of employment	1	2	3	8	26/
G. The availability of public transportation	1	2	3	8	27/
H. The likelihood that property values will go up	1	2	3	8	28/
I. Having neighbors mostly of your own race	1	2	3	8	29/
J. Good quality housing for the money	1	2	3	8	30/

-2- DECK 01

INSTRUCTIONS FOR PERSONS NOT FAMILIAR WITH CORRECT NEIGHBORHOOD NAME (Q. 1A)

1B. IF NAME ON LABEL IS:	RESPONDENT SAYS:	READ:
1 Portage Park	Jefferson Park / Northwest Side →	(JEFFERSON PARK, etc.) is a very large area in Chicago, but—
	Anything else or no name →	We're (just) studying the area from Narragansett on the west to Cicero on the east, and from Montrose on the north to Belmont on the south. Some people have called this Portage Park, and we'd like to use this name occasionally during the interview.
2 Lincoln Park	Park West / Sheffield / Neighborhood / Old Town →	(PARK WEST, etc.) is just a part of the area we're interested in.
	Anything else or no name →	We're studying the area from Diversey Parkway on the north, to North Avenue on the south, and from Ashland Avenue to the lake. Some people have called this Lincoln Park, and we'd like to use this name occasionally during the interview.
3 Austin	Anything or no name →	We're studying the area on the far west side of Chicago which some people have called Austin. We'd like to use this name occasionally during the interview.
4 Back of the Yards	Anything or no name →	We're studying the area from 47th Street to Garfield Blvd., and from Western Avenue on the west to Halsted on the east. Some people have called this Back of the Yards, and we'd like to use this name occasionally during the interview.
5 Beverly	Anything or no name →	We're studying the area from 87th Street west of the railroad tracks to 107th Street west of the railroad tracks. Some people have called this Beverly, and we'd like to use this name occasionally during the interview.
6 Hyde Park-Kenwood	Kenwood →	Kenwood is just part of the area we're interested in.
	Anything else or no name →	We're studying the area from 47th Street to 60th Street, and from Cottage Grove on the west to the lake. Some people have called this Hyde Park-Kenwood, and we'd like to use this name occasionally during the interview.
7 South Shore	Anything or no name →	We're studying the area from 67th Street to 83rd Street, and from Stony Island to the lake. Some people have called this South Shore, and we'd like to use this name occasionally during the interview.
8 East Side	Anything or no name →	We're studying the area south and east of the Calumet River. Some people have called this East Side, and we'd like to use this name occasionally during the interview.

-4-

DECK 01

4. We'd like to know how satisfied you are right now with various things in your neighborhood. First, the quality of public schools. Are you very satisfied, somewhat satisfied, somewhat dissatisfied, or very dissatisfied? CIRCLE ONE CODE ON EACH LINE.

	Very satis- fied	Somewhat satis- fied	Somewhat dissatis- fied	Very dissatis- fied	Don't know	
A. The quality of public schools	1	2	3	4	8	31/
B. The general appearance of the streets, grounds, and buildings in the area	1	2	3	4	8	32/
C. The reputation of your neighborhood	1	2	3	4	8	33/
D. The availability of convenient shopping	1	2	3	4	8	34/
E. The way property values are going	1	2	3	4	8	35/
F. The safety of the neighborhood	1	2	3	4	8	36/
G. The convenience of the neighborhood to place of employment	1	2	3	4	8	37/
H. The availability of public transportation	1	2	3	4	8	38/
I. The racial make-up of the neighborhood	1	2	3	4	8	39/
J. The quality of housing for the money	1	2	3	4	8	40/

5. On the whole, are you very satisfied with your neighborhood, somewhat satisfied, somewhat dissatisfied, or very dissatisfied?

Very satisfied 1   41/

Somewhat satisfied 2

Somewhat dissatisfied . 3

Very dissatisfied 4

Don't know 8

-5-

DECK 01

6. How likely is it that you might move out of (NEIGHBORHOOD ON COVER) within the next year? Will you definitely move, probably move, is there a fifty-fifty chance of moving, will you probably not move, or will you definitely not move?

Definitely move 1   42/

Probably move 2

Fifty-fifty chance 3

Probably not move 4

Definitely not move 5

7. Overall, in the past two years, would you say your neighborhood has become a better place to live, has gotten worse, or is it about the same as it used to be?

Better 1   43/

Worse 2

About the same 3

Don't know 8

8. All things considered, what do you think the neighborhood will be like two years from now? Will it be a better place to live, will it have gotten worse, or will it be about the same as it is now?

Better 1   44/

Worse 2

About the same 3

Don't know 8

9. Some people feel their neighborhood is a real home to them, a place where they have roots. Other people think of their neighborhood as just a place where they happen to be living. Which one of those comes closest to the way you consider your neighborhood?

Real home 1   45/

Just place to live 2

10. Suppose a family had saved its money and was thinking about buying a house in your neighborhood. In your opinion, would they be making a good financial investment, or would they be better off investing their money in another neighborhood?

Good investment 1   46/

Better off in another neighborhood 2

Don't know 8

-6-

11. I'm going to read a list of things that are sometimes problems in neighborhoods. Please tell me if they are a big problem, somewhat of a problem, or not a problem at all to you in your neighborhood.

	Big problem (ASK A)	Somewhat problem	Not a problem	
a) Noisy neighbors; people who play loud music, have late parties, or have noisy quarrels	1	2	3	47/
b) Dogs barking loudly or relieving themselves near your home	1	2	3	57/
c) People not disposing of garbage properly or leaving litter around the area	1	2	3	67/
d) Poor maintenance of property and lawns	1	2	3	09/
e) People who say insulting things or bother people as they walk down the street	1	2	3	19/
f) Landlords who don't care about what happens to the neighborhood	1	2	3	29/
g) Purse snatching and other street crimes	1	2	3	38/
h) Presence of drugs and drug users	1	2	3	47/
i) Abandoned houses or other empty buildings	1	2	3	56/
j) Vacant lots filled with trash and junk	1	2	3	65/

-7-

DECKS 01-02

FOR EACH BIG PROBLEM MENTIONED IN Q. 11, ASK:

A. Now I'm going to read you a list of what people might do when faced with such problems. Some people take no action at all. Others may talk directly to the neighbor involved, or get together with other neighbors to try to solve the problem, or call the police, or call their alderman or precinct captain, or call a city agency, or do something else. First (READ FIRST BIG PROBLEM). Have you ever taken any action to try to solve the problem? IF YES, READ ACROSS OTHER READINGS IN ROW. CIRCLE ONE CODE FOR EACH. IF NO, GO ON TO NEXT BIG PROBLEM.

	(1) Taken any action to try to solve this problem? Yes / No	(2) Talked directly with neighbor involved Yes / No	(3) Gotten together with other neighbors to try to solve the problem Yes / No	(4) Called the police Yes / No	(5) Called your alderman or city precinct captain Yes / No	(6) Called a city agency Yes / No	(7) Taken some other action* Yes / No	
a)	1 2 48/	1 2 49/ *Other (SPECIFY)	1 2 50/	1 2 51/2	1 2 52/	1 2 53/2	1 2 54/2	55-56/
b)	1 2 58/	1 2 59/ *Other (SPECIFY)	1 2 60/	1 2 61/2	1 2 62/	1 2 63/2	1 2 64/2	65-66/
c)	1 2 68/	1 2 69/ *Other (SPECIFY)	1 2 70/	1 2 71/2	1 2 72/2 BEGIN DECK 02 .07-08/	1 2 73/2	1 2 74/2	
d)	1 2 10/	1 2 11/ *Other (SPECIFY)	1 2 12/	1 2 13/2	1 2 14/2	1 2 15/2	1 2 16/2	17-18/
e)	1 2 20/	1 2 21/ *Other (SPECIFY)	1 2 22/	1 2 23/2	1 2 24/2	1 2 25/2	1 2 26/2	27-28/
f)	1 2 30/	NOT APPLICABLE *Other (SPECIFY)	1 2 31/	1 2 32/2	1 2 33/2	1 2 34/2	1 2 35/2	36-37/
g)	1 2 39/	NOT APPLICABLE *Other (SPECIFY)	1 2 40/	1 2 41/2	1 2 42/2	1 2 43/2	1 2 44/2	45-46/
h)	1 2 48/	NOT APPLICABLE *Other (SPECIFY)	1 2 49/	1 2 50/2	1 2 51/2	1 2 52/2	1 2 53/2	54-55/
i)	1 2 57/	NOT APPLICABLE *Other (SPECIFY)	1 2 58/	1 2 59/2	1 2 60/2	1 2 61/2	1 2 62/2	63-64/
j)	1 2 66/	NOT APPLICABLE *Other (SPECIFY)	1 2 67/	1 2 68/2	1 2 69/2	1 2 70/2	1 2 71/2	72-73/

-8-

BEGIN DECK 03

12. Please tell me if the following statements about your immediate neighbors are true or false.

	True	False	Don't know	
A. If I were sick, I could count on my neighbors to shop for me at the supermarket, go to the drugstores, and so on.	1	2	8	07/
B. When I'm away from home, I can count on some of my neighbors to keep their eyes open for possible trouble.	1	2	8	08/
C. If I had to borrow about $25 for an emergency, I could turn to one of my neighbors.	1	2	8	09/
D. It's pretty easy to tell a stranger from someone who lives in my immediate neighborhood.	1	2	8	10/

13. Do you ever read a local neighborhood newspaper to learn what's happening in your neighborhood?

Yes ...(ASK A) .. 1
No 2   11/

A. IF YES: About how often? Would you say nearly every week, once every few weeks, or less often than that?

Nearly every week 1
Every few weeks 2
Less often 3   12/

14. Do any of your relatives live in (NEIGHBORHOOD ON COVER)?

Yes 1
No 2
Don't have any relatives 3   13/

15. Do any of your good friends live in (NEIGHBORHOOD ON COVER)?

Yes 1
No 2
Don't have any good friends 3   14/

-9-

DECK 03

16. Please tell me how often you usually do the following things. First, spend a social evening with relatives—do you do this once a week or more, about once a month, less than once a month, or never? REPEAT ANSWER CATEGORIES AS NECESSARY AND CIRCLE ONE CODE ON EACH LINE.

	Once a week or more	About once a month	Less than once a month	Never	Not applicable	
A. Spend a social evening with relatives	1	2	3	4	5	15/
B. Spend a social evening with one of your neighbors	1	2	3	4	5	16/
C. Spend an evening with friends who live outside of (NEIGHBORHOOD)	1	2	3	4	5	17/
D. Spend some time with the people you work with away from the job	1	2	3	4	5	18/
E. Chat with your neighbors when you run into them on the street	1	2	3	4	5	19/

17. I'd like you to tell me where you do the following things. First, grocery shopping. Do you do this usually in (NEIGHBORHOOD), or usually outside the area?

	Usually in neighborhood	Usually outside	Not applicable	
A. Grocery shopping	1	2	3	20/
B. Go to restaurants	1	2	3	21/
C. Go to religious services	1	2	3	22/
D. Do your banking	1	2	3	23/
E. Go to a doctor or other medical facility	1	2	3	24/
F. Buy clothing	1	2	3	25/
G. Take your car for repairs	1	2	3	26/

-10-   DECK 03

18. We're interested in the groups and organizations that individuals belong to. Please tell me whether or not you are a member of . . . ASK EACH ITEM. FOR EACH "YES" IN A, ASK B: Does it ever meet in your neighborhood?

	A. Belong?		IF YES IN A, ASK: B. Does it ever meet in your neighborhood?	
	Yes	No	Yes	No
1) A PTA or local school council.	1	2 27/	1	2 28/
2) Any group connected with your religion or church.	1	2 29/	1	2 30/
3) Any group of renters or homeowners.	1	2 31/	1	2 32/
4) Any other group concerned with quality of community life.	1	2 33/	1	2 34/
5) Any recreational group or club, such as a bowling league, the YMCA, or something like that.	1	2 35/	1	2 36/
6) Any ethnic or nationality group.	1	2 37/	1	2 38/
7) Any other kind of group.	1	2 39/	1	2 40/

-11-   DECK 03

19. Do you live in a house or an apartment?

        House ...... (ASK A) 1
        Apartment ... (ASK B) 2
        Other (SPECIFY AND ASK B)
        _____ 3   41/

A. IF HOUSE: (HOUSE INCLUDES DETACHED SINGLE FAMILY HOUSE, ROW HOUSE, TOWN HOUSE, DUPLEX)

   Are you an owner or a renter?

        Owner ... (GO TO Q. 20) ... 1
        Renter .. (GO TO Q. 20) ... 2   42/

B. IF APARTMENT OR OTHER:

   (1) Does your building have seven or more units?

        Yes 1
        No 2   43/

   (2) Are you an owner or a renter?

        Owner ... (ASK (a)) 1
        Renter .. (ASK (b)) 2   44/

   (a) FOR OWNERS IN APARTMENT BUILDINGS:
       Is it a condominium, or is it a cooperative, or do you own the entire building?

        Condominium 1
        Cooperative 2
        Entire building 3   45/

   (b) FOR HYDE PARK-KENWOOD RENTERS ONLY: OTHERWISE GO TO Q. 20.
       Do you live in any kind of university housing, either staff or student subsidized housing?

        Yes 1
        No 2
        Uncertain ... (ASK (c)) ... 8   46/

   (c) IF UNCERTAIN: Describe name of building or type of arrangements.

-12-   DECK 03

ASK EVERYONE:

20. In what year did you move into this (house/apartment)?

RECORD YEAR: 19 [ ]   47-48/

Lived here all my life ... 85

21. What is the total number of people who live in your household? Please count any boarders, any college students who live there at least part of the year, and anyone else who normally lives there but is away now. (Make sure you count yourself.)

RECORD NUMBER: [ ]   49-50/

NOTE: IF R OWNS SINGLE FAMILY HOME, ASK Q. 22.

IF R OWNS CONDOMINIUM, COOPERATIVE, OR APARTMENT BUILDING, GO TO Q. 23.

IF R RENTS APARTMENT, GO TO Q. 24.

IF R RENTS SINGLE FAMILY HOME, GO TO Q. 27.

IF R OWNS SINGLE FAMILY HOME:

22. In the past two years or so, have you made any improvements or any necessary repairs on your home? That is, such things as painting, a new roof, new storm windows, or adding a porch or new room.

Yes .... (ASK A) 1   51/
No 2

A. IF YES: During the past two years, have you spent less than $1,000, between $1,000 and $2,000, or more than $2,000 on these improvements or repairs?

Less than $1,000 1   52/
Between $1,000 and $2,000 .. 2
More than $2,000 3

NOW SKIP TO Q. 27

IF R OWNS CONDOMINIUM, COOPERATIVE, OR APARTMENT BUILDING:

23. In the past two years or so, have you made any improvements or any necessary repairs on your home? That is, such things as painting, new storm windows, or modernizing your kitchen?

Yes .... (ASK A) 1   53/
No 2

A. IF YES: During the past two years, have you spent less than $500, between $500 and $1,000, or more than $1,000 on these improvements or repairs?

Less than $500 1   54/
Between $500 and $1,000 2
More than $1,000 3

NOW SKIP TO Q. 27

-13-   DECK 03

IF R RENTS APARTMENT:

24. As far as you know, in the past two years or so, has your landlord made any improvements in your apartment or building? That is, such things as modernizing your kitchen or bathroom, fixing up the public spaces, or improving security?

Yes 1   55/
No 2

25. In the past two years or so, have you made any improvements in your apartment? That is, such things as refinishing floors or building a closet?

Yes 1   56/
No 2

26. Please tell me whether the following things are a big problem in your building, somewhat of a problem, or not at all a problem.

	Big problem	Somewhat problem	Not a problem	
A. The amount of heat you get in the winter	1	2	3	57/
B. Roaches, mice, or rats	1	2	3	58/
C. Bad plumbing or not enough hot water	1	2	3	59/
D. Peeling paint or loose plaster	1	2	3	60/
E. Broken windows	1	2	3	61/
F. Building security	1	2	3	62/

-15-   BEGIN DECK 04

30. Do you know of any special efforts or programs going on in your neighborhood to prevent or reduce crime?

        Yes ... (ASK A AND B) 1   07/
        No 2

IF YES:
A. What are they?
                                                        08-09/
                                                        10-11/
                                                        12-13/

B. Do you actively participate in any of these programs?

        Yes 1   14/
        No 2

31. In order to avoid crime, have you ever . . .

	Yes	No
A. avoided using public transportation	1	2	15/
B. engraved identification on valuables	1	2	16/
C. arranged to go out with someone so you wouldn't have to be alone when going somewhere in the neighborhood	1	2	17/
D. installed a burglar alarm in your home	1	2	18/
E. taken other security measures such as using timers on your lights, putting bars on windows, or adding new locks	1	2	19/
F. selected a residence because of its particular safety features	1	2	20/
G. turned down a job because of its unsafe location	1	2	21/
H. kept a watchdog	1	2	22/
I. kept a gun or other weapon at home	1	2	23/

-14-   DECK 03

ASK EVERYONE:

27. Now I'd like to ask you some questions about crime. How much crime would you say there is in your own immediate neighborhood—a lot, some, or only a little?   63/

        A lot ..... (ASK A) 1
        Some .... (GO TO Q. 28) ... 2
        Only a little(ASK A) 3
        None ...... (ASK A) 4
        (IF VOLUNTEERED) ....
        Don't know (GO TO Q. 28) ... 8

A. IF A LOT, ONLY A LITTLE, OR NONE: What do you think accounts for the fact that there is (AMOUNT OF CRIME) in your neighborhood?
                                                        64-65/
                                                        66-67/
                                                        68-69/

28. Would you say that the likelihood you will be a victim of a crime in your neighborhood during the coming year is high, moderate, or low?   70/

        High 1
        Moderate 2
        Low 3
        Don't know 8

29. How much information do you get about crime in your neighborhood from each of the following sources? First, do you get a great deal of information, some information, or no information at all about crime in your neighborhood from local neighborhood newspapers? CIRCLE ONE CODE ON EACH LINE.

	Great deal	Some	None	
A. Local community newspapers	1	2	3	71/
B. Conversations with neighbors	1	2	3	72/
C. Just keeping your eyes and ears open	1	2	3	73/
D. City newspapers, radio or television	1	2	3	74/

-16-
DECK 04

32. Is there any area right around here—that is, within a mile—where you would be afraid to walk alone at night?

Yes 1   24/

No 2

33. I'm going to read some statements people have made about crime. For each one please tell me if it's mostly true in your case or mostly false.

	Mostly true	Mostly false
A. I'm often a little worried that I will be the victim of a crime in my neighborhood.	1	2	25/
B. I would probably not be afraid if a stranger stopped me at night in my neighborhood to ask for directions.	1	2	26/
C. I'm not as afraid for my own safety as I am for the people close to me	1	2	27/
D. When I have to be away from home for a long time, I worry that someone might try to break in.	1	2	28/
E. When I hear footsteps behind me at night in my neighborhood, it makes me feel uneasy.	1	2	29/

-17-
DECK 04

34. Now I'd like to ask you about some things that might have happened to you or to members of your household since the beginning of 1978. I'd like you to think back to January 1978, about 14 months ago.

Since January 1978, did anyone break into your (house/apartment) or steal anything from inside your (house/apartment)? Even someone you knew?

Yes .... (ASK A AND B) 1

No 2   30/

IF YES:
A. Did that happen once or more than once?

Once 1

More than once 2   31/

B. Did you know the person who broke into your (house/apartment)?

Yes 1

No 2

Both 3

Don't know 8   32/

35. Since January of 1978, did anyone take money or other belongings from you or from other members of your household by force? For example, did someone use a gun or knife, or in any other way force one of you to give them something that did not belong to them? Even someone you knew?

Yes .... (ASK A, B, C, D) .. 1

No 2   33/

IF YES:
A. Did that happen to you or to someone else in your household?

Respondent 1

Someone else 2

Both 3   34/

B. Did that happen once or more than once?

Once 1

More than once 2   35/

C. Did that happen in (NEIGHBORHOOD) or elsewhere?

In neighborhood 1

Elsewhere 2

Both 3

Don't know 8   36/

D. Did you/they know the person who robbed you/them?

Yes 1

No 2

Both 3

Don't know 8   37/

-18-   DECK 04

36. Other than what has been mentioned, has anyone stolen anything else from you or someone in your household during the time since January, 1978? Perhaps a bicycle, clothing, tools, wallet, money, or anything else?

    Yes .. (ASK A, B, C, D) 1   38/
    No 2

    IF YES:
    A. Did that happen to you or to someone else in your household?   39/
       Respondent 1
       Someone else 2
       Both 3

    B. Did that happen once or more than once?   40/
       Once 1
       More than once 2

    C. Did that happen in (NEIGHBORHOOD) or elsewhere?   41/
       In neighborhood 1
       Elsewhere 2
       Both 3
       Don't know 8

    D. Did you/they know the person who stole these things?   42/
       Yes 1
       No 2
       Both 3
       Don't know 8

37. Since January, 1978, has anyone damaged or defaced the building you live in, for example, by writing on the walls, breaking windows, setting fires, or anything like that?

    Yes .... (ASK A AND B) 1   43/
    No 2

    IF YES:
    A. Did that happen once or more than once?   44/
       Once 1
       More than once 2

    B. Did you know the person who damaged your building?   45/
       Yes 1
       No 2
       Both 3
       Don't know 8

-19-   DECK 04

38. Since January of 1978, was anyone in your household the victim of a rape or sexual assault, even by someone she knew?

    Yes ...(ASK A, B, C, D) 1   46/
    No 2

    IF YES:
    A. ASK FEMALE ONLY; MALE GO TO B.
       Were you the victim, or was it another member of your household?   47/
       Respondent 1
       Someone else 2
       Both 3

    B. Sometimes people are the victim of the same crime more than once during a year. Did that happen once or more than once?   48/
       Once 1
       More than once 2

    C. Did that happen in (NEIGHBORHOOD) or elsewhere?   49/
       In neighborhood 1
       Elsewhere 2
       Both 3
       Don't know 8

    D. Was the attacker someone you/she knew?   50/
       Yes 1
       No 2
       Both 3
       Don't know 8

-20-   DECK 04

ASK EVERYONE:

39. Other than what you have already mentioned, since January, 1978, did anyone, including someone you knew, use violence against you or members of your household in an argument or quarrel, or in any other way attack or assault one of you?

Yes .. (ASK A, B, C, D) ... 1   51/
No ... 2

IF YES:

A. Did that happen to you or to someone else in your household?

Respondent ... 1   52/
Someone else ... 2
Both ... 3

B. Did that happen once or more than once?

Once ... 1   53/
More than once ... 2

C. Did that happen in (NEIGHBORHOOD) or elsewhere?

In neighborhood ... 1   54/
Elsewhere ... 2
Both ... 3
Don't know ... 8

D. Was the attacker someone you/they knew?

Yes ... 1   55/
No ... 2
Both ... 3
Don't know ... 8

IF VOLUNTEERED THAT VICTIM WAS KILLED, CHECK HERE ..... [ ]   56/

-21-   DECK 04

40. Now I have just a few questions about yourself. First, in what year were you born?   57-58/

41. What is your religion--is it Protestant, Catholic, Jewish, Muslim, some other religion, or no religion?

Protestant ... 01   59-60/
Catholic ... 02
Jewish ... 03
Muslim ... 04
None ... 05
Other (SPECIFY RELIGION AND/OR CHURCH AND DENOMINATION) ... 06

42. For statistical purposes, we would like to know what racial group you belong to. Are you black, white, hispanic, or something else?

Black ... 1   61/
White .... (ASK A) ... 2
Hispanic ... 3
Other (SPECIFY) _____ 4
Refused ... 7
Don't know ... 8

A. IF WHITE:
What is your ethnic background? For example, is it Irish, Italian, Polish, or what?

Polish ... 01   62-63/
Italian ... 02
Irish ... 03
German ... 04
Other or more than one _____ 05
(RECORD)
None ... 06

-22-   DECK 04

43. What is the highest regular school certificate, diploma, or degree that you have gotten?

64-65/

None ever 01
8th grade; Jr. high 02
High school diploma; GED 03
A.A.; Junior College 04
B. A. or B. S. 05
Masters 06
Ph.D. 07
Degree in law or medicine ... 08
Other (SPECIFY) _____ 09

44. Last week were you working full time, part time, keeping house, or what?
CIRCLE ONE CODE ONLY. IF MORE THAN ONE RESPONSE, GIVE PREFERENCE TO SMALLEST CODE NUMBER THAT APPLIES AND RECORD OTHER RESPONSES VERBATIM.

66-67/

Working full time (35 hours or more) .. 01
Working part time (1-34 hours) 02
With a job, but not at work because of illness, vacation, strike .. (ASK A) . 03
Unemployed, laid off, looking for work .... (ASK A) . 04
Retired 05
In school only .... (SKIP TO Q. 46) 06
Keeping house only (SKIP TO Q. 46) 07
Other (SPECIFY) _____ 08

A. IF NOT WORKING AT PRESENT:
When you do work, is that usually full time or part time?

68/

Full time 1
Part time 2
Varies 3

-23-   DECKS 04-05

45. A. What kind of work do you (did you normally) do? That is, what is (was) your job called? IF MORE THAN ONE JOB, ASK ABOUT MAIN JOB HERE.

OCCUPATION: _____ 69-73/

IF NECESSARY, ASK: What are (were) some of your main duties? What do (did) you actually do in that job?

B. Where is your (main) place of work? Is it in (NEIGHBORHOOD), downtown Chicago, elsewhere in Chicago, in the suburbs, or where?

74/

(NEIGHBORHOOD) 1
Downtown Chicago 2
Elsewhere in Chicago 3
Suburbs 4
Other (SPECIFY) _____ 5

BEGIN DECK 05

ASK EVERYONE

46. What is your current marital status? Are you married, living with someone, widowed, divorced, separated, or have you never been married?

07/

Married 1
Living with someone 2
Widowed 3
Divorced 4   SKIP
Separated 5   TO
Never been married. 6   Q.50

-25-   DECK 05

49. A. What kind of work does he/she (did he/she normally) do? That is, what is (was) his/her job called? IF MORE THAN ONE JOB, ASK ABOUT MAIN JOB HERE.

OCCUPATION: _____   13-17/

IF NECESSARY, ASK: What are (were) some of his/her main duties? What does (did) he/she actually do in that job?

B. Where is his/her (main) place of work? Is it in (NEIGHBORHOOD), downtown Chicago, elsewhere in Chicago, in the suburbs, or where?

(NEIGHBORHOOD) 1   18/
Downtown Chicago 2
Elsewhere in Chicago 3
Suburbs 4
Other (SPECIFY) _____ 5

-24-   DECK 05

47. What is the highest regular school certificate, diploma, or degree that your husband/wife (or the person you're living with) has ever gotten?   08-09/

None ever 01
8th grade; Jr. high 02
High school diploma; GED 03
A.A.; Junior college 04
B.A. or B.S. 05
Masters 06
Ph.D. 07
Degree in law or medicine 08
Other (SPECIFY) _____ 09

48. Last week was he/she working full time, part time, keeping house, or what? CIRCLE ONE CODE ONLY. IF MORE THAN ONE RESPONSE, GIVE PREFERENCE TO SMALLEST CODE NUMBER THAT APPLIES AND RECORD OTHER RESPONSES VERBATIM.   10-11/

Working full time - (35 hours or more) .. 01
Working part time - (1-34 hours) 02
With a job, but not at work because of illness, vacation, strike .. (ASK A) .. 03
Unemployed, laid off, looking for work .... (ASK A) .. 04
Retired 05
In school only .... (SKIP TO Q. 50) .. 06
Keeping house only - (SKIP TO Q. 50) 07
Other (SPECIFY) _____ 08

A. IF NOT WORKING AT PRESENT:
When he/she does work, is that usually full time or part time?   12/

Full time 1
Part time 2
Varies 3

-26-   DECK 05

ASK EVERYONE:
50. Do you have any children under 19 living at home with you? This includes adopted
    children, foster children, and children from a previous marriage.

                                    Yes ..... (ASK A) 1
                                    No .... (SKIP TO Q. 56) ... 2   19/

A. IF YES: I'm interested in the ages of your children and where they go to school.
            First, how old is the oldest child living at home with you?
            (RECORD AGE. IF 5 YEARS OF AGE OR OLDER, ASK B. CONTINUE FOR
            REMAINING CHILDREN.)

    A.   IF 5 YEARS OF AGE OR OLDER, ASK:
    Age of child   B. What is the name of the school this child attends?
    (IF 5 YEARS OF AGE
    OR OLDER, ASK B)

    1. _____ 20-21/ 1.   22-24/
    2. _____ 25-26/ 2.   27-29/
    3. _____ 30-31/ 3.   32-34/
    4. _____ 35-36/ 4.   37-39/
    5. _____ 40-41/ 5.   42-44/
    6. _____ 45-46/ 6.   47-49/
    7. _____ 50-51/ 7.   52-54/
    8. _____ 55-56/ 8.   57-59/

    IF MORE THAN EIGHT CHILDREN, ENTER # OF ADDITIONAL CHILDREN [   ]   60/

            IF NO CHILDREN 5 YEARS OF AGE OR OLDER, SKIP TO Q. 56

C. I'm going to read a list of statements that apply to some families with school
   age children. Please tell me if each statement is mostly true or mostly false
   in your family.

	Mostly true	Mostly false	Not applicable
1) My children are not allowed to watch television until their homework is done on school nights.	1	2	3	61/
2) There are certain areas in the neighborhood where my children are not allowed to walk.	1	2	3	62/
3) I worry about my children's safety at school.	1	2	3	63/
4) My children are allowed to go to the park without adult supervision.	1	2	3	64/
5) My children stay up as late as they want to on weekends.	1	2	3	65/
6) I know the parents of most of my children's friends.	1	2	3	66/
7) I worry about my children getting involved in gangs.	1	2	3	67/
8) It frightens me when my children are late getting home and don't call me.	1	2	3	68/

-27-   DECKS 05-06

51. Have you heard about the Access to Excellence program in the city of Chicago?

                                    Yes 1
                                    No .. (SKIP TO Q. 56) .. 2   69/

52. Is your child (are any of your children) in an Access to Excellence program?

                                    Yes ..... (ASK A) 1
                                    No .... (SKIP TO Q. 56) .. 2   70/

    A. IF YES: What program is that? CIRCLE APPROPRIATE CODES.

        Preschool program 01   71-72/
        Basic skills program 02   73-74/

                                                           BEGIN DECK 06
        Classical schools 03   07-08/
        Elementary School Language Center 04   09-10/
        Centers for Languages 05   11-12/
        High School Bilingual Center 06   13-14/
        High School Performing and Creative
            Arts Centers 07   15-16/
        Career Development Centers 08   17-18/
        Technical Centers—High Schools 09   19-20/
        City-wide Permissive Enrollment 10   21-22/
        District selected programs 11   23-24/
        Advanced placement 12   25-26/
        Von Humboldt Child Parent Center 13   27-28/
        Other (SPECIFY)

        _____   14   29-30/

        Don't know 98   31-32/

53. How satisfied are you with the Access to Excellence program? Are you very satis-
    fied, somewhat satisfied, somewhat dissatisfied, or very dissatisfied?

        Very satisfied 1   33/
        Somewhat satisfied 2
        Somewhat dissatisfied 3
        Very dissatisfied 4
        Don't know 8

-28- DECK 06

54. Here are some ways the Access to Excellence program might affect your child/children. First, in helping your child to learn more quickly--is the program having a great effect, a moderate effect, hardly any effect, or no effect at all?

	Great	Moderate	Hardly any	None	Don't know	
A. Helping your child to learn more quickly	1	2	3	4	8	34/
B. Helping your child to understand students of other cultural backgrounds	1	2	3	4	8	35/
C. Helping your child to learn to work with other races	1	2	3	4	8	36/
D. Allowing you to play a more active role in school	1	2	3	4	8	37/
E. Preparing your child for a future occupation	1	2	3	4	8	38/
F. Improving your child's speaking ability	1	2	3	4	8	39/

55. Last year, did (your child/all your children) attend the same school(s) they do now?

Yes ... (GO TO Q. 56) ... 1
No .... (ASK A) 2   40/

A. IF DIFFERENT SCHOOLS, ASK FOR EACH:
I'd like to know what schools they attended. First, (the child/the oldest child) who goes to (NAME OF SCHOOL IN Q. 50) went to what school last year? (GO DOWN THE LIST)

1. Child/oldest child in Q. 50   (RECORD SCHOOL ATTENDED LAST YEAR)   41-43/

2. Second oldest in Q. 50   (RECORD SCHOOL ATTENDED LAST YEAR)   44-46/

3. Third oldest in Q. 50   (RECORD SCHOOL ATTENDED LAST YEAR)   47-49/

4. Fourth oldest in Q. 50   (RECORD SCHOOL ATTENDED LAST YEAR)   50-52/

-29- DECK 06

ASK EVERYONE:
56. Please tell me which category represents your family's total income before taxes and other deductions during 1978. (INCLUDE ALL SOURCES) Was it less than $10,000, between $10,000 and $30,000, or was it $30,000 or more?
IF EXACTLY $10,000, CIRCLE 20 AND 21; IF EXACTLY $30,000, CIRCLE 30 and 31.

A. Less than $10,000 10   53-54/
   Was it between $5,000 and $10,000?
      Yes 11
      No 12
      Refused 17
B. Between $10,000 and $30,000 20
   Was it between $10,000 and $20,000?
      Yes 21
      No 22
      Refused 27
C. $30,000 or more 30
   Was it between $30,000 and $40,000?
      Yes 31
      No 32
      Refused 37
D. Refused 97

57. I am now going to read a number of statements dealing with beliefs and feelings. Would you tell me whether you agree strongly, agree somewhat, disagree somewhat, or disagree strongly with each of these statements?

	Strongly agree	Agree somewhat	Disagree somewhat	Strongly disagree	Don't know	
A. Everytime I try to get ahead something or somebody stops me.	1	2	3	4	8	55/
B. Everything changes so quickly these days that I often have trouble deciding which are the right rules.	1	2	3	4	8	56/
C. Planning only makes a person unhappy, since plans hardly ever work out anyway.	1	2	3	4	8	57/
D. On the whole, I am satisfied with myself.	1	2	3	4	8	58/
E. People were better off in the old days when everyone knew just how he was expected to act.	1	2	3	4	8	59/

-31- DECK 06

61. Thinking about the races of the people who live in (NEIGHBORHOOD)--that is, whether they're black, white, or hispanic--would you say the racial composition is pretty stable or would you say the racial composition is changing?

Stable 1
Changing 2
Don't know 8   67/

Thank you very much for your help. I just have one more question we have to ask for statistical purposes.

62. Please tell me, are there any other telephones in your household that have a different phone number than this one?

Yes ..... (ASK A AND B) ... 1
No 2   68/

IF YES:
A. How many different numbers are there?

One 1
More than one 2   69/

B. What is that/are those number(s)?

_____
_____
_____

63. DATE OF INTERVIEW

Month: February 2
       March 3
       April 4   70/

Day: [ ]   71-72/

64. INTERVIEWER ID NUMBER   [ ]   73-74/

-30- DECK 06

58. in general, do you favor or oppose the busing of school children from one district to another to achieve racial balance?

Favor 1
Oppose .. (SKIP TO Q. 60) . 2
Don't know 8   60/

59. Would you yourself favor or oppose the busing of your children to achieve racial balance?

Favor 1
Oppose 2
Don't know 8   61/

60. I am going to read some statements that people have made about what happens when a few black families move into an all white neighborhood. For each statement, please tell me if you think it's mostly true or mostly false.

	Mostly true	Mostly false	Don't know	
A. When a few black families move into an all white neighborhood, they usually have the same income and education as the people who live there.	1	2	8	62/
B. When a few black families move into an all white neighborhood, realtors urge the people who live there to move,	1	2	8	63/
C. When a few black families move into an all white neighborhood, the black families are often harrassed and attacked.	1	2	8	64/
D. When a few black families move into an all white neighborhood, crime rates usually go up.	1	2	8	65/
E. When a few black families move into an all white neighborhood, property values are sure to go down.	1	2	8	66/

Appendix C

Shopping Strip Quality Rating Instrument;

Housing and Neighborhood Appearance Rating Instrument

SHOPPING STRIP QUALITY RATING INSTRUMENT

COMPUTER CODE	FIELD CODE	BUSINESS TYPE
		FINANCIAL:
11	F1	BANKS AND SAVINGS AND LOANS
12	F2	CURRENCY EXCHANGES
13	F3	FINANCE COMPANIES (HFC, other companies)
		CHAIN STORES:
21	C1	CHAIN FOOD STORES (A&P, Jewel, etc.), i.e. supermarkets
22	C2	OTHER CHAIN STORES (Ace Hardware, Wickes Furniture, Carpetland, Zayre, Community, Woolworth's, Walgreen's, Osco, Hallmark, Casual Corner, etc.) LIST IF IN DOUBT.
23	C3	DEPARTMENT STORES (Marshall Field, Wieboldt's, Goldblatt's, Sears, Penney's) LIST ALL OTHERS.
		AUTOMOTIVE:
31	A1	GAS/REPAIR/MOTORCYCLES
32	A2	CAR SALES
		RECREATION:
41	R1	LIQUOR STORES/BARS/COCKTAIL LOUNGES
42	R2	RESTAURANTS (sit-down)
43	R3	CHAIN RESTAURANTS (McDonald's, Arthur Treacher's, Pizza Hut)
44	R4	TAKE-OUTS (with little or no room to eat in store)
45	R5	OTHER RECREATION (theaters, bowling alleys, etc.) Also VFW, Eagles, Posts.
		OTHER STORES:
51	S1	NON-CHAIN FOOD STORES (bakeries, Mom & Pop, fish markets, produce, etc.)
52	S2	SERVICES (shoe repair, cleaners, appliance repair, tailors, barbers, beauticians, photography studios, sign painters, printers, travel agencies, newspaper distribution centers, caterers, aluminum siding, business machine sales and service)
53	S3	RETAIL I (clothing, shoes, jewelry, sporting goods, office supplies, florists, non-porno books, pets, camera shops, coin shops, drug stores, art galleries)
54	S4	RETAIL II (non-chain card shops, records, "head" stores, wigs, souvenirs, non-chain trinkets) LIST IF IN DOUBT.
61	U1	USED CLOTHING, SECOND-HAND STORES, PAWNSHOPS
62	U2	UNDESIRABLES (porno shops, reader-adviser, massage parlors, coin amusements)

CODE SHEET
SHOPPING STRIP QUALITY RATING INSTRUMENT

Street Name _____ Block _____

Time and Date _____

DETERIORATION

STORE CODE	BURGLAR BARS	BROK. WINDW. DOORS	GRAF.	LITTER	CANS/BOTTLES	STOREFRONT SIZE 2-3	STOREFRONT SIZE 4+	STORE REHAB	FOR. LANG.
1.									
2.									
3.									
4.									
5.									
6.									
7.									
8.									
9.									
10.									
11.									
12.									
13.									
14.									
15.									
16.									
17.									
18.									
19.									
20.									

COMMENTS - BLOCK CHARACTERISTICS

Number of times questioned _____

Special image features (list) _____

Sidewalk/Store integration (list) _____

Comments on people _____

Other Comments:

COMPUTER CODE	FIELD CODE	BUSINESS TYPE
		OTHER LAND USE:
71	01	PUBLIC (Post Office, Board of Education public schools, ward offices, welfare agencies, public clinics)
72	02	PROFESSIONAL/OFFICE (medical/dental/optical, clinics if private, legal offices, accountants, insurance, real estate, vocational/dance/driving schools, contractors, union headquarters, funeral homes)
73	03	CHURCH (include parochial schools)
74	04	STOREFRONT CHURCHES
75	05	FACTORY/WAREHOUSE/WHOLESALE DISTRIBUTORS
76	06	PRIVATE DWELLING
77	07	STOREFRONT DWELLING (storefront converted to private dwelling on 1st floor)
78	08	VACANT BUILDING
79	09	OTHER (list)
		LAND:
81	L1	ALLEYS
82	L2	VACANT LOT (unpaved)
83	L3	PARKING LOT/GARAGE (paved or graveled)
84	L4	PARK/PLAYLOT
85	L5	SIDE YARDS TO DWELLINGS
99	99	UNKNOWN

CODING POINTS

BURGLAR BARS (do not include silver alarm tape)

BROKEN/BOARDED WINDOWS OR DOORS, BROKEN OR CARDBOARD SIGNS (identifying the store)

LITTER: More than 6 pieces of litter on street and sidewalk in front of store, or at least 2 pieces, one of which is larger than a newspaper.

LIQUOR BOTTLES OR CANS (may be broken or crushed) COUNT IF IN GUTTER, TOO!

SPECIAL IMAGE FEATURES: Special decorative lights, sidewalks, landscaping/trees the whole block or major part of it; central square in middle of street, uniform exterior decoration/lack of extending signs; block is part of a shopping mall.

SIDEWALK/STORE INTEGRATION: Outside stands, racks; open doors

Count private dwelling only if living space on ground floor or if entry takes up space to an entire storefront.

Do not count parking lots behind stores or those in front of supermarkets. Count only if the parking lot is between stores.

Include the 2 blocks contiguous (ending) to each end of the shopping strip--even if less than 75% business.

Count the one store on side streets.

Don't count back and side yards of houses on side streets as to litter and graffiti, but do count the distance in determining if the block is more than 75% business.

Don't count the side of corner businesses for litter and graffiti unless the business district extends up that side street for at least one more store.

HOUSING AND NEIGHBORHOOD APPEARANCE RATING INSTRUMENT: KEY

A. TYPE OF STRUCTURE

1. LAND USE
   1 = Single-family home, either attached or detached (D)
   2 = 2-6 flat (F)
   3 = Multiple-unit dwelling of more than 6 units (MUD)
   4 = Vacant lot
   5 = Park/playlot/garden
   6 = Store/store with apartments above
   7 = School
   8 = Church
   9 = Office, public/professional/private; institutions (e.g. hospital)
   10 = Industrial/warehouse/factory
   11 = Parking lot (paved)
   12 = Building facing other street (do not rate further)
   13 = Side yard, back yard, other yard (rate condition of grounds items)
   14 = Alley, private street (rate for litter only; code under "Parkway")
   15 = Gas station/other automotive
   20 = Other (list on back)
   97 = Not ascertained/not visible

NOTE: For all remaining items, code 7 if feature is not present or not visible.

2. FRONT WALL MATERIAL
   1 = Brick or stone
   2 = Siding, shingles, or stucco
   3 = Mixture of 1 and 2
   4 = Concrete
   5 = Other (list on back)

3. REHABILITATION
   1 = Building permit is visible or there is other evidence of work being done on property, including the presence of workmen, ladders, or stacks of building materials. Do not code routine yard work.

4. ABANDONMENT
   1 = Building is boarded up, burned out, partially demolished, has an FBI sign, or has all windows broken out.

B. CONDITION OF STRUCTURE

1. ROOF
   1 = Missing material 1 foot in any direction

2. FACADE
   1 = Absent or peeling paint or flaking stucco over 25% of an area
   One patch missing material 6" by 6" or 1 foot in any direction
   Three patches missing material 3" by 3" or 6" in any direction
   Misalignment of balconies

3. WINDOW TRIM
   1 = Absent or peeling paint on 25% of windows
   Chunk of window sill or window ornamentation missing - 6" by 6"
   Shutter or awning missing or broken - collapsed, hanging, misaligned

4. WINDOW GLASS
   1 = For D, one pane broken or boarded up
   For F/MUD, 25% of panes broken or boarded up

5. INSIDE WINDOWS
   1 = For D, one window makeshift covered or 50% of windows bare
   For F, one flat's windows makeshift covered or 50% of windows bare
   For MUD, 50% of windows makeshift covered or bare

6. ENTRYWAY
   1 = Absent or peeling paint over 25% of an area
   Broken or missing steps
   Chunk of missing material 6" by 6"
   Misalignment of porch
   Broken railings or awnings
   Broken door

7. PATHWAYS
   1 = Chunk of concrete missing 1 foot in any direction
   Grass or weeds growing 10" or higher between segments

8. JERRY-BUILT REPAIRS
   1 = Sloppy or nonmatched repair, 1 foot in any direction

C. CONDITION OF GROUNDS

1. NEGLECT
   1 = Grass or weeds 10" high over 25% of area
   Bare spot over 25% of area

2. LANDSCAPING AND DECORATION
   1 = Cleared beds with flowers, plants, pieces of bark, or colored pebbles
   Flower boxes or planters with intentional plants
   Pruned bushes showing design in placement (see specs)
   Lawn ornaments such as statues or birdbaths

3. LITTER ON LAWN
   1 = 3-6 pieces of size 2" by 2"
   2 = 7 or more pieces 2" by 2"

4. CANS ON LAWN
   1 = 1 beer can or liquor bottle

5. LARGE LITTER ON LAWN
   1 = 1 abandoned large object

6. LITTER ON PARKWAY
   1 = 3-6 pieces of size 2" by 2"
   2 = 7 or more pieces 2" by 2"

HOUSING AND NEIGHBORHOOD APPEARANCE RATING INSTRUMENT

CODING SPECIFICATIONS

A. TYPE OF STRUCTURE

1. LAND USE

Single-family homes which are attached, such as row houses and townhouses, should be scored separately for each dwelling unit. If it is ambiguous whether townhouses are owned or rented, and especially if they are arranged around a private courtyard, code as either F (single-family) or MID (multiple-unit dwelling), according to number of units.

Two-six flat--includes two-story houses designed for occupancy by two families, as are common in Back of the Yards.

Multiple-unit dwelling--includes the type of building, whether arranged around a courtyard or parallel to the street, which has different entrances but a continuous physical structure. Rate this type of building as one unit unless there is a strong probability that the structure is joining several different buildings; in that case, rate each separately.

Vacant lot--includes only lots serving no established purpose. Unpaved lots used for parking are included here. Vacant lots should be rated on large litter and parkway items ONLY.

Land uses 5-20 should be rated on whichever instrument items apply. Be sure to code 7 for any items which do not apply.

Code 12 when a building facing another street abuts the street.

Side yard--includes yards of buildings facing another street and yards which do not clearly belong to any particular structure. Side yards which do belong to a particular structure should be considered along with the rest of its grounds.

2. FRONT WALL MATERIAL

In determining the composition of the front exterior wall, exclude entryways, foundations, eaves, window trims. If the structure is clearly 75% category 1 or 75% category 2, code as such. Mixture of 1 and 2 (category 3) means less than 75% of each material.

3. REHABILITATION

This item is intended to pick up ongoing maintenance and rehabilitation activity. If it is ambiguous whether work is ongoing or not, score the building for rehabilitation and make a

---

7. CANS ON PARKWAY AND IN GUTTER
   1 = 1 beer can or liquor bottle

8. LARGE LITTER ON PARKWAY AND IN GUTTER
   1 = 1 abandoned large object

D. BLOCK-LEVEL CHARACTERISTICS

Record anything unusual or noteworthy at the bottom of the coding sheet, particularly in regard to the following items:

1. Physical characteristics - distinctive topography, housing stock, or ornamentation

2. Social characteristics - presence of block-club signs, unusual kinds or levels of activity

3. Impressions - record any unusual questions, reactions, or happenings; note if rater's subjective impressions of block appearance do not seem to correspond to its rating

note on the back of the exact address to permit checking later. Do not score for rehab if someone is removing dirt (washing windows, sweeping steps, etc.), although sandblasting would count. Do not score large litter if it is clearly rehab-related.

4. ABANDONMENT

Do not code MUDs with some occupants remaining or buildings that are being reclaimed and undergoing rehabilitation. Do not rate abandoned buildings on any succeeding items--except parkway items.

B. CONDITION OF STRUCTURE

There are eight components to this item. Because our interest is in appearance, the general coding criterion is to code what you can see. This does not mean craning, peering under bushes, etc., to capture each and every little defect; rather, the method of looking should generally be that of the "sweeping glance." The size, proportion, and number guidelines that have been provided should generally be considered the lower limits of what to code--we don't want a single bullet hole, for example, even if some of you eagle-eyes can spot it. Similarly, if you have to spend more than a few seconds deciding whether an item is big enough to count, it isn't; and if you find only one borderline flaw with one part of a building feature, don't count it. Exceptions to and clarifications of these general instructions will be provided in the specs for the individual items.

1. ROOF

Rate the main roof of the building if any part of it is visible. Do not consider the porch roof here unless it is an extension of the main roof.

2. FACADE

Facade is the front exterior wall(s) of the building parallel to the public sidewalk. The facade includes the soffits of the roof and that portion of the exterior wall which forms the back of the porch. The facade also includes balconies which are not part of the entryway. The facade does not include roofs, windows, entryways, or foundations.

Absent or peeling paint means paint which is damaged such that the material underneath is visible over 25% of the affected portion of the facade.

Missing material includes both the outer wall covering material and the ornamentation frequently found on brick or stone Fs and MUDs. Do not, however, include ornamentation around windows and doors--these will be picked up later. The material may be completely missing or deeply eroded.

Misalignment means obvious crookedness, sloping, or sagging--one end is 1 foot higher than the other or sagging in the middle so as to form a U-shape.

3. WINDOW TRIM

A window is affected by peeling paint if the material underneath is visible along one whole side of the window. Do not consider basement windows.

4. WINDOW GLASS

Do not consider basement windows. Broken means that a piece of glass larger than a bullet hole is missing. Do not count windows that are cracked, taped, or covered with plastic unless missing glass is visible.

5. INSIDE WINDOWS

Do not consider basement, attic, and sunporch windows. Makeshift covered means covered inside with newspaper, a torn sheet, etc. Bare means no curtain, shade, blind, plants, etc., are visible. This item is intended to pick up vacancy or lack of concern about appearance. If a structure, particularly a house, technically qualifies to be scored on this item while it clearly does not indicate vacancy or lack of concern, do not count.

6. ENTRYWAY

Entryway means all building parts which one must cross over and/or pass through to get from the path to the inside of the building and which, taken together, form a whole. Thus, an entryway may include a porch, stoop, or landing; have stairs; or consist simply of a door. Include porch ceiling and roof unless it is an extension of the main roof--then rate under "Roof." Rate any portion of the entryway visible from the sidewalk, even if it is on the side of the building.

Missing material can be any type of material--roof shingles, concrete from the landing, wood from a wall, etc. Exception: do not code missing material for steps unless a whole step is broken or missing. Do not code missing material for removable items such as porch furniture--code only for permanent building parts.

Misalignment is as defined above for facade. Count severely rippled or wavy porch roofs as misaligned.

Broken door includes broken door frame and broken glass in or next to the door.

7. PATHWAYS

Pathways are those portions of the concrete walkway(s) leading from the public sidewalk up to the building. Rate walkways leading to the back and driveways only if the building has no walkway up to its main entrance.

Missing concrete may be completely absent or deeply eroded.

8. JERRY-BUILT REPAIRS

Sloppy repairs includes smeared cement as a consequence of bad tuckpointing, etc. Nonmatched repairs includes red bricks on a yellow building, etc. Count only mismatching where approximate matching would have been feasible—not, for example, slight differences in color of bricks. Do not count repairs using appropriate materials which are neat but unpainted.

C. CONDITION OF GROUNDS

For items 1-5, rate the area from the inner edge of the public sidewalk to the structure. Item 6 is to be rated for the area from the inner edge of the sidewalk to the curb; for items 7 and 8, include the gutter also. If the property is bounded by a hedge or a fence, count litter outside it with the parkway and consider only the area inside the hedge or fence as the lawn. For MDUs with just a small concrete apron between the structure and the public sidewalk, record a 7 for neglect and count litter on the apron with the parkway.

1. NEGLECT

Do not count cleared areas of beds as bare spots.

2. LANDSCAPING AND DECORATION

Do not consider the parkway on this item. Do not count beds overgrown with weeds or flowers growing randomly. Do not count bushes along the foundation of the structure unless they are set off by bricks, stones, etc. Do not count privet hedges if they are the only items present; but other species of hedge and individual bushes in beds count. Do not count vegetable gardens. Because buildings without lawns still have the opportunity to score on this item, it should never be coded as 7 under normal circumstances.

3. LITTER ON LAWN

Be sure to include large refuse like newspapers, paper bags, etc., and cans in the count of pieces of litter.

4. LARGE LITTER

Large litter includes noncombustible items like mattresses, refrigerators, tires, furniture, and abandoned cars, which can be recognized by missing license plates, two or more flat or missing tires, two or more tickets. Do not count large litter which is rehab-related.

D. BLOCK-LEVEL CHARACTERISTICS

1. PHYSICAL CHARACTERISTICS

Distinctive topography includes such facts as that the block is a cul-de-sac, abuts railroad tracks, is located atop a hill, etc.

Distinctive housing stock means that the buildings differ from those of adjacent areas in their age, material, or architectural style, e.g., a block of Victorian mansions amidst two-flats.

Distinctive ornamentation includes items like brick sidewalks, identical light fixtures, bright paint, trendy large house numbers, etc., which are common to or prevalent on the whole block.

2. SOCIAL CHARACTERISTICS

Record the text of block-club signs (name of block club and rules of the block).

Unusual kinds or levels of activity includes numbers of people loitering, sitting on stoops, working on lawns, leaning out windows, children playing in the street, etc.

3. IMPRESSIONS

Raters should note if they feel eyes staring at them from behind windows, even if no one appears to question them.

_____ (street) _____ (block) _____ (side) _____   1-16/ _____

_____ (day) _____ (month/date) _____ (time) _____ (# questions)   17-25/ _____

26-7	TYPE OF STRUCTURE				CONDITION OF STRUCTURE								CONDITION OF GROUNDS							
	Land Use	Wall	Rehab	Aban	Roof	Fac	Window Trim	Window Glass	Ins Window	Entry	Paths	Jerry Built	Neglect	Land-scape	Lawn: Litter	Cans	Large	Parkway: Litter	Cans	Large
	28-9	30	31	32	33	34	35	36	37	38	39	40	41	42	43	44	45	46	47	48
01																				
02																				
03																				
04																				
05																				
06																				
07																				
08																				
09																				
10																				
11																				
12																				
13																				
14																				
15																				
16																				
17																				
18																				
19																				
20																				

-2-

26-7	TYPE OF STRUCTURE				CONDITION OF STRUCTURE								CONDITION OF GROUNDS							
	Land Use	Wall	Rehab	Aban	Roof	Fac	Window Trim	Window Glass	Ins Window	Entry	Paths	Jerry Built	Neglect	Land-scape	Lawn: Litter	Cans	Large	Parkway: Litter	Cans	Large
	28-9	30	31	32	33	34	35	36	37	38	39	40	41	42	43	44	45	46	47	48
21																				
22																				
23																				
24																				
25																				
26																				
27																				
28																				
29																				
30																				
31																				
32																				
33																				
34																				
35																				
36																				
37																				
38																				
39																				
40																				

Appendix D

Demographics by Race

Back of the Yards and Austin, tables D.1–D.6

Beverly, Hyde Park–Kenwood, and Lincoln Park, tables D.7–D.12

Table D.1 Type of Dwelling Unit, by Race—Back of the Yards and Austin (percentage)

	House	Apartment
Back of the Yards		
White	47.0	53.0
Black	50.6	49.4
Hispanic	35.8	64.2
Austin		
White	53.4	46.6
Black	25.9	74.1

Table D.2 Ownership Status, by Race—Back of the Yards and Austin (percentage)

	Owner	Renter
Back of the Yards		
White	42.3	57.7
Black	49.4	50.6
Hispanic	30.3	69.7
Austin		
White	58.9	41.1
Black	29.3	70.7

Table D.3 Respondents' Occupation, by Race—Back of the Yards and Austin (percentage)

	Professional-Technical	Managers-Administrators	Clerical-Sales	Craftsmen	Operatives	Laborers	Service Workers
Back of the Yards							
White	13.1	4.9	38.5	13.9	11.5	9.0	9.0
Black	15.7	3.9	25.5	5.9	9.8	13.7	25.5
Hispanic	3.9	3.9	10.5	17.1	30.3	28.9	5.3
Austin							
White	23.8	9.5	26.2	9.5	2.4	9.5	19.0
Black	12.3	8.0	25.7	11.8	16.6	8.0	17.6

Table D.4 Educational Attainment, by Race—Back of the Yards and Austin (percentage)

	Less than High School	High School	More than High School
Back of the Yards			
White	37.4	55.6	7.0
Black	32.9	52.4	14.6
Hispanic	60.5	36.7	2.8
Austin			
White	21.6	58.1	20.3
Black	30.2	54.4	15.4

Table D.5 Total Family Income during 1978, by Race—Back of the Yards and Austin (percentage)

	$10,000 or less	$10,001–$20,000	$20,001–$30,000	$30,001 or more
Back of the Yards				
White	43.5	40.4	13.0	3.1
Black	54.8	24.7	11.0	9.6
Hispanic	31.6	53.1	11.2	4.1
Austin				
White	29.5	54.1	13.1	3.3
Black	51.3	32.1	8.3	8.3

Table D.6 Age Composition and Median Age, by Race—Back of the Yards and Austin (percentage)

	17–30	31–45	46–60	61 and Over	Median Age
Back of the Yards					
White	21.0	22.9	27.1	29.0	51
Black	25.9	42.0	27.2	4.9	37
Hispanic	48.6	39.4	11.9	0.0	31
Austin					
White	15.5	32.4	25.4	26.8	47
Black	32.2	44.3	18.0	5.5	36

Table D.7 Type of Dwelling Unit, by Race—Beverly, Hyde Park–Kenwood, and Lincoln Park (percentage)

	House	Apartment
Beverly		
White	87.4	12.6
Black	86.4	13.6
Hyde Park–Kenwood		
White	12.6	87.4
Black	5.0	95.0
Lincoln Park		
White	16.1	83.9
Black	11.6	88.4

Table D.8 Ownership Status, by Race—Beverly, Hyde Park–Kenwood, and Lincoln Park (percentage)

	Owner	Renter
Beverly		
White	85.3	14.7
Black	80.3	19.7
Hyde Park–Kenwood		
White	36.1	63.9
Black	22.9	77.1
Lincoln Park		
White	26.9	73.1
Black	2.3	97.7

Table D.9 Respondents' Occupation, by Race—Beverly, Hyde Park–Kenwood, and Lincoln Park (percentage)

	Professional-Technical	Managers-Administrators	Clerical-Sales	Craftsmen	Operatives	Laborers	Service Workers
Beverly							
White	42.3	14.6	28.2	5.2	2.3	0.9	6.6
Black	36.0	10.0	20.0	6.0	6.0	4.0	18.0
Hyde Park–Kenwood							
White	61.5	13.8	14.9	1.1	0.6	1.1	6.9
Black	38.7	11.8	21.0	3.4	5.9	2.5	16.8
Lincoln Park							
White	45.7	24.2	19.1	3.8	2.4	0.7	4.1
Black	30.0	13.3	26.7	6.7	10.0	0.0	13.3

Table D.10 Educational Attainment, by Race—Beverly, Hyde Park–Kenwood, and Lincoln Park (percentage)

	Less than High School	High School	More than High School
Beverly			
White	5.6	45.5	48.9
Black	4.7	50.0	45.3
Hyde Park–Kenwood			
White	4.2	16.5	79.3
Black	7.1	44.0	48.9
Lincoln Park			
White	4.1	25.8	70.1
Black	21.4	52.4	26.2

Table D.11 Total Family Income during 1978, by Race—Beverly, Hyde Park–Kenwood, and Lincoln Park (percentage)

	$10,000 or less	$10,001– $20,000	$20,001– $30,000	$30,001 or More
Beverly				
White	10.8	32.2	28.3	28.7
Black	11.1	33.3	25.9	29.6
Hyde Park–Kenwood				
White	32.5	31.1	14.0	22.4
Black	26.3	36.1	18.8	18.8
Lincoln Park				
White	17.1	36.0	21.4	25.5
Black	30.8	41.0	10.3	17.9

Table D.12 Age Composition and Median Age, by Race—Beverly, Hyde Park–Kenwood, and Lincoln Park (percentage)

	17–30	31–45	46–60	61 and Over	Median Age
Beverly					
White	17.9	32.1	25.5	24.5	46
Black	25.0	54.7	17.2	3.1	38
Hyde Park–Kenwood					
White	41.4	21.5	18.1	19.0	35
Black	26.3	42.3	16.8	14.6	38
Lincoln Park					
White	45.1	36.1	10.4	8.4	33
Black	35.7	40.5	14.3	9.5	35

Appendix E

Estimating Standardized, Regression-Adjusted Scores with the General Linear Model

Introduction

Chapters 6, 7, and 8 use tables of predicted scores to explain regression findings. The tables show the predicted scores on a dependent variable referred to here as $\hat{y}_i$ as a function of one or two predictor variables, x_i. In some cases y is a continuous variable and predicted scores fall along a broad range, in other cases y is a dichotomy with predicted scores between zero and one. In some cases the x variables are continuous, in other cases one or both of the x variables shown in the table is a dichotomy, and in other cases one or both are polytomies measured at the nominal or ordinal level. Finally, in certain analyses there are more than two predictor variables in the regression equation even though the tables of predicted scores only show the "partial" effects of one or two x's. In this case the predicted scores in the tabular displays are referred to as "regression-adjusted means" or "standardized scores" because the effects of some predictor variables have been controlled for or adjusted for even though these variables do not explicitly appear in the tables.

The purpose of this appendix is to describe the methodology used to calculate the predicted scores in each of the circumstances alluded to in the previous paragraph. Although each of these situations seems to present a unique problem, in fact one general model is used to derive the predicted scores in all types of circumstances. What we present here is an application of the general linear model to show how to estimate regression-adjusted or standardized scores (and their standard errors, to allow estimation of confidence intervals) in all types of data-analysis situations, as defined by (1) the level of measurement of each variable in the analysis, and (2) the number of predictors in the regression equation.

The next section of this appendix is an exposition of the model for estimating regression-adjusted scores and their standard errors. The third section presents two detailed empirical examples.

Estimating Regression-adjusted Scores

The Bivariate Case

We begin by considering the prediction problem in a bivariate regression. None of the predicted scores analyzed in chapters 6, 7, or 8 are calculated from bivariate models. However, the example is worth pursuing because the statistical theory here provides the basis for the extensions that follow.

We begin by assuming the usual bivariate regression model:

(1) $$y_i = \alpha + \beta x_i + \epsilon_i.$$

We also assume the usual estimators for α and β and the following estimated regression line:

(2) $$\hat{y}_i = \hat{a} + \hat{B} x_i.$$

We note the formula yielding the estimator for the intercept:

(3) $$\bar{y} = \hat{a} + \hat{B}\bar{x}.$$

We re-express the estimated regression line by subtracting equation (3) from equation (2):

(4) $$\hat{y}_i - \bar{y} = \hat{B}(x_i - \bar{x})$$

and rearrange to obtain the following prediction equation:

(5) $$\hat{y}_i = \bar{y} + \hat{B}(x_i - \bar{x}).$$

In the bivariate case, the predicted $\hat{y}_i$ is a function of the mean of y, the mean of x, the difference between x_i and the mean of x, and the regression slope. When y is a dichotomous variable scored $(0,1)$, the predicted score is the estimated proportion in the category scored 1, given the group's score on x. In some cases the predicted scores for a dichotomous y are also interpreted as rates or probabilities. When x is a dichotomous variable scored $(0,1)$, the mean is the proportion of the sample in category 1. The difference $(x_i - \bar{x})$ takes two possible values— one positive, one negative—depending on whether the group score on x is zero or one. When x is a dichotomous variable scored $(0,1)$ and y is continuous, the slope B is a difference in mean-y scores. When both x and y are dichotomies scored $(0,1)$, the means on y are proportions and so the slope B is a difference in proportions.

The variance of $\hat{y}_i$ in the bivariate case is estimated as (Kmenta 1971, 228):

(6) $$s_{\hat{y}i}^2 = s^2\left[\frac{1}{n} + \frac{(x_i - \bar{x})^2}{\Sigma_i(x_i - \bar{x})^2}\right]$$

where s^2 is the estimate of $E(\epsilon_i^2)$. When y is a continuous variable, s^2 is estimated by (Kmenta 1971, 215):

$$(7) \qquad s^2 = \frac{\Sigma_i(y_i - \hat{y}_i)^2}{n}.$$

The standard error of $\hat{y}_i$ is a function of the variability of y, the standard error of the slope, the distance between x_i (the x value used to generate the predicted score on y) and the mean-x score, and the sample size (c.f. Kmenta 1971, 240–41). The procedure for estimating s^2 when y is a dichotomous variable is a little different in principle and will be discussed at the end of this section.

A confidence interval for $\hat{y}_i$ is constructed using Student's t distribution. The interval for the $(1 - \alpha)$ level of confidence is (Kmenta 1971, 228):

$$(8) \qquad \hat{y}_i \pm t(n - 2, \alpha/2) * s_{\hat{y}i}.$$

For large n (i.e. over 30) the t value for a 95-percent confidence interval is 1.96. The interval $\hat{y}_i \pm s_{\hat{y}i}$ approximately corresponds to a 68-percent confidence interval.

Example 1 shows how to estimate regression-adjusted scores and their standard errors for a bivariate regression.

More Than One Predictor

The next set of formulas extends the results in equations (1)–(8) to the general case where there are k-predictor variables. The general model subsumes any combination of the following situations:

1. one or more of the x_k are dichotomies;
2. one or more of the x_k are polytomies measured at the nominal or ordinal level;
3. there are one or more significant higher-order multiplicative interactions among the x_k in predicting y;
4. there are more than two significant predictor variables in the regression equation.

We begin the discussion of the general case by assuming the usual multiple-regression model with k predictors:

$$(9) \qquad y_i = \alpha + \beta_1 x_1 + \ldots + \beta_k x_k + \epsilon_i$$

or, in matrix notation:

$$(10) \qquad y = \alpha + \beta X + \underset{\sim}{\epsilon}.$$

Some of the x_k may be dichotomies or interaction terms. When one of the predictor variables is a polytomy with c categories measured at the nominal or ordinal level then $(c - 1)$ of the x_k predictors are dummy variables scored $(0, 1)$ and constructed to measure whether or not a sample member belongs to one of the nonreference categories (c.f. Suits 1957; Cohen 1968; Fennessey 1968). The dependent variable may be a dichotomy scored $(0, 1)$ or a continuous variable. When y is a dichotomy, additional steps must be taken to correctly calculate the standard errors and confidence intervals. These steps are described at the end of this section.

We assume the usual estimated regression:

$$(11) \qquad \hat{y}_i = \hat{a} + \underline{\hat{B}}\underline{X}_i.$$

We note the multivariate formula yielding the estimator for the intercept:

$$(12) \qquad \bar{y} = \hat{a} + \underline{\hat{B}}\underline{\bar{X}}.$$

By a substitution and subtraction similar to step 4 in the bivariate case, we obtain the following prediction equation:

$$(13) \qquad \hat{y}_i = \bar{y} + \hat{B}(\underline{X}_i - \underline{\bar{X}}),$$

where
$$(\underline{X}_i - \underline{\bar{X}}) = \begin{bmatrix} X_{i1} - \bar{X}_1 \\ \vdots \\ X_{ik} - \bar{X}_k \end{bmatrix}.$$

In the multivariate case the predicted $\hat{y}_i$ is a function of the mean of y, and the mean of each x_k the difference between each x_{ik} and $\bar{x}_k$ and the k regression slopes.

Equation (13) applies when y is a continuous variable and also exactly applies when y is a dichotomous variable scored $(0, 1)$ if we adopt the (OLS) regression model. This model is used in Rosenberg's articles illustrating regression adjustment of proportions, which he refers to as "standardization" (Rosenberg 1962).

Equation (13) also applies regardless of the level of measurement of any of the x variables and/or the number of categories for any polytomous x measured at the nominal or ordinal level:

1. When one of the x_k is a dichotomy scored $(0, 1)$, the mean x is the proportion of the sample in category 1. The x_i score is either zero or one.
2. When there is a significant higher-order interaction among two (or more) x_k predicting y, then one of the predictor variables is a measure of the respondent's score on this interaction term. The mean for this

variable is the average sample score for the constructed interaction term. The x_i score is the individual's score on this constructed variable.

3. When one of the predictor variables is a polytomy with c categories then $(c - 1)$ of the predictors are dummy variables scored $(0, 1)$ as described earlier. The mean on each of these dummy variables can also be interpreted as the sample proportion in the particular non-reference category designated by each dummy variable. The $(0, 1)$ x_i scores for each dummy variable show whether the individual is or is not a member of the designated nonreference category. A person who is a member of the reference category receives a score of zero on each of the $(c - 1)$ dummy variables.

Equation (13) is the general expression used to predict scores on y for any number of x independent variables. When the regression model involves a single dichotomous or continuous predictor variable X_i, $\bar{X}$ and B are 1×1 matrices. With these constraints equation (13) can be seen as an alternate expression for equation (5). When there is one polytomous x variable, X_i and $\bar{X}$ are matrices of dimension $(c - 1) \times 1$ and B is a $1 \times (c - 1)$ dimensional vector. When there is a single polytomous predictor it is necessary to move to a multiple-regression framework to analyze the data.

When there is more than one predictor variable, it is useful to distinguish display variables from control variables. Most of the tables in chapters 6, 7, and 8 show the predicted scores on y as a function of one or two x variables controlling for the effects of other x variables that are not explicitly shown in the table but that are part of the full estimated-regression equation. The x variables explicitly appearing in the table are the display variables. These are the variables whose effects on y are shown "adjusting for," "standardizing for," or "controlling for" the effects of the other x variables in the equation but not appearing in the table. This second set of variables, the x's whose effects are regression adjusted, are the control variables.

Regression-adjusted scores are the predicted values of y for groups differentiated by their scores on the display variables, holding constant the control variables. The control variables are held constant by assuming that whatever the scores are for the display variables, the score for any individual on each control variable is the same as the sample average for that variable. When one or more of the control variables is a dichotomy, individuals' scores on these variables are set to the overall sample proportion, rate, or probability.

Regression-adjusted scores are calculated using equation (13). To calculate the regression-adjusted score for a particular group, one performs the following steps:

1. Build the $(X_i - \bar{X})$ matrix by inserting the appropriate scores for the display variables and the sample averages for the control variables.
2. Perform the numerical calculation shown in equation (13).

The regression-adjusted scores are a function of the mean on y, the partial regression slopes for the display variables, and the distance between the x_i scores for the display variables and the sample averages for these measures. The control variables do not contribute to the calculation of the predicted scores because the corresponding rows of the $(X_i - \bar{X})$ matrix are zero. The predicted scores on y are adjusted for the effects of the control variables, however, because the partial regression slopes used to calculate the predicted scores in equation (13) are estimated taking into account the effects of the control variables. Davis (1982) uses the logic of causal diagrams and path analysis to explain some implications of using partial regression slopes to calculate regression-adjusted means.

The variance of $\hat{y}_i$ in the multivariate case is estimated as (Kmenta 1971, 363):

$$(14) \qquad s_{\hat{y}_i}^2 = s^2[1/n + (\underline{X}_i - \bar{X})'(X'X)^{-1}(\underline{X}_i - \underline{\bar{X}})]$$

where s^2 is the estimate of $E(\epsilon_i^2)$ and $(X'X)$ is the matrix of sums of squares and crossproducts for the predictor variables. When y is continuous, s^2 is estimated by formula (7). When y is a $(0,1)$ dichotomy, other steps must be followed to estimate s^2. These steps are described below.

With a single dichotomous or continuous x variable $(X_i - \bar{X})$ and $(X'X)$ are 1×1 matrices. With these constraints, equation (14) can be seen as an alternate expression for equation (6). When there is more than one predictor variable, the standard error of $\hat{y}_i$ depends on the variability of y, the sample size, the distance between each x_i score and the sample mean for the display variables, and the sampling errors for the slope coefficients (c.f. Kmenta 1971, 240–41, 375).

A confidence interval for $\hat{y}_i$ in the multivariate case is constructed using Student's t distribution. The formula is basically the same as equation (8) except that the t value should be chosen based on $(n - k)$ degrees of freedom instead of $(n - 2)$. In most survey applications—i.e., with a sample of more than 30—the t value for a 95-percent confidence interval is 1.96, and a t value of 1.0 approximately corresponds to a 68-percent confidence interval.

Y Dichotomous

When y is a $(0,1)$ dichotomy, some modifications are usually made in the formulas for estimating the error variance and confidence intervals. The primary reason for making an adjustment is that $\hat{y}_i$ is not homoscedastic, as formulas (6) and (4) assume; rather, the variance depends on the predicted mean. One may use the following formula to estimate s^2 when y is dichotomous:

$$(15) \qquad s_i^2 = (\hat{y}_i)(1 - \hat{y}_i).$$

The variance is estimated separately for each estimated regression-adjusted score. This variance estimate is then used in place of s^2 in formula (6), or formula (14) for the multivariate case, to calculate the variance of each estimated regression-adjusted score. This correction should be applied to estimated confidence intervals for standardized proportions arising from Rosenberg's model (1962) or for any regression-adjustment technique that implicitly uses an OLS weighting (e.g. Coleman 1964). After making this correction in each estimated variance, confidence intervals for the regression-adjusted scores are estimated as before. The impact of the correction for heteroscedasticity is to change the formula for the variance. This done, the formula for the confidence interval will yield the correct calculation.

Some regression models for qualitative data use a non-OLS weighting scheme for estimating the regression parameters (e.g. Nelder and Wedderburn 1972; Grizzle, Starmer, and Koch 1969; Davis 1975; Kmenta 1971, 250–67). The non-OLS weights used in calculating the regression parameters affect the calculation of the sums of squares in the denominator of formula (6) and the $(X'X)$ matrix in formula (14). When non-OLS models are used to estimate the regression parameters, then the weighted sums of squares in $(X'X)$ should be used in formula (6) or formula (14). The "two round" GLS estimators recommended by Kmenta (1971, 264) and Achen (forthcoming) involve an explicit calculation of the weighted sums-of-squares matrix; therefore this might be the best computational procedure to use when one is interested in calculating regression-adjusted scores with confidence intervals for a dichotomous dependent variable. The sums-of-squares correction applies to the term inside the brackets in formula (6) and formula (14). When estimating confidence intervals for standardized proportions with a non-OLS regression model, one makes the sums-of-squares correction noted in this paragraph as well as the variance correction noted in the previous paragraph.

Illustrative Empirical Examples

This section presents two detailed examples that show how to estimate regression-adjusted scores and their standard errors. Example 1 is a bivariate regression with interval-level x and y variables. Example 2 includes a dichotomy and an ordinal polytomy as predictors and an interval-level standardizing variable.

Each example follows the same steps showing how to go from regression output (as might be produced by a package program such as SAS or SPSS) to tables of estimated regression-adjusted scores and standard errors, as displayed in chapters 6, 7, and 8 of this book. The steps for estimating regression-adjusted scores and their standard errors in any data-analysis situation are:

1. Note the sample size. Since we are working with hypothetical data, we assume $N = 1000$ for each example.
2. Calculate univariate statistics for each variable. Distinguish between interval-level variables, dichotomous variables, and nominal-level or ordinal-level polytomous variables. Also distinguish between $(0,1)$ dummy variables used to operationalize polytomies and natural dichotomies that are scored $(0,1)$. In each example the nature of each variable is listed under the heading "Level of Measurement," although this term does not have quite that precise meaning.
3. Calculate the variance-covariance matrix and the matrix of sums of squares and cross products. In each example the correlation matrix is shown along with the formulas used to derive the other two matrices.
4. Estimate the regression equation by OLS or GLS.
5. Determine which x variables are the display variables and decide which values (x_i) of these variables are to appear as the rows and columns in the table of estimated regression-adjusted scores.
6. Rewrite the regression equation to show estimated regression-adjusted scores as a function of the mean on y, the partial regression slopes for the display variables, and the deviations between x_i and the mean for each of the display variables.
7. Estimate the standard error for each regression-adjusted score.
8. Display the results—the estimated regression-adjusted score and its estimated standard error within each combination of categories of the display variables.

The examples analyzed here are based on hypothetical data. The numerical calculations for intermediate results are carried out with more significant digits than shown here.

Example 1: A Bivariate Regression

1. $N = 1000$.

2. Variables	Range	Level of Measurement	Mean	Std. Dev.	Variance	Sum of Squares
y	$(-3, +3)$	interval	-1.0	1.5	2.25	2,250
X_1	$(0, 50)$	interval	25.0	10	100	100,000

Note: In this example and in all following examples we take the sum of squares as $N*(\text{Variance})$.

3. Correlation matrix:

$$
\begin{array}{c|cc}
 & y & X_1 \\
\hline
y & 1 & .20 \\
X_1 & & 1
\end{array}.
$$

4. Regression equation:

$$\hat{y} = -1.75 + .03(X_1),$$
$$R^2 = .04,$$
$$S^2 = (1 - R^2) * 2.25 = 2.16.$$

Note: In this and in all following examples we use the unadjusted R^2 for calculating the mean squared residual.

5. Values of X for display: (10, 20, 25, 30, 40);
Note: One should choose values centered around the mean(s) of the predictor variable(s). See the note to step 8 for explanation.

6. Equation for predicting display values of y:

$$\hat{y}_i = -1.0 + .03(X_{i1} - \bar{X}_1).$$

Note: See equation (5) in text.

7. Equation for the standard error of $\hat{y}_i$:

$$s_{\hat{y}_i} = \left[2.16 * \left(.001 + \frac{(X_{i1} - 25)^2}{100,000} \right) \right]^{1/2}.$$

Note: See equation (6) in text.

8. Results:

Predicted Values of y as a Function of X_1
(standard errors in parentheses)

10	20	25	30	40
-1.45	-1.15	-1.00	$-.85$	$-.25$
(.08)	(.05)	(.05)	(.05)	(.08)

Note: The standard error of the predicted value increases as X_{i1} is taken further away from the mean of X_1.

Example 2: Categorical Data

y is a $(0, 1)$ dichotomy, one dichotomous X, one ordinal polytomous X, and an interval-level standardizing variable.

1. $N = 1000$.

2.

Variables	Range	Level of Measurement	Mean	Std. Dev.	Variance	Sum of Squares
y	$(0,1)$	dichotomy	.45	.4975	.2475	247.5
X_2	$(0,1)$	dichotomy	.60	.4899	.2400	240.0
X_3	$(0,10)$	interval	4.0	3.0	9.0	9,000
X_{4a}	$(0,1)$	dummy	.30	.4583	.2100	210.0
X_{4b}	$(0,1)$	dummy	.40	.4899	.2400	240.0
X_4	$(0,2)$	ordinal polytomy	-------------------- [see note] --------------------			

Note: X_{4a} and X_{4b} are dummy variables for membership in categories 1 and 2, respectively, of X_4.

3. Correlation matrix:

	y	X_2	X_3	X_{4a}	X_{4b}
y	1	.30	.30	.20	.30
X_2		1	.20	.10	.20
X_3			1	.20	.15
X_{4a}				1	−.5435
X_{4b}					1

Note: Cohen (1968, 429) discusses the following formula for the correlation between dummy variable i and dummy variable j, when i and j have a common-reference category:

$$r_{ij} = -1 * [n_i n_j / ((N - n_i)(N - n_j))]^{1/2}$$

where n_i is the number of cases scored 1 on i,
n_j is the number of cases scored 1 on j.

4. Regression equation:

$$\hat{y} = -.043 + .142(X_2) + .019(X_3) + .454(X_{4a}) + .486(X_{4b}).$$

Notes: s^2 is not calculated in this step because a dichotomous y is heteroscedastic. s^2 is estimated separately for each predicted value of y using equation (14) in the text.

When y is a dichotomy, there are several alternative methods recommended for calculating the regression results. Rosenberg's model for standardization implicitly assumes sample observations are equally weighted, and, therefore, the model can be derived as a special case of the one presented here which is based on OLS methods and an unweighted correlation matrix.

Other methods recommend differentially weighting observations when regression models are used to predict a standardized dichotomous y. The Grizzle-Starmer-Koch technique for estimating weighted regression slopes does not explicitly calculate a weighted correlation matrix or a weighted sums-of-squares and cross-products matrix and so should not be used when standard errors for predicted values of y are desired.

Other generalized-least-squares techniques do calculate weighted correlations and cross-products, but involve several more computational steps than the GSK technique. (See text for references and further discussion.)

This example assumes Rosenberg's model and unweighted statistics.

5. X Variables for display: X_2 and X_4.
   Values of X variables for display: $X_2\ (0,1)$,
   $\qquad\qquad\qquad\qquad\qquad\qquad\qquad X_4\ (0,1,2)$.

6. Equation for predicting display values of y:

$$\hat{y}_i = .45 + .142(X_{i2} - .6) + .454(X_{i4a} - .3) + .486(X_{i4b} - .4).$$

Note: See equation (11) in text.

The effect of X_4 is modeled using two dummy variables, X_{4a} and X_{4b}, described in the previous example.

X_3 is a standardizing variable, always assumed to be measured at its mean. Therefore, $(X_{i3} - 4)$ is always zero and does not explicitly appear in the equation predicting display values of y.

7. Calculating the standard error of $\hat{y}_i$:
   a. $\qquad\qquad [X_i - \bar{X}]' = [X_{i2} - .6\ \ X_{i3} - 4\ \ X_{i4a} - .3\ \ X_{i4b} - .4]$.

   Note: Because X_3 is a standardizing variable, $X_{i3} - 4$ is always zero in this expression.

   b. Inverse of matrix of sums of squares and crossproducts for X variables.

	X_2	X_3	X_{4a}	X_{4b}
X_2	.004680	-.000078	-.001200	-.001500
X_3		.000129	-.000300	-.000300
X_{4a}			.007840	.004450
X_{4b}	(symmetric)			.006930

   c. s^2 is estimated separately for each predicted value of y as $(\hat{y}_i)(1 - \hat{y}_i)$. (See equation (14) in text.)

   d. $\qquad s\hat{y}_i = [((\hat{y}_i)(1 - \hat{y}_i)) * (.001 + [X_i - \bar{X}]'[X'X]^{-1}[X_i - \bar{X}])]^{1/2}$

8. Results:

Predicted Proportion on y, as a Function of X_2
and X_4, Controlling for Effects of X_3
(standard errors in parentheses)

	X_4		
X_2	0	1	2
0	.03 (.011)	.49 (.037)	.52 (.035)
1	.18 (.028)	.63 (.031)	.66 (.026)

Notes

Chapter 1

1. We do not want to give the impression that gentrification represents the general urban future. Taken as some proportion of total urban housing, its impact appears to be quite small. We focus on it, however, because it helps to underline certain theoretical and empirical issues.

2. This is a simplification. Alonso (1980) and others (e.g., Goetze 1976) have argued that the large baby-boom cohort now entering the housing market and the life-style changes that have led to more singles, unmarried couples, divorced people, and, hence, to smaller households, make urban living more attractive and appropriate housing units scarce, forcing relative low-income (young) professionals into new marginal markets. In addition, the small number of children such households produce reduces the significance of an inadequate school system for these families, and the many childless households do not have to worry about the impact of crime on the young.

3. In the short run, it should be added, pioneering blacks may be the ones who bolster an otherwise weak market.

Chapter 2

1. Crimes are located by axial coordinates, making it impossible to determine on which side of the street a crime took place. Since streets form the boundaries of many of our communities, we had to allocate the crime statistics for these border areas proportionately to the area falling within the community. Because our community areas are large, however, these allocated crimes represent a very small proportion of all crimes.

2. We limited our calculations to single-family houses because they seem to be more comparable on average and to represent clearly defined submarkets in each of our communities. We thus excluded not only multiple-family dwellings, but also condominiums.

3. For similar batteries of questions, see Andrews and Withey 1976; Taylor 1980, 1981b.

4. The development of this instrument was one of our most challenging tasks—the construction of an instrument that was not culturally or class biased and that could be completed quickly and reliably was a formidable undertaking. Our review of the literature on this issue and an interview with a contractor-developer led us to conclude that we could

not measure absolute levels of physical decay of buildings by rating only the outsides of them. What we have measured, then, is the *appearance* of building deterioration and neglect of property.

Chapter 3

1. Paradoxically, although it has not been physically or socially distinctive, Austin has spawned some of the nation's most well-known leaders in the neighborhood-preservation movement and was one of the first areas in the nation to make "redlining," the practice of denying mortgages to an area because of its racial composition, a major political and social issue. That issue and the calling for changes in FHA housing policies because of their negative consequences, particularly in Austin, subsequently became cornerstones of efforts to develop a national neighborhoods program.

2. It would be difficult to estimate how many whites did pass through South Shore between the close of the Second World War and 1970, but the numbers must have been large. If one estimates an annual turnover of about 10 percent, the number would be 200,000. One of our white field workers, meeting a present-day black South Shore resident outside of the neighborhood and expressing strong interest in the area, was asked with a faintly irritated tone, "And when did *you* live in South Shore?"

3. Indirect confirmation of this impression comes from a white shopkeeper on the Beverly strip who reports that his business consists almost exclusively of selling designer suits to black youth—he claims to have the largest selection of such items in Illinois.

4. We first ranked the neighborhoods on each item according to the percentage of respondents who reported an item to be a big problem or somewhat of a problem. The Kendall coefficient of concordance (W) was calculated to determine the relation among the rankings. Since the W of .69 was significant ($p < .001$), we summed the ranks across the ten items for each neighborhood and used these sums, which range theoretically from 10 to 80, as the basis for a second overall ranking (Siegel 1956).

Chapter 4

1. Significantly, a few of the people at the meeting did telephone us subsequently to apologize for the behavior of the group as a whole. One of them was a young woman who was one of the few of her high-school class to leave the community to attend college. She wanted us to know that people were very warm and friendly to each other, but that the outside world made them nervous. She hoped we would see their better side.

Chapter 5

1. BAPA is the lead organization among many, including Beverly Improvement Association, West Beverly Homeowners, Beverly Woods' Kennedy Park, Beverly Ridge Homeowners, East Beverly Association, Ridge Hills Civic Association, and Vanderpoel Improvement Association.

2. See Spear (1967) for an account of resistance, sometimes violent, to black in-migration in Hyde Park during the early 1900s.

Chapter 6

1. Granovetter does not explicitly discuss neighborhood investment. The suggestion that the threshold model might be appropriate here is our own.

2. The city of Waukegan can be classified as an older, industrial satellite city in the Chicago SMSA (Murphy and Rehfuss 1976, chap. 4). The Waukegan Community Survey, a block-quota personal-interview sample of five hundred adult residents of the city, was conducted by the National Opinion Research Center under contract with the mayor's office of the city of Waukegan.

3. According to Abelson and Tukey (1970), the threat from converting ordinal to metric information arises when the distance in the first and/or last interval is actually on the order of five-times larger than assumed. There is no way to use the data to check this threat to the validity of our coding. The comments by Abelson and Tukey suggest, however, the approach one might take to improve the measurement of threshold scores in this kind of analysis. The results reported here do not vary significantly for two other choices of the coding scheme.

4. The dependent variable used here is based on questions 22 and 23 from the Chicago Neighborhood Survey questionnaire.

5. The variables in the equation were chosen by: (1) a priori inclusion of a measure of neighborhood racial concentration referred to in the table as the black-white demand ratio; (2) a priori inclusion of marital-status, family-size, income, and housing-deterioration measures; (3) forward-stepwise selection procedures for the remaining variables; and (4) to facilitate discussion, any variable included in the equation for one racial group was automatically included in the equation for the other.

6. The block-deterioration scale adds together three components. Observers from our research project rated a sample of respondents' blocks with respect to the number of residential structures that were abandoned and the number of residential structures that visibly needed maintenance and repair. Respondents also rated their block as to the degree of problems posed by poor property maintenance, abandoned buildings, and other signs of lack of upkeep. The scale is formed by determining for each respondent whether his block is above or below the median on each measure of deterioration. The three measures are then added. The range for the block-deterioration scale is from 0 to 3. The average score for white homeowners is about .8, the average for nonwhite homeowners is about 1.5. The components of the block-deterioration scale are described more fully in appendix C.

7. The control variable in table 6.6 is a summary measure of neighborhood housing-market evaluations based on statements of satisfaction with the appearance of housing, the quality of housing for the money, and the investment opportunities in the neighborhood. The range for this variable is from −6 (negative evaluation) to +6 (positive). The median score for whites is between 3 and 4; the median for nonwhites is between 2 and 3. The control variable in table 6.7 is a single question measuring respondent satisfaction with the way property values are going in the neighborhood. The range for this variable is from 1 (very dissatisfied) to 4 (very satisfied). The median score for whites is between 3 and 3.5; the median for nonwhites is between 2.5 and 3. The results in tables 6.6 and 6.7 illustrate the effects of adding interaction terms for the variables shown to the equation described in table 6.5. Each interaction term is statistically significant at the .01 level.

8. Note, however, that neighborhood variation in income levels *among homeowners* is much less than neighborhood variation in income for all adult residents taken together. Therefore, adjustments for income levels do not affect neighborhood-investment predictions as much as one might first expect.

Chapter 7

1. The exact methods and questions asked were necessarily different because the DAS was a personal interview and the Omaha survey was done by telephone. In the DAS, respondents were shown a series of cards with fifteen houses, some of which were colored

black. Respondents were asked if they would try to move out of a neighborhood with designated racial composition. In the Omaha survey, neighborhoods were described as "so-many black and so-many white" where the number of blacks and whites added up to ten. Respondents were then asked if they would try to move out of their neighborhood if it changed to the situation described in the question. One potential difficulty in interpreting the Detroit data is that we do not know what kind of area respondents have in mind when they answer—if they are thinking of their own neighborhood or some other area in the city.

2. This is explicitly the case in the Omaha data where 28 percent of whites said they would stay in all-black areas. The suggestion from table 7.3 is that the tolerant core is smaller in Detroit, although the differences in wording and administrative procedures mentioned in the previous footnote suggest caution in coming to such conclusions.

3. Schelling argues that the bounded-neighborhood model can accommodate a preference for integration. He states that for some people, their point on the tolerance schedule reflects the "upper limits to the ratios at which people's preference for integrated residence is outweighed by their extreme minority status. . . . We [do] not postulate a lower limit to the acceptable proportion of opposite color, i.e., an upper limit to the proportion of like color in the neighborhood" (1978, 165). To accurately model a preference for integration, however, there must be some account taken of the lower limit. A preference for integration means precisely that people will try to live in neighborhoods that are neither too white nor too black. To model a preference for integration, it is necessary to work with some kind of unfolding scale of individual tolerance for neighborhoods of different degrees of integration (c.f. Coombs 1964). This type of preference structure can be empirically estimated, but it is not compatible with a formal requirement of the bounded-neighborhood model which assumes a monotonic relationship between tolerance and amount of integration for each neighborhood resident.

4. The white curves in figure 7.2 also stop short of the x axis. The questions in the survey were not well-enough tuned to estimate the shape of the graph in this region. In the simulations that follow, we assume the white curve stops just above the x axis—the least-tolerant white person could accept 1-percent blacks in the neighborhood. The exact shape of the graph in this region is of little consequence for the substantive conclusions we draw from our examination of the bounded-neighborhood model.

5. The nonoverlap of curves holds for almost any assumption about relative numbers of blacks and whites who are assumed to be interested in living in the neighborhood.

6. In the bounded-neighborhood model, Schelling is actually interested in studying tipping in all kinds of group situations, most of which do not have a practical restriction on occupancy. Therefore, most of the models and conclusions do not take into account the implications of a limited supply of housing. In the cases where he does introduce a supply constraint, he notes that there can be (and in all of his examples there is) "a kind of neutral equilibrium" (1971, 173). In other words, the neighborhoods do not tip, and the reader notes that compared to the unconstrained models, equilibrium conditions do not seem so hard to achieve.

7. This quotation is not a finding, it is a research hypothesis. In its formal definition, the bounded-neighborhood model contains no explicit provision for expectation or speculation: "[We assume] people do not know the intentions of others and do not project future turnover" (Schelling 1978, 156).

8. In her study of the Russel Woods neighborhood in Detroit, Wolf notes that "white demand . . . declined markedly before a single Negro family had moved in. . . . One might say that the tip-point, in the sense of white willingness to enter . . . had already been reached at that time" (1963, 220).

9. "It is hard to pinpoint a precise date when the probability of Negroes moving into the neighborhood became real. . . . Some residents showed concern ten years before the first house was sold to Negroes. . . . As early as [three years before the first Negro family

moved in] it was apparent . . . that neighborhoods adjacent on three sides were becoming racially mixed. . . . The selling of the third house [to a Negro] convinced everyone that the neighborhood was destined to become mixed. During the ensuing year . . . about 40 houses were sold to Negroes, with perhaps another 100 for sale. During this time about five white families also moved into the area" (Mayer 1960, 202–4).

10. Exploratory analyses showed that fear of tipping is a meaningful concept for black and Hispanic residents as well. As we discussed in previous chapters, however, the focus of these fears is less a matter of racial coding and more an apprehension about change in the social-class composition of the neighborhood. Middle-class blacks, for instance, are worried about "the element" moving in. Demographic studies of decline in areas after they are re-segregated suggest reasons for this concern among blacks and Hispanics (e.g., Duncan and Duncan 1957).

11. The low ratio itself, however, reflects concern about racial change among East Siders—they have worked diligently to keep blacks out.

12. The effect of market evaluations on the expectation of tipping was analyzed separately for homeowners and renters. The relationships are somewhat stronger for owners than for renters. The pattern of relationships involving this scale and all other variables is, however, similar for both groups. The substantive gains from presenting analyses for each group separately are small compared to the costs.

Chapter 8

1. Following Campbell's work, we employ satisfaction scales to measure net judgments of the seriousness of the crime problem. See question 4f in appendix B. To improve reliability in certain analyses, responses to this question sometimes are scaled with a similar measure of satisfaction with the reputation of the neighborhood. See question 4c in appendix B.

2. Using panel data collected in South Shore, we have found that intentions to move, measured as we have done, are strongly related to actual moves.

3. The demographic variables included in the first equation in table 8.3 are those that remain significant when measures of the crime problem and the deterioration problem are added as predictors—c.f. equation (2) in table 8.3.

4. Inspection of standard errors and other "troubleshooting" statistics (Draper and Smith 1966) shows that the pattern of regression results is not a superficial result of multicollinearity and instability of coefficients.

Chapter 9

1. We do note that in their pathbreaking work, the Duncans (1957) frequently argue that the invasion-deterioration-succession syndrome does not move at the same rate of speed in all neighborhoods. But they do anticipate that ultimately it will always take place.

2. On the basis of limited experimentation, it appears that vouchers do not work quite the way one would hope. Many users opt to take their augmented income in ways other than improved housing, and the market is so large and diffuse, and the subsidies so small, that very little impact on the housing market has been observable (e.g., see Struyk and Bendick 1981). Even so, the potential gains from such a system seem worth additional efforts in this direction.

3. In this case, local residents organized by an outside group of community organizers fought back, mitigating the worst evils of General Motors' massive displacement program.

Appendix A

1. An unpublished study, cited by Judd (1966), done by Illinois Bell showed that 20 percent of all Chicago customers of the Bell company were not listed.

References

Abelson, R., and J. Tukey. 1970. Efficient conversion of non-metric information into metric information. In *The quantitative analysis of social problems*, ed. E. Tufte, 407–17. Reading, Mass.: Addison-Wesley.

Achen, C. (Forthcoming.) *Quasi-experimentation*. Berkeley: University of California Press.

Alonso, William. 1980. The population factor and urban structure. In *The prospective city*, ed. Arthur P. Solomon, 32–51. Cambridge: M.I.T. Press.

Andrews, Frank, and Stephen Withey. 1976. *Social indicators of well-being*. New York: Plenum Press.

Barry, Brian, and Russell Hardin, eds. 1982. *Rational man and irrational society? An introduction and sourcebook*. Beverly Hills: Sage Publications.

Berry, Brian J. L., and John D. Kasarda. 1977. *Contemporary urban ecology*. New York: Macmillan.

Bordley, R. 1982. Public perceptions of crime: A derivation of Warr's power function from the Bayesian odds relations. *Social Forces* 61:134–43.

Bradbury, Katharine, Anthony Downs, and Kenneth Small. 1982. *Urban decline and the future of American cities*. Washington, D.C.: Brookings.

Burgess, Ernest W. 1925. The growth of the city. In *The city*, ed. Robert E. Park, Ernest W. Burgess, and Roderick D. McKenzie. Chicago: University of Chicago Press.

Campbell, Angus. 1981. *The sense of well-being in America*. New York: McGraw-Hill.

Chicago Sun-Times. 1977. *Chicago area shopping centers*. Market research department of the *Chicago Sun-Times*.

Cohen, J. 1968. Multiple regression as a general data-analytic system. *Psychological Bulletin* 70:426–43.

Coleman, J. 1964. *Introduction to mathematical sociology*. New York: Free Press.

Condit, Carl W. 1973. *Chicago, 1910–1929: Building, planning, and urban technology*. Chicago: University of Chicago Press.

Coombs, Clyde. 1964. *A theory of data*. New York: John Wiley.

Courant, P., and J. Yinger. 1977. On models of racial prejudice and urban residential structure. *Journal of Urban Economics* 4:272–91.

Davis, J. 1975. Analyzing contingency tables with linear flow graphs: D-systems. In *Sociological Methodology 1976*, ed. D. Heise. San Francisco: Jossey-Bass.

———. 1982. Extending Rosenberg's technique for standardizing percentage tables. Department of Sociology, Harvard University. Typescript.

Davis, Otto, and A. Whinston, 1961. The economics of urban renewal. *Law and Contemporary Problems* 26:105–17.

Downs, Anthony. 1978. Urban policy. In *Setting national priorities: The 1979 budget*, ed. Joseph A. Pechman, 161–94. Washington, D.C.: Brookings.

Draper, N., and H. Smith. 1966. *Applied regression analysis*. New York: John Wiley.

DuBow, Fred, and Aaron Podolefsky. 1980. Citizen participation in collective responses to crime. Typescript.

Duncan, Otis Dudley, and Beverly Duncan. 1957. *The Negro population of Chicago: A study of residential succession*. Chicago: University of Chicago Press.

Faris, Robert E. L. 1970. *Chicago sociology, 1920–1932*. Heritage of Sociology. Chicago: University of Chicago Press.

Farley, Reynolds. 1979. Racial progress in the last two decades: What can we determine about who benefited and why? Paper presented at the meeting of the American Sociological Association, Boston.

Farley, Reynolds, Howard Schuman, Suzanne Bianchi, Diane Colasanto, and Shirley Hatchett. 1978. Chocolate city, vanilla suburbs: Will the trend toward racially separate communities continue? *Social Science Research* 7:319–44.

Fennessey, J. 1968. The general linear model: A new perspective on some familiar topics. *American Journal of Sociology* 74:1–27.

Fontaine, Roger. 1942. Beverly. In *Forty-four cities in the city of Chicago*. Chicago: Chicago Plan Commission.

Garofalo, James, and John Laub. 1978. The fear of crime: Broadening our perspective. *Victimology: An International Journal* 3:242–53.

Glazer, Nathan. 1975. *Affirmative discrimination*. New York: Basic Books.

Goetze, Rolf. 1976. *Building neighborhood confidence: A humanistic strategy for urban housing.* Cambridge: Ballinger.

Goodwin, Carole. 1979. *The Oak Park strategy.* Chicago: University of Chicago Press.

Granovetter, Mark. 1978. Threshold models of collective behavior. *American Journal of Sociology* 83(6):1420–43.

———. 1983. Personal communication, June 1983.

Greeley, Andrew. 1977. *Neighborhood.* New York: Seabury.

Grizzle, J., F. Starmer, and G. Koch. 1969. Analysis of categorical data by general linear models. *Biometrics* 25:489–504.

Grodzins, Morton. 1957. *Metropolitan segregation.* Chicago: University of Chicago Press.

Groves, R. M. 1978. An empirical comparison of two telephone sample designs. *Journal of Marketing Research* 15:622–31.

Hakim, Simon. (Forthcoming.) *Crime in the metropolis.* Cambridge: Lexington Books.

Harris, Chauncy P., and Edward L. Ullman. 1957. The nature of cities. In *Cities and society: The revised reader in urban sociology*, ed. Paul K. Hatt and Albert J. Reiss, Jr., 237–247. New York: Free Press.

Hauck, Matthew, and Michael Cox. 1974. Locating a sample by random digit dialing. *Public Opinion Quarterly* 38:253–60.

Hawley, Amos. 1981. Human ecology: Persistence and change. *American Behavioral Scientist* 24(3):423–44.

Holt, Glen E., and Dominic A. Pacyga. 1979. *Chicago: A historical guide to the neighborhoods.* Chicago: Chicago Historical Society.

Hoyt, Homer. 1937. City growth and mortgage risk. *Insured Mortgage Portfolio* 1:6–10.

———. 1942a. South Shore. In *Forty-four cities in the city of Chicago.* Chicago: Chicago Plan Commission.

———. 1942b. Hyde Park, Kenwood, and Oakland. In *Forty-four cities in the city of Chicago.* Chicago: Chicago Plan Commission.

Hunter, Albert. 1974. *Symbolic communities: The persistence and change of Chicago's local communities.* Chicago: University of Chicago Press.

Hyman, Herbert, and Paul B. Sheatsley. 1964. Attitudes toward desegregation. *Scientific American* 211(1):16–23.

Jacob, Herbert. 1982. Policy responses to crime in ten U.S. cities, 1948–1978. Paper presented at "The Future of Our City" conference, University of Chicago.

Janowitz, Morris. 1952. *The community press in an urban setting.* Chicago: University of Chicago Press.

Judd, Robert C. 1966. Telephone usage and survey research. *Journal of Advertising Research* 6:38–39.

Karlen, David H. 1968. Racial integration and property values in Chicago. *Urban Economics Report No. 7* (Apr.). Chicago: University of Chicago.

Kasarda, John D. 1982. Adapting policy to new urban realities. Paper presented at "The Future of Our City" conference, University of Chicago.

Kasarda, John D., and Morris Janowitz. 1974. Community attachment in mass society. *American Sociological Review* 39 (June):328–39.

Kitagawa, Evelyn M., and Karl E. Taeuber. 1963. *Local community fact book: Chicago metropolitan area, 1960.* Chicago: University of Chicago.

Klove, Robert C. 1942. Austin. In *Forty-four cities in the city of Chicago.* Chicago: Chicago Plan Commission.

Kmenta, J. 1971. *Elements of econometrics.* New York: Macmillan.

Lewis, Dan A. 1981. *Reactions to Crime.* Beverly Hills: Sage Publications.

Lewis, Dan A., and Michael G. Maxfield. 1978. Fear in the neighborhoods: A preliminary investigation of the impact of crime in Chicago. Center for Urban Affairs, Northwestern University, Evanston, Illinois. Unpublished.

Lucas, William A., and William C. Adams. 1977. An assessment of telephone survey methods. Santa Monica, Calif.: RAND Corporation, R-2135-NSF.

McIntyre, Jennie. 1967. Public attitudes toward crime and law enforcement. *Annals of the American Academy of Political and Social Science* 374:34–46.

Marans, Robert, and Willard Rodgers. 1974. Toward an understanding of community satisfaction. In *Metropolitan America: Papers on the state of knowledge,* ed. A. Hawley and V. Rock. Washington, D.C.: National Academy of Sciences.

Marshall, Alfred. 1920. *Principles of economics.* 8th ed. London: Macmillan.

Marx, Gary. 1969. *Protest and prejudice.* New York: Harper and Row.

Mayer, Albert. 1960. Russel Woods: Change without conflict. In *Studies in housing and minority groups,* ed. Nathan Glazer and Davis McEntire. Berkeley: University of California Press.

Milbrath, L. W., and R. C. Sahr. 1975. Perceptions of environmental quality. *Social Indicators Research* 1:397–438.

Molotch, Harvey. 1972. *Managed integration: Dilemmas of doing good in the city.* Berkeley: University of California Press.

———. 1976. The city as a growth machine: Toward a political economy of place. *American Journal of Sociology* 82(2):309–32.

Murphy, Thomas, and John Rehfuss. 1976. *Urban politics in the suburban era.* Homewood, Ill.: Dorsey Press.

Myrdal, Gunnar. 1944. *An American dilemma.* New York: Harper and Row.

National Research Council. 1976. *Surveying crime: Report of the Panel for the Evaluation of Crime Surveys*. Washington, D.C.: National Academy of Sciences.

Nelder, J., and R. Wedderburn. 1972. Generalized linear models. *Journal of the Royal Statistical Society* 135 (series A):370–84.

Olson, Mancur. 1965. *The logic of collective action*. Cambridge: Harvard University Press.

Pettigrew, Thomas. 1973. Attitudes on race and housing: A social psychological view. In *Segregation in residential areas*, ed. A. Hawley and V. Rock. Washington, D.C.: National Academy of Sciences.

Riker, William, and Peter Ordeshook. 1973. *An introduction to positive political theory*. Englewood Cliffs, N.J.: Prentice-Hall.

Rosenberg, M. 1962. Test factor standaridzation as a method of interpretation. *Social Forces* 41:53–61.

Rossi, Peter H., and Robert A. Dentler. 1961. *The politics of urban renewal: The Chicago findings*. Glencoe, Ill.: Free Press.

Schelling, Thomas. 1971. Dynamic models of segregation. *Journal of Mathematical Sociology* 1:143–86.

———. 1978. *Micromotives and macrobehavior*. New York: W. W. Norton.

Schuman, H., and B. Gruenberg. 1970. The impact of city on racial attitudes. *American Journal of Sociology* 76:213–61.

Siegel, Sidney. 1956. *Nonparametric statistics for the behavioral sciences*. New York: McGraw-Hill.

Silberman, Charles E. 1978. *Criminal violence, criminal justice*. New York: Random House.

Skogan, Wesley G. 1976. *Sample surveys of the victims of crime*. Cambridge, Mass.: Ballinger.

———. 1981. Issues in the measurement of victimization. Bureau of Justice Statistics, U.S. Department of Justice. Washington, D.C.: Government Printing Office.

Skogan, Wesley G., and Michael G. Maxfield. 1981. *Coping with crime: Victimization, fear, and reactions to crime*. Beverly Hills: Sage Publications.

Sparks, Richard, Hazel G. Genn, and David J. Dodd. 1977. *Surveying victims*. New York: John Wiley.

Spear, Allan H. 1967. *Black Chicago: The making of a Negro ghetto, 1890–1920*. Chicago: University of Chicago Press.

Stegman, Michael. 1972. *Housing investment in the inner city: The dynamics of decline*. Cambridge: M.I.T. Press.

Sternlieb, George. 1966. *The tenement landlord*. New Brunswick, N.J.: Rutgers University Press.

Stinchcombe, A. L., R. Adams, C. Heimer, K. Scheppele, T. Smith, and D. G. Taylor. 1980. *Crime and punishment: Changing attitudes in America*. San Francisco: Jossey Bass.

Struyk, Raymond J., and Marc Bendick, Jr. 1981. *Housing vouchers for the poor: Lessons from a national experiment*. Washington, D.C.: Urban Institute.

Suits, D. 1957. Use of dummy variables in regression equations. *Journal of the American Statistical Association* 52:548–51.

Taub, Richard P., George P. Surgeon, Sara Lindholm, Phyllis Betts Otti, and Amy Bridges. 1977. Urban voluntary associations, locality based and externally induced. *American Journal of Sociology* 83(2): 425–42.

Taub, Richard P., D. Garth Taylor, and Jan D. Dunham. 1981. Neighborhoods and safety. In *Reactions to Crime*, ed. Dan A. Lewis. Beverly Hills: Sage Publications.

Taylor, D. Garth. 1979. Housing, neighborhoods and race relations: Recent survey evidence. *Annals of the American Academy of Political and Social Science* 441:26–40.

———. 1980. Social indicators and rural development policy. *Review of Public Data Use* 8:225–35.

———. 1981a. Racial preferences, housing segregation and the causes of school segregation: Recent evidence from a social survey used in civil litigation. *Review of Public Data Use* 9:267–82.

———. 1981b. Waukegan in the present and the future. Chicago: National Opinion Research Center.

———. 1982. Trends in black educational attainment and other causes of revisionism in American ethnic studies. Paper presented at the meeting of the Midwest Political Science Association.

———. (Forthcoming.) City residents and aggregate social theorists: Some microanalytic surprises on crime and the causes of neighborhood decline. In *Crime in the metropolis*, ed. S. Hakim. Cambridge: Lexington Books.

Taylor, D. G., K. L. Scheppele, and A. L. Stinchcombe. 1979. Salience of crime and support for harsher criminal sanctions. *Social Problems* 26:412–24.

Taylor, D. G., P. Sheatsley, and A. Greeley. 1978. Attitudes toward desegregation. *Scientific American* 238:42–49.

Treiman, Donald. 1966. Status discrepancy and prejudice. *American Journal of Sociology* 71:651–64.

Warner, Margaret S. 1979. The renovation of Lincoln Park: An ecological study of neighborhood change. Ph.D. diss., University of Chicago.

Warr, M. 1980. The accuracy of public beliefs about crime. *Social Forces* 59:456–70.

Where blacks live. 1978. Chicago: Chicago Urban League.

Wilson, William J. 1979. *The declining significance of race.* Chicago: University of Chicago Press.

————. (Forthcoming.) *The Hidden Agenda*. New York: Macmillan.

Wiseman, Frederick. 1972. Methodological bias in public opinion surveys. *Public Opinion Quarterly* 36:105–8.

Wittberg, Patricia. 1982. Neighborhood shopping areas in eight Chicago neighborhoods: An exploration of variations. Ph.D. diss., University of Chicago.

Wolf, Eleanor. 1963. The tipping point in racially changing neighborhoods. *Journal of the American Institute of Planners* 29(3):217–22.

Index